Gateshead
Council

S

Due for Return	Due for Return	Due for Return
1 7 AUG 2017		
2 7 DEC 2018		

Visit us at:
www.gateshead.gov.uk/books

Tel: 0191 433 8410

THE BIG BOOK OF
LITTLE CAKES

240 delectable recipes for bars, cupcakes, muffins, brownies, pastries, tarts and confectionery, shown in 240 photographs

Edited by Catherine Atkinson

southwater

This edition is published by Southwater, an imprint of
Anness Publishing Ltd, Blaby Road, Wigston, Leicestershire LE18 4SE
Email: info@anness.com
Web: www.southwaterbooks.com; www.annesspublishing.com

If you like the images in this book and would like to investigate using
them for publishing, promotions or advertising, please visit our
website www.practicalpictures.com for more information.

Publisher: Joanna Lorenz
Editorial Director: Helen Sudell
Editor: Simona Hill
Recipes: Pepita Aris, Catherine Atkinson, Alex Barker,
Ghillie Basan, Angela Boggiano, Carol Bowen, Georgina Campbell,
Elizabeth Wolf-Cohen, Carla Capalbo, Maxine Clark,
Carole Clements, Matthew Drennan, Tessa Evelegh, Joanna Farrow,
Christine France, Brian Glover, Nicola Graimes, Carole Handslip,
Biddy White Lennon, Sara Lewis, Gilly Love, Lesley Mackley,
Norma MacMillan, Sue Maggs, Sally Mansfield, Jane Milton,
Sally Morris, Anna Mosesson, Janice Murfitt, Rena Salaman,
Anne Sheasby, Young Jin Song, Marlena Spieler, Christopher Trotter,
Laura Washburn, Kate Whiteman, Judy Williams, Jeni Wright,
Carol Wilson, Annette Yates
Photographers: Karl Adamson, Edward Allwright, Martin Brigdale,
James Duncan, John Freeman, Michelle Garrett, Amanda Heywood,
David Jordan, William Lingwood, Debbie Patterson, Sam Stowell
Editorial Reader: Molly Perham
Production Controller: Christine Ni

ETHICAL TRADING POLICY
At Anness Publishing we believe that business should be conducted
in an ethical and ecologically sustainable way, with respect for the
environment and a proper regard to the replacement of the natural
resources we employ.
As a publisher, we use a lot of wood pulp in high-quality paper for
printing, and that wood commonly comes from spruce trees. We are
therefore currently growing more than 750,000 trees in three
Scottish forest plantations: Berrymoss (130 hectares/320 acres),
West Touxhill (125 hectares/305 acres) and Deveron Forest
(75 hectares/185 acres). The forests we manage contain more than
3.5 times the number of trees employed each year in making paper
for the books we manufacture.
Because of this ongoing ecological investment programme, you, as
our customer, can have the pleasure and reassurance of knowing
that a tree is being cultivated on your behalf to naturally replace the
materials used to make the book you are holding.
Our forestry programme is run in accordance with the UK
Woodland Assurance Scheme (UKWAS) and will be certified by the
internationally recognized Forest Stewardship Council (FSC). The
FSC is a non-government organization dedicated to promoting
responsible management of the world's forests. Certification ensures
forests are managed in an environmentally sustainable and socially
responsible way. For further information about this scheme,
go to www.annesspublishing.com/trees

A CIP catalogue record for this book is available from the
British Library.

Previously published as part of a larger volume,
500 Cookies, Biscuits and Bakes.

NOTES
Bracketed terms are intended for American readers.

For all recipes, quantities are given in both metric and imperial
measures and, where appropriate, in standard cups and spoons.
Follow one set of measures, but not a mixture, because they
are not interchangeable.

Standard spoon and cup measures are level. 1 tsp = 5ml,
1 tbsp = 15ml, 1 cup = 250ml/8fl oz.

Australian standard tablespoons are 20ml. Australian readers should
use 3 tsp in place of 1 tbsp for measuring small quantities.

American pints are 16fl oz/2 cups. American readers should use
20fl oz/2.5 cups in place of 1 pint when measuring liquids.

Electric oven temperatures in this book are for conventional ovens.
When using a fan oven, the temperature will probably need to be
reduced by about 10–20°C/20–40°F. Since ovens vary, you should
check with your manufacturer's instruction book for guidance.

The nutritional analysis given for each recipe is calculated per cake,
unless otherwise stated. The analysis does not include optional
ingredients, such as salt added to taste.

Medium (US large) eggs are used unless otherwise stated.

Granulated (white) sugar is used unless otherwise stated.

Main front cover image shows Chocolate Muffins
– for recipe, see page 70

PUBLISHER'S NOTE
Although the advice and information in this book are believed to be
accurate and true at the time of going to press, neither the authors
nor the publisher can accept any legal responsibility or liability for
any errors or omissions that may have been made nor for any
inaccuracies nor for any loss, harm or injury that comes about
from following instructions or advice in this book.

Contents

Introduction

A sweet treat is a pleasure to savour, whether it's the finale to a meal, a simple offering to be shared over morning coffee or afternoon tea, a special reward, or a well-earned treat. Satisfying to make and gratifying to eat, little cakes and bakes are all about pleasure.

WHAT'S IN THE BOOK

This divine collection contains more than 240 recipes for every kind of individual cake portion and is sure to include everybody's favourites. There are bars, squares, slices and brownies of every description, with low-fat and no-bake options included. These recipes range from quick-and-easy fare, such as flapjacks that can be made with minimal ingredients in no time at all, to sophisticated bars with complex flavours and contrasting textures that are topped with drizzled icing, melted chocolate, crunchy crumble or a sprinkling of chopped nuts. Many would make delightful desserts if served with custard, cream or ice cream; for example, try creamy fig and peach squares or apple crumble and custard slices. Wholesome offerings packed

Above: *Bars are perfect for the cake stall and for packing in lunchboxes.*

with nutritious dried fruits, oats and spices that make perfect lunchbox fillers are included too. These chewy bars are guaranteed to satisfy the appetite as well as provide sustaining energy.

A chapter on cakes, scones and muffins follows. There are hearty confections that are suitable for afternoon tea and guaranteed to appeal to traditionalists, such as old-fashioned gingerbread and sticky treacle squares, and also blueberry muffins and daisy cakes, which might win the day with a younger generation. Light and airy sponge drops, moreish madeleines, sweet drop scones and winning combinations of cocoa and fruits, together with a whole range of familiar and appealing flavours make up this chapter.

Pastry makes the most convenient package in which to serve a sweet treat. Made into tarts, éclairs, profiteroles and turnovers, sweet shortcrust, puff, filo and choux pastries can be used to make everyday recipes as well as indulgent offerings to serve at special celebrations. Churros, doughnuts and Chelsea buns are just a few of the sweet breads that are included.

Below: *Morsels of sweet pastry encasing fruity fillings are tasty served with tea.*

Above: *Plain sponge filled with sweet and light cream and a helping of fresh fruit make a mid-afternoon snack.*

For those who like to bake treats that are a little less sweet, a chapter on savoury recipes is included. Scones and muffins flavoured, for example, with cheese, ham and herbs, make fabulous accompaniments to salads, simple omelettes and soups in place of bread rolls, and are delicious for an alternative weekend breakfast. Try cheese and pineapple wholemeal scones for brunch, or ham and potato scones with summer salad.

Finally, a chapter on sweets and candies includes a delightful selection of tried-and-tested recipes that make great gift solutions. Rich chocolate truffles, moulded marzipan fruits, sweet fudge, soft marshmallows and chewy nougat are just a few of the fabulous confections on offer.

BEFORE YOU BEGIN

Many of these little cakes can be made with standard store-cupboard ingredients and none of them are difficult to make. Just a few baking methods are used for the majority, so once you've mastered the techniques, a whole host of recipes will be at your

Right: *Meringues are a fabulous sweet treat – they're low in fat and just large enough to provide a sugary taste.*

fingertips. The most complex method is to make choux pastry for profiteroles and éclairs. Step-by-step photographs show you how to achieve results you can be proud of.

Before beginning, read the recipe through to ensure that you understand every stage. Assemble all of the ingredients just to be doubly sure that you have them all before you begin, and (unless otherwise stated) for best results allow eggs and butter to come to room temperature before using them.

Check that your bakeware is the correct size and in good order, and buy a reliable oven thermometer to test the temperature of your oven, if you are unsure of its accuracy. When possible bake the mixture in the centre of the oven where the heat is more likely to be constant. If you are using a fan-assisted oven, follow the manufacturer's guidelines for baking. Finally, if you are baking more than one item at the same time, swap the positions midway through the baking time to ensure an even distribution of heat. Test to ensure the goods are baked through before removing them from the oven – they should be golden brown on top and have a 'set' appearance. Once out of the oven leave the bakes to go cold on a wire rack before storing them in an airtight container. Most baked goods will taste fresh for up to 3–4 days.

Measuring Ingredients

Cooks with years of experience may not need to measure ingredients, but if you are a beginner or are trying a new recipe for the first time, it is best to follow instructions carefully. Also, measuring ingredients precisely will ensure consistent results. Always use the best quality ingredients that are within their "use-by" date.

1 For liquids measured in pints or litres, use a glass or clear plastic meauring jug (cup). Put it on a flat surface and pour in the liquid. Check that the liquid is level with the marking specified in the recipe.

2 For liquids measured in spoons, pour the liquid into the measuring spoon, to the brim, and then pour it into the mixing bowl. Do not measure it over the mixing bowl in case of spillages.

3 For measuring dry ingredients in a spoon, fill the spoon, scooping up the ingredients. Level the surface with the straight edge of a knife.

4 For measuring dry ingredients by weight, scoop or pour on to the scales, watching the dial and reading carefully. Balance scales give more accurate readings than spring scales.

5 For measuring syrups, set the mixing bowl on the scales and turn the gauge to zero, or make a note of the weight. Pour in the required weight of syrup.

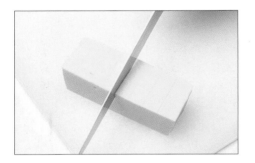

6 For measuring butter, cut with a sharp knife and weigh, or cut off the specified amount following the markings on the wrapping paper.

Making Cookies with the Beating Method

When baking with the beating method, the fat and sugar are beaten together before the eggs and dry ingredients are added. The fat (usually butter) should be soft enough to be beaten so, if necessary, remove it from the refrigerator and leave for at least 30 minutes. For best results, the eggs should be at room temperature too.

1 Put the fat in a bowl and beat with an electric mixer or a wooden spoon until soft and pliable. Add the sugar and beat until the mixture is pale and fluffy. Add the eggs or egg yolks, one at a time, beating well after each addition.

2 Sift in the flour with the salt, raising agent, spices or unsweetened cocoa powder. Beat at low speed just until smoothly combined, or fold in with a large metal spoon. Add any other dry ingredients, beating with a wooden spoon.

3 If the recipe calls for any liquid, add it in small quantities. Add the cake batter to muffin or cupcake cases, or to a lined baking tin (pan). Cake-like batters made by this method are also used as toppings for bars and slices.

Making Cookies with the Rubbing in Method

Many traditional cookies, such as shortbread are made by rubbing the fat, which can be butter, margarine, white vegetable fat or lard, into the flour. The fat should be firm and cool but not straight from the refrigerator, so leave the fat at room temperature before using. Beaten eggs, milk or water may be added to bind the mixture.

1 Sift the flour and salt into a large bowl. Dice the fat and add it to the bowl. Use your fingertips to rub the fat into the flour, lifting each handful as you work to incorporate air. Shake the bowl so that large lumps rise to the surface.

2 Stir in the sugar and any other dry ingredients. Sprinkle the cold liquid evenly over the mixture. Mix lightly with a metal table knife, fork or spoon until the mixture forms lumps. Alternatively, use cold hands.

3 Use one hand to press the lumps together. If it is too dry, add a little more water. If the mixture is too wet, add a little more flour. Incorporate all the ingredients into a ball, then wrap in clear film and chill.

Making Choux Pastry

Light and crispy, choux pastry puffs up during baking to at least double its original size, creating a hollow centre that is perfect for filling with cream. Making choux pastry is a cooking skill that requires confidence, since the stages happen very quickly and need immediate action. However, the results are worth the effort.

1 Sift the flour and salt on to a small sheet of baking parchment. Set aside. Beat the eggs and set aside. Put the butter and water into a heavy pan and heat very gently until the butter has melted.

2 Increase the heat and bring to a rolling boil. Remove from the heat. Add all the flour and beat vigorously with a wooden spoon until the flour is mixed into the liquid. Beat out any lumps.

3 Return the pan to a low heat and beat the mixture vigorously until it begins to form a ball and leave the sides of the pan. This will take about 1 minute.

4 Remove the pan from the heat and leave for 2–3 minutes to cool slightly. Add the beaten egg a little at a time. Beat well until the paste is smooth and the egg has all been incorporated.

5 Spoon walnut-sized quantities on to a greased baking sheet or a baking sheet lined with dampened baking parchment. Alternatively, fill a piping (pastry) bag and pipe lengths of pastry.

6 Bake as directed in the recipe and leave to cool on a wire rack. Use a clean, sharp implement to puncture a hole in the base of each choux bun to let steam escape and to fill with cream.

Fruity Muesli Bars

These fruity muesli bars make an appetizing treat for a takeaway snack.

Makes 10–12
115g/4oz/½ cup butter
75g/3oz/⅓ cup soft light brown sugar
45ml/3 tbsp golden (light corn) syrup

150g/5oz/1¼ cups Swiss-style muesli (granola)
150g/2oz/½ cup rolled oats
5ml/1 tsp ground mixed spice (apple pie spice)
50g/2oz/⅓ cup sultanas (golden raisins)
50g/2oz/½ cup chopped ready-to-eat dried pears

1 Preheat the oven to 180°C/350°F/Gas 4. Lightly grease an 18cm/7in square cake tin (pan).

2 Put the butter, sugar and syrup in a pan and heat gently until melted, stirring.

3 Remove the pan from the heat and add the muesli, rolled oats, spice, sultanas and dried pears. Mix well with a wooden spoon until thoroughly combined.

4 Transfer the mixture to the prepared tin and level the surface, pressing down.

5 Bake for 20–30 minutes, until golden brown. Cool slightly into the tin, then mark into bars using a sharp knife.

6 When firm, remove the muesli bars from the tin and cool on a wire rack.

Variations
• A combination of rolled oats and oatmeal can be used instead of muesli (granola) for a delicious change.
• Try using different dried fruits instead of sultanas (golden raisins) and pears – papaya and mango for a tropical taste, cranberries and apple for a hint of autumn or apricots and dates for a Middle Eastern flavour.

Fruity Breakfast Bars

Instead of buying fruit and cereal bars from the supermarket, try making this quick and easy version – these are much tastier and more nutritious than most of the commercially-made ones. They can be stored in an airtight container for up to four days.

Makes 12
270g/10oz/1¼ cups ready-made apple sauce
115g/4oz/½ cup ready-to-eat dried apricots, chopped

115g/4oz/¾ cup raisins
50g/2oz/¼ cup demerara (raw) sugar
50g/2oz/scant ½ cup sunflower seeds
25g/1oz/2 tbsp sesame seeds
25g/1oz/¼ cup pumpkin seeds
75g/3oz/scant 1 cup rolled oats
75g/3oz/¾ cup self-raising (self-rising) wholemeal (whole-wheat) flour
50g/2oz/⅔ cup desiccated (dry unsweetened shredded) coconut
2 eggs

1 Preheat the oven to 200°C/400°F/Gas 6. Lightly grease a 20cm/8in square shallow baking tin (pan) and line with baking parchment.

2 Put the apple sauce in a large bowl with the apricots, raisins, sugar and the sunflower, sesame and pumpkin seeds and stir together with a wooden spoon until thoroughly mixed.

3 Add the oats, flour, coconut and eggs to the fruit mixture and gently stir together until evenly combined.

4 Turn the mixture into the tin and spread to the edges in an even layer. Bake for about 25 minutes, or until golden and just firm to the touch.

5 Leave to cool in the tin, then lift out on to a board and cut into bars.

Cook's Tip
It's best to sift the flour before adding it to the mixture.

Fruity Breakfast Bars Energy 207kcal/871kJ; Protein 4.9g; Carbohydrate 29.3g, of which sugars 19.2g; Fat 8.7g, of which saturates 3g; Cholesterol 32mg; Calcium 65mg; Fibre 2.8g; Sodium 24mg.
Fruity Muesli Bars Energy 221kcal/927kJ; Protein 3.2g; Carbohydrate 32.1g, of which sugars 17.2g; Fat 9.8g, of which saturates 5.1g; Cholesterol 20mg; Calcium 32mg; Fibre 2g; Sodium 122mg.

Oaty Muesli Slices

Oaty muesli is said to be an excellent anti-aging food, so it makes a great ingredient in these chewy slices. As well as adding flavour, the dried apricots and apples provide an extra boost of the valuable antioxidant vitamin E.

Makes 8
75g/3oz/⅓ cup ready-to-eat dried apricots, chopped
I eating apple, cored and grated
150g/5oz/1¼ cups Swiss-style muesli (granola)
150ml/¼ pint/⅔ cup apple juice
15g/½ oz/1 tbsp soft butter

1 Preheat the oven to 190°C/375°F/Gas 5.

2 Place all the ingredients together in a large bowl and mix well with a wooden spoon until combined.

3 Press the mixture into a 20cm/8in non-stick sandwich tin (layer cake pan) with the back of a wooden spoon and bake for 35–40 minutes, until lightly browned and firm.

4 Using a sharp knife, mark the fruit muesli slice into eight equal-size wedges while it is still hot. Leave to cool in the tin.

Wholewheat Seed Slices

This wholewheat slice contains ingredients that are rich in nutrients, making it a healthy snack to eat.

Makes 7 slices
115g/4oz/1 cup soya flour
115g/4oz/1 cup wholemeal (whole-wheat) flour
115g/4oz/generous 1 cup rolled oats
5cm/2in preserved stem ginger, chopped
25g/1oz/2 tbsp sesame seeds
25g/1oz/¼ cup pumpkin seeds
75g/3oz/scant 1 cup rolled oats
2.5ml/½ tsp ground ginger
2.5ml/½ tsp nutmeg
2.5ml/½ tsp cinnamon
200g/7oz/1½ cups raisins
115g/4oz linseeds
50g/2oz sunflower seeds
50g/2oz sliced almonds
300ml/½ pint soya milk
15ml/1 tbsp malt extract

1 Sift the flours into a large bowl. Tip in any bran left in the sieve (strainer).

2 Add all the dry ingredients, seeds and spices to the flour, and mix well to combine thoroughly. Slowly add the milk and malt extract, stirring well after each addition.

3 Cover the bowl for one hour, leaving the dry ingredients to soak.

4 Preheat the oven to 190°C/370°F/Gas 5. Lightly grease and line a 1lb/500g loaf tin.

5 Spoon the soaked ingredients into the cake tin and bake for up to 1 hour 15 minutes, or until golden. Leave to cool, then remove from the tin and serve cut into bars. Store in an airtight container for up to 7 days.

Sultana and Cinnamon Chewy Bars

These spicy, chewy bars are hard to resist and make a great treat, especially for children and teenagers.

Makes 16
115g/4oz/½ cup butter
25g/1oz/2 tbsp light soft brown sugar
25g/1oz plain toffees
50g/2oz/¼ cup clear honey
175g/6oz/generous 1 cup sultanas (golden raisins)
10ml/2 tsp ground cinnamon
175g/6oz/6 cups crisped rice cereal

1 Lightly grease a shallow rectangular 23 × 28cm/9 × 11in cake tin (pan).

2 Place the butter, sugar, toffees and honey in a pan and heat gently until melted, stirring. Bring to the boil, then remove the pan from the heat.

3 Stir in the sultanas, cinnamon and crisped rice cereal and mix well. Transfer the mixture to the prepared tin and spread the mixture evenly, pressing it down firmly.

4 Leave to cool, then chill until firm. Once firm, cut into bars, remove from the tin and serve. Store the bars in an airtight container in the refrigerator.

> **Cook's Tip**
> *Take care when melting the butter, sugar, toffees and honey and stir constantly to prevent the mixture from catching.*

> **Variation**
> *For an extra-special treat, melt 75g/3oz plain (semisweet) or milk chocolate in a heatproof bowl over a pan of gently simmering water, then spread it over the cold crisped rice cereal mixture. Alternatively, using a teaspoon or a paper piping (pastry) bag, drizzle it decoratively over the mixture. Leave to set for about 1 hour before cutting into bars.*

Oaty Muesli Slices Energy 107kcals/452kJ; Protein 2.3g; Carbohydrate 19.6g; of which sugars 10.9g; Fat, total 2.7g; saturated fat 1.2g; Fibre 1.9g. **Wholewheat Seed Slices** Energy 107kcals/452kJ; Protein 2.3g; Carbohydrate 19.6g; of which sugars 10.9g; Fat, total 2.7g; saturated fat 1.2g; Fibre 1.9g. **Sultana and Cinnamon Chewy Bars** Energy 145kcal/608kJ; Protein 1.1g; Carbohydrate 22.2g, of which sugars 12.8g; Fat 6.4g, of which saturates 3.9g; Cholesterol 16mg; Calcium 60mg; Fibre 0.3g; Sodium 122mg.

Spicy Fruit Slices

A double-layered sweet cookie in which the topping combines dried fruit with grated carrot to keep it moist. A truly indulgent teatime treat.

Makes 12–16
90g/3¹/₂oz/7 tbsp butter
75g/3oz/scant ¹/₂ cup caster (superfine) sugar
1 egg yolk
115g/4oz/1 cup plain (all-purpose) flour
30ml/2 tbsp self-raising (self-rising) flour
30ml/2 tbsp desiccated (dry unsweetened shredded) coconut
icing (confectioners') sugar, for dusting

For the topping
30ml/2 tbsp ready-to-eat prunes, chopped
30ml/2 tbsp sultanas (golden raisins)
50g/2oz/¹/₂ cup ready-to-eat dried pears, chopped
25g/1oz/¹/₄ cup walnuts, chopped
75g/3oz/³/₄ cup self-raising (self-rising) flour
5ml/1 tsp ground cinnamon
2.5ml/¹/₂ tsp ground ginger
175g/6oz/generous 1 cup grated carrots
1 egg, beaten
75ml/5 tbsp vegetable oil
2.5ml/¹/₂ tsp bicarbonate of soda (baking soda)
90g/3¹/₂oz/scant ¹/₂ cup dark muscovado (molasses) sugar

1 Preheat the oven to 180°C/350°F/Gas 4. Line a 28 × 18cm/ 11 × 7in shallow baking tin (pan) with baking parchment.

2 In a large mixing bowl, beat together the butter, sugar and egg yolk until smooth and creamy.

3 Stir in the plain flour, self-raising flour and coconut and mix together well. Press into the base of the prepared tin, using your fingers to spread the dough evenly.

4 Bake for about 15 minutes, or until firm to the touch and light golden brown.

5 To make the topping, mix together all the ingredients and spread over the cooked base. Bake for about 35 minutes, or until firm. Cool completely in the tin before cutting into bars or squares. Dust with icing sugar.

Lemon-iced Date Slices

Lemon-flavoured icing tops these scrumptious, low-fat bars, which are full of succulent fruit and crunchy seeds – the perfect mid-morning pick-me-up with a cup of decaf.

Makes 12–16
175g/6oz/³/₄ cup light muscovado (brown) sugar
175g/6oz/1 cup ready-to-eat dried dates, chopped
115g/4oz/1 cup self-raising (self-rising) flour
50g/2oz/¹/₂ cup muesli (granola)
30ml/2 tbsp sunflower seeds
15ml/1 tbsp poppy seeds
30ml/2 tbsp sultanas (golden raisins)
150ml/¹/₄ pint/²/₃ cup natural (plain) low-fat yogurt
1 egg, beaten
200g/7oz/1³/₄ cups icing (confectioners') sugar, sifted
lemon juice
15–30ml/1–2 tbsp pumpkin seeds

1 Preheat the oven to 180°C/350°F/Gas 4. Line a 28 × 18cm/ 11 × 7in shallow baking tin (pan) with baking parchment.

2 In a bowl mix together the muscovado sugar, dates, flour, muesli, sunflower seeds, poppy seeds, sultanas, yogurt and beaten egg until thoroughly combined.

3 Spread in the tin and bake for about 25 minutes, until golden brown. Leave to cool.

4 To make the topping, put the icing sugar in a bowl and stir in just enough lemon juice to make a spreading consistency.

5 Spread the icing evenly over the baked date mixture and sprinkle generously with pumpkin seeds. Leave to set before cutting into squares or bars.

> **Variation**
> Pumpkin seeds can sometimes be rather fibrous, so if you prefer, you could substitute other seeds, such as sesame, or flaked (sliced) almonds.

Spicy Fruit Slices Energy 228kcal/955kJ; Protein 2.7g; Carbohydrate 29.7g, of which sugars 13.9g; Fat 11.8g, of which saturates 3.8g; Cholesterol 25mg; Calcium 34mg; Fibre 1.1g; Sodium 55mg.
Lemon-iced Date Slices Energy 211kcal/893kJ; Protein 3.6g; Carbohydrate 43.6g, of which sugars 35.5g; Fat 3.6g, of which saturates 0.5g; Cholesterol 12mg; Calcium 56mg; Fibre 1.3g; Sodium 18mg.

Date and Orange Slices

These tempting wholesome slices make a tasty treat.

Makes 16
350g/12oz/2⅓ cups stoned
    (pitted) dried dates, chopped
200ml/7fl oz/scant 1 cup freshly
    squeezed orange juice
finely grated rind of 1 orange
115g/4oz/1 cup plain
    (all-purpose) wholemeal
    (whole-wheat) flour

175g/6oz/1¾ cups rolled oats
50g/2oz/½ cup fine oatmeal
pinch of salt
175g/6oz/¾ cup butter
75g/3oz/⅓ cup soft light
    brown sugar
10ml/2 tsp ground cinnamon

1 Preheat the oven to 190°C/375°F/Gas 5. Lightly grease an 18 × 28cm/7 × 11in non-stick cake tin (pan).

2 Put the dates in a pan with the orange juice. Cover, bring to the boil and simmer for 5 minutes, stirring occasionally. Stir in the orange rind and set aside to cool completely.

3 Put the flour, oats, oatmeal and salt in a bowl and mix together. Lightly rub in the butter.

4 Stir in the sugar and cinnamon. Press half the oat mixture over the base of the prepared tin. Spread the date mixture on top and sprinkle the remaining oat mixture evenly over the dates to cover them completely. Press down lightly.

5 Bake for about 30 minutes, until golden brown.

6 Leave to cool slightly in the tin and mark into 16 bars, using a sharp knife. When firm, remove from the tin and cool completely on a wire rack.

> **Variation**
> *Ready-to-eat dried apricots or prunes used in place of the dates in this recipe make equally tasty slices.*

Tropical Fruit Slices

Densely packed dried exotic fruits make the filling for these deliciously moist bars. Vary the tropical fruits in different areas of the baking tray for differently-tasting snacks from the same batch.

Makes 12–16
175g/6oz/1½ cups plain
    (all-purpose) flour, plus extra
    for dusting
90g/3½oz/generous ½ cup white
    vegetable fat (shortening)
60ml/4 tbsp apricot jam or
    ready-made apricot glaze

For the filling
115g/4oz/½ cup unsalted
    butter, softened
115g/4oz/generous ½ cup caster
    (superfine) sugar
1 egg, beaten
25g/1oz/¼ cup ground almonds
25g/1oz/2½ tbsp ground rice
300g/11oz/scant 2 cups
    ready-to-eat mixed dried
    tropical fruits, chopped

1 Preheat the oven to 180°C/350°F/Gas 4. Lightly grease a 28 × 18cm/11 × 7in tin (pan).

2 Sift the flour into a bowl and add the vegetable fat. Cut it into the flour, then rub in with your fingertips until the mixture resembles fine breadcrumbs. Gradually add just enough water to mix to a firm dough.

3 Roll out to a rectangle on a lightly floured surface and use to line the base of the prepared tin, trimming off any excess. If using apricot jam, pass it through a sieve (strainer) and then spread 30ml/2 tbsp of the jam or glaze over the dough base.

4 To make the filling, beat together the butter and sugar in a bowl until light and creamy. Beat in the egg, then stir in the ground almonds, ground rice and mixed fruits. Spread the mixture evenly in the tin.

5 Bake for about 35 minutes, until firm and golden. Remove from the oven and brush with the remaining apricot jam or glaze. Leave to cool completely in the tin before cutting into bars.

Tropical Fruit Slices Energy 220kcal/921kJ; Protein 2.7g; Carbohydrate 26.9g, of which sugars 17.3g; Fat 12g, of which saturates 6g; Cholesterol 28mg; Calcium 41mg; Fibre 1.7g; Sodium 98mg.
Date and Orange Slices Energy 197kcals/829KJ; Protein 4.02g; Fat 5.76g of which saturates 1.48g; Carbohydrate 34g; Fibre 1.76g; Sodium 0.08g.

Spiced Raisin Squares

Moist and aromatic, these tasty fruit bars make great any-time-of day snacks and are the perfect choice for a summer picnic basket.

Makes 30

115g/4oz/1 cup plain
  (all-purpose) flour
7.5ml/1½ tsp baking powder
5ml/1 tsp ground cinnamon
2.5ml/½ tsp freshly grated
  nutmeg
1.5ml/¼ tsp ground cloves
1.5ml/¼ tsp ground allspsice
200g/7oz/1½ cups raisins
115g/4oz/½ cup butter,
  at room temperature
90g/3½oz/½ cup caster
  (superfine) sugar
2 eggs
165g/5½oz/scant ½ cup black
  treacle (molasses)
50g/2oz/½ cup walnuts, chopped

1 Preheat the oven to 180°C/350°F/Gas 4. Line a 33 × 23cm/13 × 9in tin (pan) with baking parchment and lightly grease the surface.

2 Sift together the flour, baking powder, cinnamon, nutmeg, cloves and allspice into a bowl.

3 Place the raisins in another bowl and toss with a few tablespoons of the flour mixture.

4 In another bowl, beat the butter and sugar together until light and fluffy. Beat in the eggs, one at a time, then the treacle. Stir in the flour mixture, raisins and walnuts.

5 Spoon the mixture into the prepared tin and spread evenly with the back of the spoon. Bake for 15–18 minutes, until just firm to the touch. Leave to cool completely in the tin before cutting into bars or squares.

Variation
You could also make these spicy bars with chopped dried figs instead of raisins and substitute pistachio nuts or hazelnuts for the walnuts.

Sticky Date and Apple Squares

Combining fresh and dried fruits gives these bars a wonderful texture and fabulous flavour – truly a winning partnership.

Makes 16

115g/4oz/½ cup butter
50g/2oz/4 tbsp soft dark
  brown sugar
50g/2oz/4 tbsp golden (light
  corn) syrup
115g/4oz/⅔ cup dried dates,
  chopped
115g/4oz/1⅓ cup rolled oats
115g/4oz/1 cup wholemeal
  (whole-wheat) self-raising
  (self-rising) flour
2 eating apples, peeled, cored
  and grated
5–10ml/1–2 tsp lemon juice
walnut halves, to decorate

1 Preheat the oven to 190°C/375°F/Gas 5. Line an 18–20cm/7–8in square or rectangle loose-based cake tin (pan).

2 Put the butter, sugar and golden syrup into a large pan and melt over a low heat, stirring occasionally, until smooth and thoroughly combined.

3 Add the dates and cook until they have softened. Gradually work in the oats, flour, apples and lemon juice until well mixed.

4 Spoon into the prepared tin and spread out evenly. Top with the walnut halves.

5 Bake for 30 minutes, then reduce the temperature to 160°C/325°F/Gas 3 and bake for 10–12 minutes more, until firm to the touch and golden.

6 Cut into squares or bars while still warm if you are going to eat them straightaway, or wrap in foil when nearly cold and keep for 1–2 days before eating.

Variation
Although not quite so sticky, these bars would also be delicious made with dried blueberries instead of dates.

Spiced Raisin Squares Energy 84kcal/353kJ; Protein 1.2g; Carbohydrate 11.4g, of which sugars 8.4g; Fat 4.1g, of which saturates 1.8g; Cholesterol 19mg; Calcium 43mg; Fibre 0.3g; Sodium 37mg.
Sticky Date and Apple Squares Energy 150kcal/631kJ; Protein 1.9g; Carbohydrate 22g, of which sugars 11.3g; Fat 6.7g, of which saturates 3.8g; Cholesterol 15mg; Calcium 21mg; Fibre 1.1g; Sodium 56mg.

Chewy Orange Flapjacks

Flapjacks are about the easiest cookies to make and, with a little guidance, can be knocked up in minutes by even the youngest cooks. This chunky, chewy version is flavoured with orange rind, but you can substitute other fruits such as a handful of raisins, chopped prunes or apricots.

Makes 18

250g/9oz/generous 1 cup unsalted (sweet) butter
finely grated rind of 1 large orange
225g/8oz/⅔ cup golden (light corn) syrup
75g/3oz/⅓ cup light muscovado (brown) sugar
375g/13oz/3¾ cups rolled oats

1 Preheat the oven to 180°C/350°F/Gas 4. Line the base and sides of a 28 × 20cm/11 × 8in shallow baking tin (pan) with baking parchment.

2 Put the butter, orange rind, syrup and sugar in a large pan and heat gently until the butter has melted.

3 Add the oats to the pan and stir to mix thoroughly. Transfer the mixture to the tin and spread into the corners in an even layer.

4 Bake for 15–20 minutes, until just beginning to colour around the edges. (The mixture will still be very soft but will harden as it cools.) Leave to cool in the tin.

5 Lift the flapjack out of the tin in one piece and cut into fingers.

Cook's Tips
• Flapjack is the British name for this traditional British cookie – in the United States, the term refers to pancakes. But whether you call them flapjacks or energy bars, these oaty treats are always delicious.
• Don't be tempted to overcook flapjacks; they'll turn crisp and dry and lose their lovely chewy texture.

Wholemeal Flapjacks

Perfect for picnics and packed lunches, these flapjacks are really crisp and crunchy.

Makes 16

115g/4oz/½ cup butter
60ml/4 tbsp rice syrup
50g/2oz/½ cup wholemeal (whole-wheat) flour
225g/8oz/2¼ cups rolled oats
50g/2oz/½ cup pine nuts

1 Preheat the oven to 180°C/350°F/Gas 4. Line a 20cm/8in shallow baking tin (pan) with oiled foil.

2 Melt the butter and rice syrup in a small pan over a low heat.

3 Add the flour, rolled oats and pine nuts and stir well until thoroughly combined.

4 Turn the mixture into the tin and pat it out evenly with the back of a spoon.

5 Bake for 25–30 minutes, until the flapjacks are lightly browned and crisp. Mark into squares while still warm.

6 Cool slightly, then lift them out of the tin and cool on a wire rack.

Cook's Tip
Rice syrup is starch- rather than sugar-based and may be available from some large supermarkets. It is also found in Japanese food stores, sometimes labelled mizuame or mizu-ame. However, this is not always made from rice and may be based on other starches from vegetable sources, such as sweet potatoes. Rice syrup is not as liquid as sugar syrups but a slightly smaller quantity of golden (light corn) syrup may be used as an alternative if you cannot find it. Whatever syrup you use, do not let the mixture boil or the flapjacks will be tacky rather than crisp.

Chewy Orange Flapjacks Energy 241kcal/1007kJ; Protein 2.7g; Carbohydrate 29.5g, of which sugars 14.3g; Fat 13.2g, of which saturates 7.2g; Cholesterol 30mg; Calcium 18mg; Fibre 1.4g; Sodium 125mg.
Wholemeal Flapjacks Energy 122kcals/513kJ; Carbohydrate 14.3g of which sugars 1.45g; Fat, 6.4g of which saturates1.2g; Fibre 1.35g Sodium 54.1mg.

Chewy Flapjacks

Flapjacks are popular with adults and children alike and they are so quick and easy to make. They are always based on rolled oats, but this standard recipe is very adaptable and all manner of variations are possible.

Makes 12
175g/6oz/¾ cup unsalted (sweet) butter
50g/2oz/¼ cup caster (superfine) sugar
150g/5oz/generous ⅓ cup golden (light corn) syrup
250g/9oz/2¾ cups rolled oats

1 Preheat the oven to 180°C/350°F/Gas 4. Line the base and sides of a 20cm/8in square cake tin (pan) with baking parchment.

2 Put the butter, sugar and golden syrup in a pan and melt over a low heat, stirring occasionally, until smooth and thoroughly combined.

3 Add the oats and stir until all the ingredients are combined. Turn the mixture into the tin and level the surface.

4 Bake the flapjacks for 15–20 minutes, until just beginning to turn golden. Leave to cool slightly in the tin, then cut into bars or squares, carefully remove from the tin and leave on a wire rack to cool completely. Store in an airtight container for 3–4 days.

Cook's Tips
• *For fruity flapjacks, stir in 50g/2oz/¼ cup finely chopped ready-to-eat dried apricots, peaches, apples or mangoes or 50g/2oz/scant ½ cup sultanas (golden raisins) with the rolled oats in step 3.*
• *Try stirring in 50g/2oz/⅔ cup desiccated (dry unsweetened shredded) coconut with the oats.*
• *For a decadent treat, melt 75g/3oz plain (semisweet) or milk chocolate in a heatproof bowl set over a pan of gently simmering water. Remove from the heat and dip the cooled flapjacks in the chocolate to half cover.*

Microwave Sticky Lemon Flapjacks

Flavoured with tangy lemon juice and grated rind, these thick and chewy flapjacks are simply scrumptious. Cooked in the microwave, they're made in minutes.

Makes 8
75g/3oz/6 tbsp butter, diced
60ml/4 tbsp golden (light corn) syrup
115g/4oz/½ cup demerara (raw) sugar
175g/6oz/1¾ cups rolled oats
juice and finely grated rind of ½ lemon

1 Put the butter, syrup and sugar in a microwave bowl. Microwave on medium (50 per cent) power for 3–4 minutes, stirring halfway through.

2 Stir in the oats, lemon rind and juice. Spoon the mixture into a 20cm/8in microwave flan dish and spread out.

3 Cook on full (100 per cent) power for 3–3½ minutes, or until bubbling all over. Remove from the oven and mark into wedges when warm. Leave to cool in the dish.

Cranberry Oat Flapjacks

Here's a real teatime treat for everybody to enjoy! With minimal ingredients it's quick to make and doesn't take long to bake in the oven, too.

Makes 14
150g/5oz/1½ cups rolled oats
115g/4oz/½ cup demerara sugar
75g/3oz/½ cup dried cranberries
115g/4oz/½ cup butter

1 Preheat the oven to 190°C/375°F/Gas 5. Grease a shallow 28 × 18cm/11 × 7in tin (pan).

2 Stir the rolled oats, demerara sugar and dried cranberries together in a bowl.

3 In a small pan, melt the butter over a low heat. Pour the melted butter on to the oat mixture and stir thoroughly until completely combined.

4 Press the oat and cranberry mixture into the prepared tin using the back of a wooden spoon. Bake in the oven for 15–20 minutes, until pale golden brown.

5 Remove the flapjack from the oven and mark into 14 bars, then leave to cool for 5 minutes, in the tin. Remove the bars and place on a wire rack to cool completely. Store for up to 5 days in an airtight container.

Cook's Tip
Dried cranberries, also known as craisins, are a relatively new product, available from larger supermarkets. They have a sweet yet slightly tart flavour and their bright red colour will add visual appeal. They can be used to replace more usual dried fruits, such as sultanas (golden raisins).

Chewy Flapjacks Energy 241kcal/1008kJ; Protein 2.7g; Carbohydrate 29.5g, of which sugars 14.3g; Fat 13.2g, of which saturates 7.2g; Cholesterol 30mg; Calcium 18mg; Fibre 1.4g; Sodium 125mg. **Microwave Sticky Lemon Flapjacks** Energy 237kcal/995kJ; Protein 2.9g; Carbohydrate 36.9g, of which sugars 21g; Fat 9.6g, of which saturates 4.9g; Cholesterol 20mg; Calcium 23mg; Fibre 1.5g; Sodium 85mg. **Cranberry Oat Flapjacks** Energy 145kcal/607kJ; Protein 1.6g; Carbohydrate 18.4g, of which sugars 10.6g; Fat 7.7g, of which saturates 4.3g; Cholesterol 18mg; Calcium 16mg; Fibre 1.1g; Sodium 55mg.

Granola Bars

A gloriously dense fruity, nutty and oaty mixture, packed with goodness and delicious too, these bars are an ideal snack and perfect to pack for a school lunch.

Makes 12
175g/6oz/³/₄ cup unsalted
  butter, diced
150g/5oz/²/₃ cup clear honey
250g/9oz/generous 1 cup
  demerara (raw) sugar
350g/12oz/3 cups jumbo oats
5ml/1 tsp ground cinnamon
75g/3oz/³/₄ cup pecan nut halves
75g/3oz/generous ¹/₂ cup raisins
75g/3oz/¹/₃ cup ready-to-eat
  dried papaya, chopped
75g/3oz/¹/₃ cup ready-to-eat
  dried apricots, chopped
50g/2oz/¹/₂ cup pumpkin seeds
50g/2oz/scant ¹/₂ cup sunflower
  seeds
50g/2oz/¹/₄ cup sesame seeds
50g/2oz/¹/₂ cup ground almonds

1 Preheat the oven to 190°C/375°F/Gas 5. Line a 23cm/9in square cake tin (pan) with baking parchment.

2 Put the butter and honey in a large heavy pan and heat gently until the butter has melted and the mixture is completely smooth.

3 Add the demerara sugar to the pan and heat very gently, stirring constantly, until the sugar has completely dissolved. Bring the butter mixture to the boil and continue to boil for 1–2 minutes, stirring the mixture constantly until it has formed a smooth caramel sauce.

4 Add the remaining ingredients and mix together. Transfer the mixture to the tin and press down with a spoon. Bake for 15 minutes, until the edges turn brown.

5 Leave to cool, then chill for 1–2 hours. Turn out of the tin, peel off the parchment and cut into bars.

Variation
You can use other dried fruits, such as mango and pear.

Apricot and Pecan Flapjacks

A tried-and-tested favourite made even more delicious by the addition of maple syrup, fruit and nuts. This is a real energy booster at any time of day – great for kids and adults alike.

Makes 10
150g/5oz/²/₃ cup unsalted
  (sweet) butter, diced
150g/5oz/²/₃ cup light
  muscovado (brown) sugar
30ml/2 tbsp maple syrup
200g/7oz/2 cups rolled oats
50g/2oz/¹/₂ cup pecan
  nuts, chopped
50g/2oz/¹/₄ cup ready-to-eat
  dried apricots, chopped

1 Preheat the oven to 160°C/325°F/Gas 3. Lightly grease an 18cm/7in square shallow baking tin (pan).

2 Put the butter, sugar and maple syrup in a large heavy pan and heat gently, stirring occasionally, until the butter has melted. Remove from the heat and stir in the oats, nuts and apricots until thoroughly combined.

3 Spread evenly in the prepared tin and, using a knife, score the mixture into ten bars. Bake for about 25–30 minutes, or until golden.

4 Remove from the oven and cut through the scored lines. Leave until completely cold before removing from the tin.

Cook's Tip
Make sure that you stir the syrup mixture quite frequently to prevent it from sticking on the base of the pan.

Variations
• You can substitute walnuts for the pecan nuts, if you like, although the nutty flavour won't be so intense.
• Try using different dried fruits instead of the apricots. Let children choose their own.

Granola Bars Energy 522kcal/2189kJ; Protein 8.4g; Carbohydrate 63.8g, of which sugars 40.9g; Fat 27.7g, of which saturates 8.9g; Cholesterol 31mg; Calcium 93mg; Fibre 4.3g; Sodium 108mg.
Apricot and Pecan Flapjacks Energy 240kcal/1000kJ; Protein 3.2g; Carbohydrate 18.3g, of which sugars 3.7g; Fat 17.6g, of which saturates 8.1g; Cholesterol 32mg; Calcium 21mg; Fibre 1.9g; Sodium 98mg.

Spiced Almond Slices

Traditionally made for Christmas, these spicy slices are rich and flavourful.

Makes 36 slices
125g/4¼oz/generous½ cup butter, diced, plus extra for greasing
breadcrumbs, for sprinkling
250g/9oz/2¼ cups plain (all-purpose) flour, plus extra for dusting
2.5ml/½tsp baking powder
2.5ml/½tsp ground nutmeg
7.5ml/1½ tsp ground cinnamon
2.5ml/½ tsp ground cardamom
2.5ml/½ tsp ground allspice
pinch of salt
1.5ml/¼ tsp crushed aniseed
150g/5oz/⅔ cup muscovado (molasses) sugar
60ml/4 tbsp milk, plus extra for brushing
400g/14oz almond paste
1 small (US medium) egg
72 split blanched almonds, to decorate

1 Preheat the oven to 180°C/350°F/Gas 4. Grease a shallow 23cm/9in square baking tin (pan) with butter. Sprinkle with breadcrumbs to coat, shake out the excess.

2 Sift the flour with the baking powder, spices and salt into a bowl. Stir in the aniseed and sugar.

3 Rub in the butter, add a little milk, then knead together until a smooth and elastic ball of dough forms.

4 Halve the dough. Roll out half on a lightly floured surface slightly larger than the baking tin. Use to line the tin, easing the dough up the sides and letting it overhang the rim. Roll out the second ball to fit the tin exactly.

5 Mix the almond paste with the egg in a bowl. Spread this over the dough with dampened fingers. Cover the paste with the second piece of dough, pressing the edges to seal. Trim off any overhanging dough. Brush the top with milk and decorate with the almonds in neat rows. Prick holes between the nuts.

6 Bake for 50 minutes, gently flattening any bubbles with the back of a spoon after 30 minutes. Remove from the oven, cover with foil and leave to cool in the tin. Cut into slices.

Apple Crumble and Custard Slices

These luscious apple slices are easy to make using ready-made sweet pastry and custard. Just think, all the ingredients of one of the world's most popular desserts – in a slice.

Makes 16
350g/12oz ready-made sweet pastry dough
1 large cooking apple, about 250g/9oz
30ml/2 tbsp caster (superfine) sugar
60ml/4 tbsp ready-made thick custard

For the crumble topping
115g/4oz/1 cup plain (all-purpose) flour
2.5ml/½ tsp ground cinnamon
60ml/4 tbsp sugar
90g/3½oz/7 tbsp unsalted butter, melted

1 Preheat the oven to 190°C/375°F/Gas 5. Lightly grease a 28 × 18cm/11 × 7in shallow cake tin (pan)

2 Roll out the dough and use to line the base of the tin. Prick the dough with a fork, line with foil and baking beans and bake blind for about 10–15 minutes. Remove the foil and baking beans and return the pastry to the oven for another 5 minutes, until cooked and golden brown.

3 Meanwhile, peel, core and chop the apple. Place in a pan with the sugar. Heat gently until the sugar dissolves, then cover with a lid and cook gently for 5–7 minutes, until a thick purée is formed. Beat with a wooden spoon and set aside to cool.

4 Mix the cold apple with the custard. Spread over the pastry base in an even layer.

5 To make the crumble topping, put the flour, cinnamon and sugar into a bowl and pour over the melted butter. Stir thoroughly until the mixture forms small clumps. Sprinkle the crumble over the filling.

6 Return to the oven and bake for about 10–15 minutes, until the crumble topping is cooked and golden brown. Leave to cool in the tin, then slice into bars to serve.

Spiced Almond Slices Energy 126kcal/527kJ; Protein 2.2g; Carbohydrate 16.2g, of which sugars 10.6g; Fat 6.3g, of which saturates 2.1g; Cholesterol 12.7mg; Calcium 0.6mg; Fibre 0.6g; Sodium 25mg.
Apple Crumble and Custard Slices Energy 196kcal/822kJ; Protein 2.1g; Carbohydrate 23.7g, of which sugars 8.1g; Fat 11g, of which saturates 4.9g; Cholesterol 15mg; Calcium 37mg; Fibre 0.9g; Sodium 124mg.

Creamy Fig and Peach Squares

A sweet cream cheese and dried fruit filling with a hint of mint makes these squares really special. They are ideal for quietening hunger pangs after school or work.

Makes 24
350g/12oz/3 cups plain
    (all-purpose) flour, plus extra
    for dusting
200g/7oz/scant 1 cup unsalted
    (sweet) butter, diced
1 egg, beaten
caster (superfine) sugar,
    for sprinkling

For the filling
500g/1¼lb/2½ cups ricotta
    cheese
115g/4oz/generous ½ cup
    caster (superfine) sugar
5ml/1 tsp finely chopped
    fresh mint
50g/2oz/⅓ cup ready-to-eat dried
    figs, chopped
50g/2oz/¼ cup ready-to-eat dried
    peaches, chopped

1 Preheat the oven to 190°C/375°F/Gas 5. Lightly grease a 33 × 23cm/13 × 9in Swiss roll tin (jelly roll pan) or shallow cake tin (pan).

2 Put the flour and butter into a bowl. Rub in the butter with your fingertips until the mixture resembles fine breadcrumbs. Add the egg and enough water to mix to a firm but not sticky dough.

3 Divide the dough into two and roll out one piece on a lightly floured surface to fit the base of the prepared tin. Place in the tin and trim.

4 To make the filling, put all the ingredients in a bowl and mix together. Spread over the pastry base.

5 Roll out the remaining dough and place on top of the filling. Prick lightly all over with a fork then sprinkle with caster sugar.

6 Bake for about 30 minutes, until light golden brown. Remove from the oven and sprinkle more caster sugar thickly over the top. Cool and cut into slices to serve.

Apricot Specials

These attractive bars taste great with tea, coffee or a cold drink and fit the bill perfectly whenever you need a nutritious snack. They're surprisingly easy to make, too.

Makes 12
90g/3½oz/generous ⅓ cup soft
    light brown sugar
75g/3oz/¾ cup plain
    (all-purpose) flour
75g/3oz/6 tbsp unsalted
    butter, chilled and diced

For the topping
150g/5oz/generous ½ cup
    ready-to-eat dried apricots
250ml/8fl oz/1 cup water
grated rind of 1 lemon
55g/2½oz/5 tbsp caster
    (superfine) sugar
10ml/2 tsp cornflour (cornstarch)
50g/2oz/½ cup chopped walnuts

1 Preheat the oven to 180°C/350°F/Gas 4.

2 In a bowl, combine the brown sugar and flour. Rub in the butter with your fingertips until the mixture resembles coarse breadcrumbs.

3 Spoon the flour and butter mixture into a 20cm/8in square baking tin (pan) and level the surface by pressing down with the back of a spoon. Bake for 15 minutes, until just set. Remove from the oven but leave the oven switched on.

4 To make the topping, put the apricots into a pan and pour in the measured water. Bring to the boil, then lower the heat and simmer for about 10 minutes, until soft. Strain, reserving the cooking liquid. Chop the apricots.

5 Return the apricots to the pan and add the lemon rind, caster sugar, cornflour, and 60ml/4 tbsp of the soaking liquid. Cook for 1 minute.

6 Cool slightly before spreading the topping over the base. Sprinkle over the walnuts and continue baking for 20 minutes more. Leave to cool in the tin before cutting into bars.

Creamy Fig and Peach Squares Energy 179kcal/747kJ; Protein 3.8g; Carbohydrate 18.8g, of which sugars 7.7g; Fat 10.3g, of which saturates 6.3g; Cholesterol 34mg; Calcium 32mg; Fibre 0.7g; Sodium 56mg. **Apricot Specials** Energy 169kcal/711kJ; Protein 1.8g; Carbohydrate 23.9g, of which sugars 18.3g; Fat 8.1g, of which saturates 3.5g; Cholesterol 13mg; Calcium 30mg; Fibre 1.1g; Sodium 41mg.

Banana Gingerbread Slices

Bananas make this spicy bake delightfully moist. The flavour develops on keeping, so store the gingerbread for a few days before cutting into slices, if possible.

Makes 20 slices
275g/10oz/2½ cups plain (all-purpose) flour
5ml/1 tsp bicarbonate of soda (baking soda)
20ml/4 tsp ground ginger
10ml/2 tsp mixed spice (apple pie spice)
115g/4oz/⅔ cup soft light brown sugar
60ml/4 tbsp sunflower oil
30ml/2 tbsp black treacle (molasses)
30ml/2 tbsp malt extract
2 eggs
60ml/4 tbsp orange juice
3 ripe bananas
115g/4oz/⅔ cup raisins or sultanas (golden raisins)

1 Preheat the oven to 180°C/350°F/Gas 4. Lightly grease and line a 28 × 18cm/11 × 7in shallow baking tin (pan).

2 Sift the flour, bicarbonate of soda and spices into a mixing bowl. Place the sugar in the sieve (strainer) over the bowl, add some of the flour mixture and rub through with a spoon.

3 Make a well in the centre of the dry ingredients. Add the oil, treacle, malt extract, eggs and juice. Mix thoroughly.

4 Mash the bananas on a plate. Add the raisins or sultanas to the gingerbread mixture, then mix in the mashed bananas.

5 Scrape the mixture into the prepared baking tin. Bake for about 35–40 minutes, or until the centre of the gingerbread springs back when lightly pressed.

6 Leave to cool for 5 minutes, then turn out on to a wire rack to cool completely. Cut into 20 slices to serve.

Cook's Tip
If your brown sugar is lumpy, mix it with a little flour and it will be easier to sift.

Blueberry Streusel Slices

The delicious melt-in-the-mouth crumbly topping on this fruity slice is packed with flavour – irresistible.

Makes about 30 slices
225g/8oz shortcrust pastry dough
50g/2oz/½ cup plain (all-purpose) flour, plus extra for dusting
1.25ml/¼ tsp baking powder
40g/1½oz/3 tbsp butter
25g/1oz/½ cup fresh white breadcrumbs
50g/2oz/⅓ cup soft light brown sugar
pinch of salt
50g/2oz/½ cup flaked (sliced) or chopped almonds
30ml/4 tbsp blackberry jelly
115g/4oz blueberries, fresh or frozen

1 Preheat the oven to 180°C/350°F/Gas 4. Lightly grease an 18 × 28cm/7 × 11in Swiss roll tin (jelly roll pan).

2 Roll out the dough on a lightly floured surface to fit the base and side of the tin. Prick the base all over with a fork.

3 Rub together the flour, baking powder, butter, breadcrumbs, sugar and salt until really crumbly, then mix in the almonds.

4 Spread the dough with the jelly, sprinkle with the blueberries, then cover evenly with the streusel topping, pressing down lightly.

5 Bake for 30–40 minutes, reducing the temperature after 20 minutes to 170°C/325°F/Gas 3.

6 Remove from the oven when golden on the top and the pastry is cooked through. Cut into slices while still hot, then leave to cool.

Cook's Tip
For best results when using frozen blueberries, leave them to thaw completely before cooking.

Banana Gingerbread Slices Energy 133kcal/563kJ; Protein 2.3g; Carbohydrate 25.9g, of which sugars 15.2g; Fat 3g, of which saturates 0.5g; Cholesterol 19mg; Calcium 37mg; Fibre 0.7g; Sodium 18mg.
Blueberry Streusel Slice: Energy 74kcal/309kJ; Protein 1.1g; Carbohydrate 8.5g, of which sugars 3g; Fat 4.2g, of which saturates 1.4g; Cholesterol 4mg; Calcium 15mg; Fibre 0.4g; Sodium 45mg.

Old-fashioned Gingerbread

Adding vinegar to the milk when making gingerbread is an old-fashioned trick. The extra acidity activates the two raising agents and this guarantees a lovely light result, without affecting the flavour.

Serves 8–10
15ml/1 tbsp vinegar
175ml/6fl oz/¾ cup milk
175g/6oz/1½ cups plain
 (all-purpose) flour
10ml/2 tsp baking powder
1.5ml/¼ tsp bicarbonate of soda
 (baking soda)

pinch of salt
10ml/2 tsp ground ginger
5ml/1 tsp ground cinnamon
1.5ml/¼ tsp ground cloves
115g/4oz/½ cup butter, at
 room temperature
115g/4oz/generous ½ cup caster
 (superfine) sugar
1 egg, at room temperature
175ml/6fl oz/¾ cup black
 treacle (molasses)
whipped cream, for serving
chopped preserved stem ginger,
 for decorating

1 Preheat the oven to 180°C/350°F/Gas 4. Line an 20cm/8in square cake tin (pan) with baking parchment and grease the parchment and the sides of the pan.

2 Add the vinegar to the milk in a small bowl and set aside. It will curdle.

3 In another mixing bowl, sift all the dry ingredients, except the caster sugar, together three times and set aside.

4 In a bowl, beat together the butter and sugar until light and fluffy. Beat in the egg until well combined. Stir in the black treacle, mixing well.

5 Fold in the dry ingredients in four batches, alternating with the milk. Mix only enough to blend.

6 Pour the mixture into the prepared tin and bake for 45–50 minutes, until firm to the touch. Cut the gingerbread into squares and serve warm with whipped cream. Decorate with preserved stem ginger.

Sticky Marmalade Squares

These baked treats have a plain lower layer supporting a scrumptious nutty upper layer flavoured with orange and chunky marmalade. Cut into squares or bars – whichever you prefer.

Makes 24
350g/12oz/3 cups plain
 (all-purpose) flour
200g/7oz/scant 1 cup unsalted
 butter, diced

150g/5oz/⅔ cup light muscovado
 (brown) sugar
2.5ml/½ tsp bicarbonate of soda
 (baking soda)
1 egg, beaten
120ml/4fl oz/½ cup single
 (light) cream
50g/2oz/½ cup pecan
 nuts, chopped
50g/2oz/⅓ cup mixed
 (candied) peel
90ml/6 tbsp chunky marmalade
15–30ml/1–2 tbsp orange juice

1 Preheat the oven to 190°C/375°F/Gas 5. Line the base of an 28 × 18cm/11 × 7in tin (pan) with baking parchment.

2 Put the flour in a bowl and rub in the butter with your fingertips. Stir in the sugar and then spread half over the base of the prepared tin. Press down firmly. Bake for 10–15 minutes, until lightly browned. Leave to cool.

3 To make the filling, put the remaining flour mixture into a bowl. Stir in the bicarbonate of soda. Mix in the egg and cream, pecan nuts, peel and half the marmalade.

4 Pour the mixture over the cooled base. Bake for 20–25 minutes, or until the filling is just firm and golden.

5 Put the remaining marmalade into a small pan and heat gently. Add just enough orange juice to make a spreadable glaze. Brush the glaze over the baked cookie mixture while it is still warm. Leave to cool. Cut into bars.

> **Variation**
> *These bars would be just as delicious made with lemon, lime, grapefruit or mixed fruit marmalade instead of orange.*

Old-fashioned Gingerbread Energy 191kcal/802kJ; Protein 1.6g; Carbohydrate 24.7g, of which sugars 24.6g; Fat 10.3g, of which saturates 6.3g; Cholesterol 45mg; Calcium 128mg; Fibre 0g; Sodium 116mg.
Sticky Marmalade Squares Energy 194kcal/809kJ; Protein 2.1g; Carbohydrate 22g, of which sugars 10.9g; Fat 11.4g, of which saturates 6.2g; Cholesterol 33mg; Calcium 36mg; Fibre 0.7g; Sodium 77mg.

Walnut and Honey Bars

A sweet, custard-like filling brimming with nuts sits on a crisp pastry base. These scrumptious bars are pure heaven to bite into.

Makes 12–14

175g/6oz/1½ cups plain (all-purpose) flour
30ml/2 tbsp icing (confectioners') sugar, sifted
115g/4oz/½ cup unsalted butter, diced

For the filling

300g/11oz/scant 3 cups walnut halves
2 eggs, beaten
50g/2oz/¼ cup unsalted butter, melted
50g/2oz/¼ cup light muscovado (brown) sugar
90ml/6 tbsp dark clear honey
30ml/2 tbsp single (light) cream

1 Preheat the oven to 190°C/375°F/Gas 5. Lightly grease a 28 × 18cm/11 × 7in shallow tin (pan).

2 Put the flour, icing sugar and butter in a food processor and process until the mixture forms crumbs. Using the pulse button, add 15–30ml/1–2 tbsp water – enough to make a firm dough.

3 Roll the dough out on baking parchment and line the base and sides of the tin. Trim and fold the top edge inwards.

4 Prick the base, line with foil and baking beans and bake blind for 10 minutes. Remove the foil and beans. Return the base to the oven for about 5 minutes, until cooked but not browned. Reduce the temperature to 180°C/350°F/Gas 4.

5 For the filling, sprinkle the walnuts over the base. Whisk the remaining ingredients together. Pour over the walnuts and bake for 25 minutes.

> **Cook's Tip**
> *Dark honey does not necessarily have a stronger flavour than paler varieties, but some types have a distinctive taste. These include chestnut, buckwheat and manuka.*

Figgy Bars

Dried figs are a traditional addition to cookies but have been a little out of fashion in recent years. These tasty bars will remind you why they were once so popular.

Makes 48

3 eggs
175g/6oz/scant 1 cup caster (superfine) sugar
75g/3oz/¾ cup plain (all-purpose) flour
5ml/1 tsp baking powder
2.5ml/½ tsp ground cinnamon
1.5ml/¼ tsp ground cloves
1.5ml/¼ tsp grated nutmeg
pinch of salt
350g/12oz/2 cups coarsely chopped dried figs
75g/3oz/¾ cup chopped walnuts
30ml/2 tbsp brandy
icing (confectioners') sugar, for dusting

1 Preheat the oven to 160°C/325°F/Gas 3. Line a 30 × 20 × 3cm/12 × 8 × 1½in tin (pan) with baking parchment and lightly grease the paper.

2 In a bowl, whisk together the eggs and sugar until pale and thoroughly blended.

3 In another bowl, sift together the flour, baking powder, cinnamon, cloves, nutmeg and salt. Using a flexible spatula, gently fold the dry ingredients into the egg mixture in several batches. Stir in the figs, walnuts and brandy.

4 Scrape the mixture into the prepared tin and bake for 35–40 minutes, until the top is firm and brown. It should still be soft underneath.

5 Leave to cool in the tin for 5 minutes, then unmould and transfer to a sheet of baking parchment lightly sprinkled with icing sugar. Cut into bars.

> **Variation**
> *If you prefer not to use brandy in these bars, you could substitute red grape juice or orange juice.*

Walnut and Honey Bars Energy 333kcal/1386kJ; Protein 5.4g; Carbohydrate 21.4g, of which sugars 11.7g; Fat 25.7g, of which saturates 7.8g; Cholesterol 53mg; Calcium 49mg; Fibre 1.1g; Sodium 85mg.
Figgy Bars Energy 53kcal/224kJ; Protein 1g; Carbohydrate 8.9g, of which sugars 7.7g; Fat 1.6g, of which saturates 0.2g; Cholesterol 12mg; Calcium 26mg; Fibre 0.7g; Sodium 9mg.

Pecan Squares

A melt-in-the-mouth base and a crunchy toffee-like topping make these richly coloured cookies totally impossible to resist.

Makes 36
225g/8oz/2 cups plain
   (all-purpose) flour
pinch of salt
115g/4oz/½ cup sugar
225g/8oz/1 cup cold butter, diced
1 egg
finely grated rind of 1 lemon

For the topping
175g/6oz/¾ cup butter
75g/3oz/⅓ cup clear honey
50g/2oz/¼ cup sugar
115g/4oz/½ cup dark
   brown sugar
75ml/5 tbsp whipping cream
450g/1lb/4 cups pecan halves

1 Preheat the oven to 190°C/375°F/Gas 5. Lightly grease a 37 × 27 × 2.5cm/15½ × 10½ × 1in Swiss roll tin (jelly roll pan).

2 Sift the flour and salt into a mixing bowl. Stir in the sugar. With your fingertips, rub in the butter until the mixture resembles coarse breadcrumbs.

3 Add the egg and lemon rind and blend with a fork until the mixture just holds together.

4 Spoon the mixture into the prepared tin. With floured fingertips, press into an even layer. Prick the pastry all over with a fork and chill for 10 minutes.

5 Bake the pastry crust for 15 minutes. Remove the tin from the oven, but keep the oven on while making the topping.

6 To make the topping, melt the butter, honey and both sugars. Bring to the boil. Boil, without stirring, for 2 minutes. Remove from the heat and stir in the cream and pecans. Pour over the crust and bake for 25 minutes. Leave to cool.

7 When cool, run a knife around the edge. Invert on to a baking sheet, place another sheet on top and invert again. Dip a sharp knife into very hot water and cut into squares for serving.

Almond-topped Squares

Slightly chewy with a crunchy top, these squares are perfect any-time-of-day cookies whenever you feel that you deserve a treat.

Makes 18
75g/3oz/6 tbsp butter
50g/2oz/¼ cup sugar
1 egg yolk
grated rind and juice of ½ lemon
2.5ml/½ tsp vanilla extract
30ml/2 tbsp whipping cream

115g/4oz/1 cup plain
   (all-purpose) flour, plus extra
   for dusting

For the topping
225g/8oz/1 cup sugar
75g/3oz/¾ cup flaked
   (sliced) almonds
4 egg whites
2.5ml/½ tsp ground ginger
2.5ml/½ tsp ground cinnamon

1 Preheat the oven to 190°C/375°F/Gas 5. Line a 33 × 23cm/13 × 9in Swiss roll tin (jelly pan) with baking parchment and grease the paper.

2 In a bowl, beat together the butter and sugar until light and fluffy. Beat in the egg yolk, lemon rind and juice, vanilla extract and cream.

3 Gradually stir in the flour. Gather into a ball of dough with your fingertips.

4 Lightly dust your fingers with flour, then gently press the dough evenly into the base of the prepared tin. Bake for about 15 minutes, until just set. Remove the tin from the oven but leave the oven switched on.

5 To make the topping, put all the ingredients into a large heavy pan. Cook over a low heat, stirring constantly, until the mixture comes to the boil. Continue to boil, without stirring, for about 1 minute, until just golden. Pour the topping over the dough base, spreading it to cover evenly with a spatula.

6 Return to the oven and bake for about 45 minutes. Remove and score into bars or squares. Cool completely.

Almond-topped Squares Energy 127kcal/531kJ; Protein 2.4g; Carbohydrate 14.9g, of which sugars 9.9g; Fat 6.8g, of which saturates 2.9g; Cholesterol 22mg; Calcium 27mg; Fibre 0.5g; Sodium 41mg.
Pecan Squares Energy 245kcal/1016kJ; Protein 2.1g; Carbohydrate 15.5g, of which sugars 10.5g; Fat 19.8g, of which saturates 7.6g; Cholesterol 33mg; Calcium 26mg; Fibre 0.8g; Sodium 71mg.

Hazelnut and Raspberry Bars

The hazelnuts make a superb sweet pastry which is baked with a layer of raspberry jam in the middle.

Makes 30
250g/9oz/2¼ cups hazelnuts
300g/10oz/2½ cups plain
   (all-purpose) flour
5ml/1 tsp mixed spice (apple
   pie spice)
2.5ml/½ tsp ground cinnamon
150g/5oz/1¼ cups golden icing
   (confectioners') sugar

15ml/1 tbsp grated lemon rind
300g/10oz/1¼ cups unsalted
   (sweet) butter, softened
3 egg yolks
350g/12oz/1¼ cups seedless
   raspberry jam

For the topping
1 egg, beaten
15ml/1 tbsp clear honey
50g/2oz/½ cup flaked
   (sliced) almonds

1 Grind the hazelnuts in a food processor and then put in a bowl. Sift in the flour, spices and icing sugar. Add the lemon rind and mix well, then add the butter and the egg yolks and, using your hands, knead until a smooth dough is formed. Wrap in clear film (plastic wrap) and chill for 30 minutes.

2 Preheat the oven to 200°C/400°F/Gas 6. Lightly grease a 33 × 23cm/13 × 9in Swiss roll tin (jelly roll pan).

3 Roll out half the dough and fit in the base of the tin. Spread the jam over the dough base. Roll out the remaining dough and place on top of the jam.

4 To make the topping, beat the egg and honey together and brush over the dough. Sprinkle the almonds evenly over the top.

5 Bake for 10 minutes, lower the oven temperature to 180°C/350°F/Gas 4. Bake for another 20–30 minutes until golden brown. Cool, then cut into bars.

> **Cook's Tip**
> *Don't use ready-ground hazelnuts for these bars.*

Lemon Bars

These luscious lemon bars really zing with flavour and go beautifully with iced tea in summer.

Makes 36
50g/2oz/½ cup icing
   (confectioners') sugar
175g/6oz/1½ cups plain
   (all-purpose) flour
pinch of salt
175g/6oz/¾ cup butter, diced

For the topping
4 eggs
350g/12oz/1¾ cups caster
   (superfine) sugar
grated rind of 1 lemon
120ml/4fl oz/½ cup fresh
   lemon juice
175ml/6fl oz/¾ cup whipping
   cream
icing (confectioners') sugar,
   for dusting

1 Preheat the oven to 160°C/325°F/Gas 3. Lightly grease a 33 × 23cm/13 × 9in baking tin (pan).

2 Sift the sugar, flour and salt together into a large bowl. Rub the butter in with your fingertips until the mixture resembles coarse breadcrumbs.

3 Press the mixture into the base of the prepared tin using the back of a metal spoon. Bake for about 20 minutes, until golden brown.

4 For the topping, whisk the eggs and sugar together until blended. Add the lemon rind and juice and mix well.

5 Lightly whip the cream until it holds its shape and fold it into the egg mixture. Pour the liquid over the still-warm base, return it to the oven and bake for about 40 minutes, until set.

6 Leave to cool completely before cutting into bars. Dust with icing sugar.

> **Variation**
> *For an equally delicious citrus boost, substitute grated orange rind and juice for the lemon.*

Hazelnut and Raspberry Bars Energy 231kcal/962kJ; Protein 2.9g; Carbohydrate 22.1g, of which sugars 14.3g; Fat 15.1g, of which saturates 5.9g; Cholesterol 41mg; Calcium 38mg; Fibre 1g; Sodium 66mg. **Lemon Bars** Energy 124kcal/519kJ; Protein 1.3g; Carbohydrate 15.7g, of which sugars 12g; Fat 6.6g, of which saturates 3.9g; Cholesterol 37mg; Calcium 20mg; Fibre 0.2g; Sodium 39mg.

Fruity Lemon Drizzle Bars

These tangy iced, spongy bars are great for popping in lunchboxes. Experiment with other filling combinations, such as orange and dried apricots and dried pineapple.

Makes 16

250g/9oz ready-made sweet shortcrust pastry dough
90g/3¼ oz/¾ cup self-raising (self-rising) flour
75g/3oz/¾ cup fine or medium oatmeal
5ml/1 tsp baking powder
130g/4½oz/generous ½ cup light muscovado (brown) sugar
2 eggs
150g/5oz/⅔ cup unsalted butter, at room temperature, diced
finely grated rind of 1 lemon
90g/3½oz/¾ cup sultanas (golden raisins)
150g/5oz/1¼ cups icing (confectioners') sugar
15–20ml/3–4 tsp lemon juice

1 Preheat the oven to 190°C/375°F/Gas 5 and place a baking sheet in the oven to heat through. Generously grease a 28 × 18cm/11 × 7in shallow baking tin (pan).

2 Roll out the dough thinly on a lightly floured, clean surface. Line the base of the baking tin, pressing the pastry up the sides.

3 Put the flour, oatmeal, baking powder, sugar, eggs, butter and lemon rind in a mixing bowl. Beat for 2 minutes with a hand-held electric whisk until pale and creamy. Stir in the sultanas.

4 Tip the filling into the pastry case (pie shell) and spread evenly. Place the tin on the heated baking sheet in the oven and bake for about 30 minutes, until pale golden and firm.

5 Put the icing sugar in a small bowl with enough lemon juice to mix to a thin paste, about the consistency of thin cream.

6 Using a teaspoon, drizzle the icing diagonally across the warm cake in thin lines. Leave to cool in the tin.

7 When the icing has set, use a sharp knife to cut the cake in half lengthways. Cut each half across into 8 even-size bars.

Luscious Lemon Bars

A crisp cookie base is covered with a tangy lemon topping. The bars make a delightful addition to the tea table on a warm summer's day in the garden.

Makes 12

150g/5oz/1¼ cups plain (all-purpose) flour
90g/3½oz/7 tbsp unsalted butter, chilled and diced
50g/2oz/½ cup icing (confectioners') sugar, sifted

For the topping

2 eggs
175g/6oz/scant 1 cup caster (superfine) sugar
finely grated rind and juice of 1 large lemon
15ml/1 tbsp plain (all-purpose) flour
2.5ml/½ tsp bicarbonate of soda (baking soda)
icing (confectioners') sugar, for dusting

1 Preheat the oven to 180°C/350°F/Gas 4. Line the base of a 20cm/8in square shallow cake tin (pan) with baking parchment and lightly grease the sides of the tin.

2 Put the flour, diced butter and icing sugar into a food processor and process until the mixture comes together as a smooth, firm dough.

3 Press evenly into the base of the tin and spread smoothly using the back of a tablespoon. Bake for 12–15 minutes, until lightly golden. Cool in the tin.

4 To make the topping, whisk the eggs in a bowl until frothy. Gradually add the caster sugar, a little at a time, whisking well after each addition. Whisk in the lemon rind and juice, flour and bicarbonate of soda until thoroughly combined, but do not overmix. Pour the topping evenly over the cookie base.

5 Bake for 20–25 minutes, until set and golden, then remove from the oven.

6 Leave to cool slightly in the tin, then cut into 12 bars and transfer to a wire rack. Dust lightly with icing sugar and leave to cool completely.

Fruity Lemon Drizzle Bars Energy 272kcal/1141kJ; Protein 3.1g; Carbohydrate 37.3g, of which sugars 22.5g; Fat 13.3g, of which saturates 6.5g; Cholesterol 46mg; Calcium 42mg; Fibre 0.9g; Sodium 132mg. **Luscious Lemon Bars** Energy 189kcal/795kJ; Protein 2.5g; Carbohydrate 30.3g, of which sugars 19.8g; Fat 7.3g, of which saturates 4.2g; Cholesterol 48mg; Calcium 35mg; Fibre 0.4g; Sodium 59mg.

Fudge Nut Bars

Although your kids will be desperate to tuck into these fudgy treats, it's well worth chilling them for a few hours before slicing so that they can be cut into neat pieces. You can use any kind of nut, from mild-flavoured almonds, peanuts or macadamia nuts to slightly stronger tasting pecans or hazelnuts.

Makes 16
150g/5oz/⅔ cup unsalted
  (sweet) butter, chilled and diced
250g/9oz/2¼ cups plain
  (all-purpose) flour
75g/3oz/scant ½ cup caster
  (superfine) sugar

For the topping
150g/5oz milk chocolate, broken
  into pieces
40g/1½oz/3 tbsp unsalted
  butter
405g/14¼oz can sweetened
  condensed milk
50g/2oz/½ cup chopped nuts

1 Preheat the oven to 160°C/325°F/Gas 3. Lightly grease a 28 × 18cm/11 × 7in shallow baking tin (pan).

2 Put the butter and flour in a food processor and process until the mixture resembles fine breadcrumbs. Add the sugar and process briefly again until the mixture starts to cling together and form a dough.

3 Transfer the mixture to the prepared baking tin and spread out with the back of a wooden spoon to fill the base in an even layer. Bake for 35–40 minutes, until the surface is very lightly coloured. Remove from the oven.

4 To make the topping, put the chocolate in a heavy pan with the butter and condensed milk. Heat gently, stirring occasionally until the chocolate and butter have melted, then increase the heat and cook, stirring constantly, for 3–5 minutes, until the mixture starts to thicken.

5 Add the chopped nuts to the pan and pour the mixture over the cookie base, spreading it in an even layer. Leave to cool, then chill for at least 2 hours until firm. Serve cut into bars.

Toffee Meringue Bars

The lovely light and airy topping with its delicious caramel flavour makes these unusual bars irresistible.

Makes 12
50g/2oz/¼ cup butter
215g/7½oz/scant 1 cup soft
  dark brown sugar
1 egg
2.5ml/½ tsp vanilla extract
65g/2½oz/9 tbsp plain
  (all-purpose) flour
pinch of salt
1.5ml/¼ tsp freshly
  grated nutmeg

For the topping
1 egg white
pinch of salt
15ml/1 tbsp golden (light
  corn) syrup
90g/3½oz/½ cup caster
  (superfine) sugar
50g/2oz/⅓ cup walnuts,
  finely chopped

1 Combine the butter and brown sugar in a pan and heat until bubbling. Set aside to cool.

2 Preheat the oven to 180°C/350°F/Gas 4. Line the base and sides of a 20cm/8in square cake tin (pan) with baking parchment and oil.

3 Beat the egg and vanilla into the cooled sugar mixture. Sift over the flour, salt and nutmeg, and fold in. Spread out evenly over the base of the tin.

4 For the topping, beat the egg white with the salt until it holds soft peaks. Beat in the golden syrup, then the sugar and continue beating until the mixture holds stiff peaks. Fold in the nuts and spread on top of the dough base.

5 Bake for 30 minutes. Cut into bars when cool.

> **Variation**
> *The topping also tastes terrific made with maple syrup.*

Fudge Nut Bars Energy 315kcal/1317kJ; Protein 4.9g; Carbohydrate 36.6g, of which sugars 24.7g; Fat 17.5g, of which saturates 9.7g; Cholesterol 37mg; Calcium 123mg; Fibre 0.7g; Sodium 116mg.
Toffee Meringue Bars Energy 189kcal/797kJ; Protein 2g; Carbohydrate 31.9g, of which sugars 27.8g; Fat 6.8g, of which saturates 2.5g; Cholesterol 25mg; Calcium 28mg; Fibre 0.3g; Sodium 42mg.

Sticky Treacle Squares

This three-layered treat of buttery cookie base, covered with a sticky dried fruit filling, followed by an oaty flapjack-style topping, is utterly delicious.

Makes 14
175g/6oz/1½ cups plain
  (all-purpose) flour
90g/3½oz/7 tbsp unsalted
  (sweet) butter, diced
50g/2oz/¼ cup caster (superfine)
  sugar

For the filling
250g/9oz/generous 1 cup mixed
  dried fruit, such as prunes,
  apricots, peaches, pears
  and apples
300ml/½ pint/1¼ cups apple or
  orange juice

For the topping
225g/8oz/⅔ cup golden (light
  corn) syrup
finely grated rind of 1 small
  orange, plus 45ml/3 tbsp juice
90g/3½oz/1 cup rolled oats

1 Preheat the oven to 180°C/350°F/Gas 4. Lightly grease a 28 × 18cm/11 × 7in shallow baking tin (pan).

2 Put the flour and butter in a food processor and process until the mixture begins to resemble fine breadcrumbs. Add the sugar and mix until the dough starts to cling together in a ball.

3 Tip the mixture into the baking tin and press down in an even layer with the back of a fork. Bake for about 15 minutes, until the surface just begins to colour.

4 Meanwhile, prepare the filling. Remove the stones (pits) from any of the dried fruits. Chop the fruit fairly finely and put in a pan with the fruit juice. Bring to the boil, reduce the heat and cover with a lid. Simmer gently for about 15 minutes, or until all the juice has been absorbed.

5 Leaving the base in the tin, tip the dried fruit filling on top and spread out in an even layer with the back of a spoon.

6 For the topping, put the golden syrup in a bowl with the orange rind and juice and oats and mix together. Spoon over the fruits, spreading it out evenly. Return to the oven for 25 minutes. Leave to cool before cutting into squares.

Marbled Caramel Chocolate Slices

The classic chocolate-topped millionaire's slice is guaranteed to make you feel like a lottery winner.

Makes about 24
For the base
250g/9oz/2¼ cups plain
  (all-purpose) flour
75g/3oz/scant ½ cup caster
  (superfine) sugar
175g/6oz/¾ cup unsalted
  butter, softened

For the filling
90g/3½oz/7 tbsp unsalted
  butter, diced
90g/3½oz/scant ½ cup light
  muscovado (brown) sugar
2 × 400g/14oz cans sweetened
  condensed milk

For the topping
90g/3½oz plain (semisweet)
  chocolate
90g/3½oz milk chocolate
50g/2oz white chocolate

1 Preheat the oven to 180°C/350°F/Gas 4. Line and lightly grease a 33 × 23cm/13 × 9in Swiss roll tin (jelly roll pan).

2 Put the flour and caster sugar in a bowl and rub in the butter until it resembles fine breadcrumbs. Work with your hands until the mixture forms a dough.

3 Turn the dough into the tin and press it out with back of a tablespoon to cover the base. Prick all over with a fork and bake for about 20 minutes, or until firm to the touch. Set aside and leave in the tin to cool.

4 To make the filling, put all the ingredients into a pan and heat gently, stirring, until the sugar has dissolved. Stirring constantly, bring to the boil. Reduce the heat and simmer the mixture very gently, stirring constantly, for about 5–10 minutes, or until it has thickened and has turned a caramel colour.

5 Pour the filling over the cookie base, spread evenly, then leave until cold.

6 To make the topping, melt each chocolate separately in a heatproof bowl set over a pan of gently simmering water. Spoon plain, milk and white chocolate over the filling. Use a skewer to form a marbled effect on top.

Sticky Treacle Squares Energy 213kcal/898kJ; Protein 2.6g; Carbohydrate 39.3g, of which sugars 25.1g; Fat 6.1g, of which saturates 3.4g; Cholesterol 14mg; Calcium 35mg; Fibre 1.8g; Sodium 88mg.
Marbled Caramel Chocolate Slices Energy 305kcal/1281kJ; Protein 4.6g; Carbohydrate 39.6g, of which sugars 31.6g; Fat 15.4g, of which saturates 9.6g; Cholesterol 37mg; Calcium 132mg; Fibre 0.4g; Sodium 120mg.

Pecan Toffee Shortbread

Coffee shortbread is topped with pecan-studded toffee. Cornflour gives it a crumbly light texture, but all plain flour can be used if you like.

Makes 20

15ml/1 tbsp ground cofee
15ml/1 tbsp near-boiling water
115g/4oz/½ cup butter, softened
30ml/2 tbsp smooth
   peanut butter
75g/3oz/scant ½ cup caster
   (superfine) sugar
75g/3oz/⅔ cup cornflour
   (cornstarch)
185g/6½oz/1⅔ cups plain
   (all-purpose) flour

For the topping

175g/6oz/1¾ cup butter
175g/6oz/¾ cup soft light
   brown sugar
30ml/2 tbsp golden (light
   corn) syrup
175g/6oz/1½ cups shelled pecan
   nuts, coarsely chopped

1 Preheat the oven to 180°C/350°F/Gas 4. Lightly grease and line the base of an 18 × 28cm/7 × 11in tin (pan) with baking parchment.

2 Put the ground coffee in a small bowl and pour the hot water over. Leave to infuse (steep) for 4 minutes, then strain through a fine sieve (strainer).

3 Put the unsalted butter, peanut butter, sugar and coffee in a large bowl and beat together until light and creamy. Sift together the cornflour and flour into the bowl and mix gently to make a smooth dough.

4 Press the dough evenly into the base of the prepared tin and prick all over with a fork. Bake for about 20 minutes, until set and very lightly coloured.

5 To make the topping, put the butter, sugar and syrup into a heavy pan and cook over a medium heat, stirring occasionally, until melted. Bring to the boil, lower the heat and simmer for 5 minutes. Stir in the chopped nuts.

6 Spread the topping over the base. Leave in the tin until cold, then cut into bars.

Chocolate Butterscotch Bars

Wonderfully sticky with their sweet toffee and chocolate double topping, these rich, nutty cookie bars will be popular.

Makes 24

225g/8oz/2 cups plain
   (all-purpose) flour
2.5ml/½ tsp baking powder
115g/4oz/½ cup unsalted
   butter, diced
50g/2oz/¼ cup light muscovado
   (brown) sugar
150g/5oz plain (semisweet)
   chocolate, melted
30ml/2 tbsp ground almonds

For the topping

175g/6oz/¾ cup unsalted butter
115g/4oz/generous ½ cup caster
   (superfine) sugar
30ml/2 tbsp golden (light
   corn) syrup
175ml/6fl oz/¾ cup unsweetened
   condensed milk
150g/5oz/1¼ cups toasted
   hazelnuts
225g/8oz plain (semisweet)
   chocolate, chopped

1 Preheat the oven to 160°C/325°F/Gas 3. Lightly grease a shallow 30 × 20cm/12 × 8in cake tin (pan).

2 Sift together the flour and baking powder into a large bowl. Add the butter and rub it in until it resembles breadcrumbs.

3 Stir in the sugar. Gradually, work in the melted chocolate and ground almonds until thoroughly combined. Press the mixture into the prepared cake tin, prick the surface all over with a fork.

4 Bake for 25–30 minutes, until firm. Place the tin on a wire rack and leave to cool.

5 To make the topping, gently heat the butter, sugar, syrup and condensed milk in a pan until melted. Simmer, stirring occasionally, until golden, then stir in the hazelnuts. Pour over the base. Leave to set.

6 Melt the chocolate in a heatproof bowl set over a pan of gently simmering water. Spread over the butterscotch layer. Leave to set, then cut into bars.

Pecan Toffee Shortbread Energy 267kcal/1112kJ; Protein 1.9g; Carbohydrate 25.5g, of which sugars 14.9g; Fat 18.2g, of which saturates 8.1g; Cholesterol 31mg; Calcium 28mg; Fibre 0.7g; Sodium 95mg.
Chocolate Butterscotch Bars Energy 305kcal/1273kJ; Protein 3.5g; Carbohydrate 30g, of which sugars 22.5g; Fat 19.8g, of which saturates 9.7g; Cholesterol 29mg; Calcium 57mg; Fibre 1.2g; Sodium 89mg.

Chocolate and Coconut Slices

Very simple to make, these slices are deliciously moist and sweet. They look very tempting, too, with their sweet coconut filling and attractive, nutty topping.

Makes 24
115g/4oz/½ cup butter diced
175g/6oz/scant 2½ cups
  crushed digestive biscuits
  (graham crackers)
50g/2oz/¼ cup caster
  (superfine) sugar
pinch of salt
75g/3oz/1 cup desiccated
  (dry unsweetened
  shredded) coconut
250g/9oz/1½ cups plain
  (semisweet) chocolate chips
250ml/8fl oz/1 cup sweetened
  condensed milk
115g/4oz/1 cup mixed nuts,
  to decorate

1 Preheat the oven to 180°C/350°F/Gas 4.

2 Melt the butter in a pan over a low heat, then remove from the heat. Mix together the biscuit crumbs, sugar and salt in a bowl and stir in the melted butter until thoroughly combined. Press the mixture evenly over the base of an ungreased 33 × 23cm/13 × 9in ovenproof dish.

3 Sprinkle the coconut, then the chocolate chips, over the base. Pour the condensed milk evenly over the chocolate. Sprinkle the walnuts on top.

4 Bake for 30 minutes. Transfer to a wire rack and leave to cool, preferably overnight. When cooled, cut into slices.

Chunky Chocolate Bars

Chocolate, nuts and dried fruit are a truly enticing combination – fabulous.

Makes 12
350g/12oz plain (semisweet)
  chocolate, broken into
  small pieces
115g/4oz/½ cup unsalted
  (sweet) butter
400g/14oz can condensed
  (sweetened) milk
225g/8oz digestive biscuits
  (graham crackers), broken
50g/2oz/⅓ cup raisins
115g/4oz/1½ cups ready-to-eat
  dried peaches, coarsely
  chopped
50g/2oz/½ cup hazelnuts or
  pecan nuts, coarsely chopped

1 Line a 28 × 18cm/11 × 7in cake tin (pan) with clear film (plastic wrap).

2 Melt the chocolate and butter in a large heatproof bowl set over a pan of simmering water. Stir until well mixed. Pour the condensed milk into the chocolate and butter mixture. Beat with a wooden spoon until creamy.

3 Add the remaining ingredients and mix until well coated in the chocolate sauce. Pour the mixture into the prepared tin. Cool, then chill until set.

4 Lift the cake out of the tin using the clear film and then peel off the film. Cut into 12 bars and serve at once.

Chocolate Walnut Bars

Once you have tasted this delicious homemade version, you will never want to eat store-bought again.

Makes 24
50g/2oz/½ cup walnuts
75g/3oz/⅓ cup sugar
75g/3oz/⅔ cup plain
  (all-purpose) flour, sifted
75g/3oz/6 tbsp cold unsalted
  (sweet) butter, diced
icing (confectioners') sugar,
  for dusting

For the topping
25g/1oz/2 tbsp unsalted
  (sweet) butter
75ml/5 tbsp water
40g/1½oz/⅓ cup unsweetened
  cocoa powder
115g/4oz/½ cup sugar
5ml/1 tsp vanilla extract
pinch of salt
2 eggs

1 Preheat the oven to 180°C/350°F/Gas 4. Lightly grease a 20cm/8in square cake tin (pan).

2 Grind the walnuts with a few tablespoons of the sugar in a food processor, blender or nut grinder.

3 Mix the ground walnuts, the remaining sugar and the flour in a bowl. Rub in the butter until the mixture resembles breadcrumbs.

4 Pat the walnut mixture into the base of the prepared tin in an even layer. Bake for 25 minutes.

5 To make the topping, melt the butter with the water in a small pan over a low heat. Whisk in the cocoa and sugar. Remove from the heat, stir in the vanilla extract and salt and leave to cool for 5 minutes. Whisk in the eggs, one at a time.

6 Remove the cake tin from the oven and pour the topping evenly over the cooked walnut mixture.

7 Return the tin to the oven and bake for about 20 minutes, until set. Set the tin on a wire rack to cool. Once cooled, cut into bars and dust with sifted icing sugar. Store the bars in the refrigerator.

Chocolate and Coconut Slices Energy 217kcal/907kJ; Protein 2.8g; Carbohydrate 20g, of which sugars 15.8g; Fat 14.6g, of which saturates 7.5g; Cholesterol 18mg; Calcium 48mg; Fibre 1g; Sodium 89mg.
Chunky Chocolate Bars Energy 462kcal/1935kJ; Protein 6.3g; Carbohydrate 53.7g, of which sugars 43g; Fat 26.2g, of which saturates 13.9g; Cholesterol 42mg; Calcium 135mg; Fibre 1.9g; Sodium 220mg.
Chocolate Walnut Bars Energy 97kcal/407kJ; Protein 1.5g; Carbohydrate 9.8g, of which sugars 6.5g; Fat 6.1g, of which saturates 2.9g; Cholesterol 26mg; Calcium 16mg; Fibre 0.3g; Sodium 45mg.

White Chocolate Macadamia Slices

Keep these luxury slices for a celebratory afternoon tea. Not only do they have a superbly rich flavour, but a crunchy texture, too. For a special occasion serve with whipped cream.

Makes 16
150g/5oz/1¼ cups macadamia nuts
400g/14oz white chocolate

50g/2oz/¼ cup ready-to-eat dried apricots
75g/3oz/⅓ cup unsalted butter
5ml/1 tsp vanilla extract
3 eggs
150g/5oz/⅔ cup light muscovado (brown) sugar
115g/4oz/1 cup self-raising (self-rising) flour

1 Preheat the oven to 190°C/375°F/Gas 5. Lightly grease two 20cm/8in sandwich tins (layer cake pans) and line the base of each with baking parchment.

2 Coarsely chop the nuts and half the white chocolate, making sure that the pieces are more or less the same size, then cut the apricots into similar-size pieces.

3 Place the remaining white chocolate and the butter in a heatproof bowl set over a pan of hot water. Melt over a gentle heat, stirring occasionally until smooth. Remove the bowl from the heat and leave to cool slightly.

4 Stir in the vanilla extract. Whisk the eggs and sugar in a mixing bowl until thick and pale, then whisk in the melted chocolate mixture.

5 Sift the flour over the mixture and fold in gently and evenly. Stir in the nuts, chopped white chocolate and apricots.

6 Spoon into the prepared tins, smooth the top level and bake for 30–35 minutes, until golden brown. Leave to cool slightly, then turn out and leave to cool on a wire rack.

7 Serve cut into slices or wedges, with a spoonful of fresh whipped cream.

Nutty Chocolate Squares

They taste wonderful and look appetizing; these cookies are sure to become a family favourite.

Makes 16
2 eggs
10ml/2 tsp vanilla extract
pinch of salt
175g/6oz/1½ cups pecan nuts, coarsely chopped

50g/2oz/½ cup plain (all-purpose) flour
50g/2oz/¼ cup caster (superfine) sugar
120ml/4fl oz/½ cup golden (light corn) syrup
75g/3oz plain (semisweet) chocolate, finely chopped
45ml/3 tbsp butter
16 pecan halves, for decorating

1 Preheat the oven to 160°C/325°F/Gas 3. Line the base and sides of a 20cm/8in square baking tin (pan) with baking parchment and grease lightly.

2 Whisk together the eggs, vanilla extract and salt. In another bowl, mix together the chopped pecan nuts and flour. Set both bowls aside.

3 In a pan, bring the sugar and golden syrup to the boil. Remove from the heat and stir in the chocolate and butter and blend thoroughly with a wooden spoon.

4 Mix in the beaten egg mixture, then fold in the pecan mixture with a flexible spatula.

5 Pour the mixture into the prepared tin and bake for about 35 minutes, until set. Leave to cool in the tin for 10 minutes before turning out. Cut into 5cm/2in squares and press pecan halves into the tops while warm. Cool completely on a rack.

Cook's Tip
The shells of pecan nuts are naturally brown but they are often sold dyed a pinkish colour, perhaps to make them more eye catching. The dye does not affect the kernels which are naturally a reddish brown colour.

White Chocolate Macadamia Slices Energy 317kcal/1326kJ; Protein 4.8g; Carbohydrate 31.6g, of which sugars 26g; Fat 20g, of which saturates 8.4g; Cholesterol 46mg; Calcium 95mg; Fibre 0.9g; Sodium 97mg. **Nutty Chocolate Squares** Energy 180kcal/749kJ; Protein 2.6g; Carbohydrate 16.1g, of which sugars 13.3g; Fat 12.1g, of which saturates 3.2g; Cholesterol 31mg; Calcium 30mg; Fibre 0.7g; Sodium 52mg.

Double Chocolate Slices

These delicious cookies have a smooth chocolate base, topped with a mint-flavoured cream and drizzles of melted chocolate. Perfect for a teatime treat – or at any time of day.

Makes 12
200g/7oz/1³⁄₄ cups plain (all-purpose) flour
25g/1oz/2 tbsp unsweetened cocoa powder
150g/5oz/²⁄₃ cup unsalted butter, diced
75g/3oz/³⁄₄ cup icing (confectioners') sugar

For the topping
75g/3oz white chocolate mint crisps
50g/2oz/1⁄4 cup unsalted butter, softened
90g/3¹⁄₂oz/scant 1 cup icing (confectioners') sugar
50g/2oz milk chocolate

1 Preheat the oven to 180°C/350°F/Gas 4. Lightly grease an 18cm/7in square shallow baking tin (pan) and line with a strip of baking parchment that comes up over two opposite sides.

2 Put the flour and cocoa powder into a food processor and add the pieces of butter. Process briefly until the mixture resembles fine breadcrumbs. Add the icing sugar and mix briefly again to form a smooth soft dough.

3 Turn the flour mixture into the prepared tin and gently press out to the edges with your fingers to make an even layer. Bake for 25 minutes, then remove from the oven and leave the base to cool completely in the tin.

4 To make the topping, put the chocolate mint crisps in a plastic bag and tap firmly with a rolling pin until they are crushed. Beat the butter and sugar together until creamy, then beat in the crushed chocolate mint crisps. Spread the mixture evenly over the cookie base.

5 Melt the milk chocolate in a small heatproof bowl set over a pan of gently simmering hot water. Carefully lift the cookie base out of the tin; and remove the paper. Using a teaspoon, drizzle the melted chocolate over the topping. Leave to set, then cut into squares.

Chocolate Raspberry Macaroon Bars

Other seedless jams, such as strawberry or plum, can be used instead of the raspberry in the topping for these flavour-packed bars.

Makes 16–18 bars
115g/4oz/1⁄2 cup unsalted butter
50g/2oz/1⁄2 cup icing (confectioners') sugar
25g/1oz/1⁄4 cup unsweetened cocoa powder
pinch of salt
5ml/1 tsp almond extract
150g/5oz/1¹⁄₄ cups plain (all-purpose) flour

For the topping
150g/5oz/scant 1⁄2 cup seedless raspberry jam
15ml/1 tbsp raspberry-flavour liqueur
175g/6oz/1 cup mini chocolate chips
175g/6oz/1¹⁄₂ cups finely ground almonds
4 egg whites
pinch of salt
200g/7oz/1 cup caster (superfine) sugar
2.5ml/1⁄2 tsp almond extract
50g/2oz/1⁄2 cup flaked (sliced) almonds

1 Preheat the oven to 160°C/325°F/Gas 3. Line a 23 × 33cm/9 × 13in cake tin (pan) with lightly greased foil.

2 In a bowl, beat together the butter, sugar, cocoa and salt. Add the almond extract and flour and stir until the mixture forms a crumbly dough. Turn the dough into the lined tin and smooth out. Prick with a fork. Bake for 20 minutes, until just set. Remove from the oven and increase the temperature to 190°C/375°F/Gas 5.

3 To make the topping, mix together the raspberry jam and liqueur in a bowl. Spread evenly over the chocolate crust, then sprinkle with chocolate chips.

4 In a food processor fitted with a metal blade, blend the almonds, egg whites, salt, sugar and almond extract until foamy. Pour over the raspberry layer. Sprinkle with flaked almonds.

5 Bake for 20–25 minutes, until the top is golden. Transfer to a wire rack to cool in the tin for 20 minutes. Remove to a wire rack to cool completely. Cut into bars.

Double Chocolate Slices Energy 299kcal/1248kJ; Protein 2.3g; Carbohydrate 34.4g, of which sugars 20.8g; Fat 17.3g, of which saturates 10.8g; Cholesterol 37mg; Calcium 28mg; Fibre 0.8g; Sodium 126mg. **Chocolate Raspberry Macaroon Bars** Energy 266kcal/1115kJ; Protein 4.5g; Carbohydrate 32.1g, of which sugars 26.6g; Fat 14.1g, of which saturates 5.7g; Cholesterol 16mg; Calcium 66mg; Fibre 1.2g; Sodium 79mg.

Vanilla Streusel Bars

The crumbly topping on this cake makes a crunchy contrast to the moist vanilla-flavoured sponge base underneath.

Makes about 25

175g/6oz/1½ cups self-raising (self-rising) flour
5ml/1 tsp baking powder
175g/6oz/¾ cup butter, softened
175g/6oz/¾ cup vanilla sugar

3 eggs, beaten
1½ tsp vanilla extract
1–2 tbsp milk

For the topping

115g/4oz/1 cup self-raising (self-rising) flour
75g/3oz/6 tbsp butter
75g/3oz/6 tbsp vanilla sugar
icing (confectioners') sugar, to finish

1 Preheat the oven to 180°C/350°F/Gas 4. Lightly grease and line a shallow rectangular 23 × 18cm/9 × 7in baking tin (pan) with baking parchment.

2 To make the topping, sift the flour into a bowl and rub in the butter until the mixture resembles coarse breadcrumbs. Stir in the vanilla sugar and set aside.

3 Sift the flour and baking powder into a bowl. Add the butter, vanilla sugar and eggs. Beat well until the mixture is smooth, adding the vanilla extract and just enough milk to give a soft dropping consistency.

4 Spoon the mixture into the prepared tin and level the surface. Sprinkle the streusel topping over the surface and press down to cover.

5 Bake for 45–60 minutes, until browned and firm. Cool in the tin for 5 minutes, then turn out on to a wire rack to cool completely. Cut into bars and dust with icing sugar.

> **Cook's Tip**
> Cover the cake loosely with foil if the topping browns too quickly.

Date and Honey Bars

Fresh dates are a good source of natural fibre, yet are kind and gentle on the digestive system. For a slightly different, more toffee flavour, replace the honey with real maple syrup.

Makes 16

175g/6oz/1 cup fresh dates, pitted (stoned) and chopped
45ml/3 tbsp clear honey

30ml/2 tbsp lemon juice
150g/5oz/1¼ cups plain (all-purpose) flour
150ml/¼ pint/⅔ cup water
1.5ml/¼ tsp freshly grated nutmeg
115g/4oz/1 cup self-raising (self-rising) flour
25g/1oz/2 tbsp brown sugar
150g/5oz/1¼ cups rolled oats
175g/6oz/¾ cup unsalted butter, melted

1 Preheat the oven to 190°C/375°F/Gas 5. Lightly grease the base of an 18cm/7in square cake tin (pan) and line with baking parchment.

2 Put the dates, honey, lemon juice, plain flour and measured water into a heavy pan. Gradually bring to the boil over a low heat, stirring constantly. Remove the pan from the heat and leave to cool.

3 Sift together the nutmeg and self-raising flour into another bowl and stir in the sugar, oats and melted butter until well combined. Spoon half the mixture into the prepared tin and spread it out evenly over the base with the back of the spoon, pressing down well.

4 Spread the date mixture over the top and finish with the remaining oat mixture, pressing evenly all over the surface with the back of a spoon. Bake for about 25 minutes until golden. Cool in the cake tin for 1 hour, then cut into bars.

> **Cook's Tip**
> To remove the stone (pit), split the date lengthways with a small sharp knife without cutting right through. Ease out the stone with the point of the knife.

Vanilla Streusel Bars Energy 162kcal/680kJ; Protein 2g; Carbohydrate 19.5g, of which sugars 10.7g; Fat 9g, of which saturates 5.4g; Cholesterol 44mg; Calcium 27mg; Fibre 0.4g; Sodium 70mg.
Date and Honey Bars Energy 203kcal/853kJ; Protein 3g; Carbohydrate 27g, of which sugars 7.5g; Fat 10g, of which saturates 5.7g; Cholesterol 23mg; Calcium 34mg; Fibre 1.4g; Sodium 71mg.

Chocolate Nut Slices

Although the unsliced bar looks small, it's very rich so is best sliced thinly. If you have any other plain cookies in the cupboard, you can use them instead of the rich tea, with equally good results.

Makes 10 slices
225g/8oz milk chocolate
40g/1½oz/3 tbsp unsalted
  butter, diced
75g/3oz rich tea biscuits
  (plain cookies)
50g/2oz/½ cup flaked
  (sliced) almonds
75g/3oz plain (semisweet)
  or white chocolate,
  coarsely chopped
icing (confectioners') sugar,
  for dusting

1 Break the milk chocolate into small pieces and place in a heatproof bowl with the butter. Set the bowl over a pan of gently simmering water and heat gently, stirring frequently until melted.

2 Dampen a 450g/1lb loaf tin (pan) and line the base and sides with clear film (plastic wrap). Don't worry about smoothing out the creases in the film.

3 When the chocolate has melted and the mixture is smooth, remove the bowl from the heat and leave for 5 minutes, until slightly cooled.

4 Break the cookies into small pieces, then stir into the melted chocolate with the almonds. Add the chopped plain or white chocolate to the bowl and fold in quickly and lightly with a flexible spatula.

5 Turn the mixture into the tin and pack down with a fork. Tap the base of the tin gently on the work surface. Chill in the refrigerator for 2 hours until set.

6 To serve, turn the chocolate loaf on to a board and peel away the clear film. Dust lightly with icing sugar and slice thinly with a serrated knife.

Chocolate Dominoes

These sweet and sugary confections are ideal for children to help to decorate.

Makes 16
175g/6oz/¾ cup butter
175g/6oz/¾ cup caster
  (superfine) sugar
3 eggs
150g/5oz/1¼ cups self-raising
  (self-rising) flour

25g/1oz/¼ cup unsweetened
  cocoa powder, sifted

For the topping
175g/6oz/¾ cup butter
25g/1oz/¼ cup unsweetened
  cocoa powder
300g/11oz/2½ cups icing
  (confectioners') sugar
a few liquorice strips
115g/4oz M&Ms, for decoration

1 Preheat the oven to 180°C/350°F/Gas 4. Lightly grease an 18 × 28cm/7 × 11in baking tin, and line the base and sides with baking parchment.

2 Put all the cake ingredients in a bowl and beat until smooth. Spoon into the prepared tin and level with a metal spatula.

3 Bake for 30 minutes, until the cake springs back when pressed with the fingertips. Cool in the tin for 5 mintues, then loosen the edges with a knife and transfer to a wire rack. Peel off the paper and leave to cool. Turn out and cut into 16 bars.

4 To make the topping, place the butter in a bowl, sift in the cocoa and icing sugar and beat until smooth. Spread the topping evenly over the cakes.

5 Decorate each with a strip of liquorice and M&Ms.

> **Variation**
> To make Traffic Light Cakes, omit the cocoa and add an extra 25g/1oz/3 tbsp plain (all-purpose) flour. Omit cocoa from the icing and add an extra 25g/1oz/4 tbsp icing (confectioners') sugar and 2.5ml/½ tsp vanilla extract. Spread over the cakes and decorate with red, yellow and green glacé cherries to look like traffic lights.

Rich Chocolate Slices Energy 326kcal/1361kJ; Protein 2.7g; Carbohydrate 29g, of which sugars 23.8g; Fat 23g, of which saturates 13.9g; Cholesterol 33mg; Calcium 44mg; Fibre 0.9g; Sodium 144mg.
Chocolate Nut Slices Energy 248kcal/1034kJ; Protein 3.7g; Carbohydrate 23.5g, of which sugars 19.4g; Fat 16.1g, of which saturates 8.2g; Cholesterol 16mg; Calcium 74mg; Fibre 0.9g; Sodium 75mg.

Rocky Road Chocolate Bars

This recipe is a dream to make with kids. They love smashing up the biscuits, and can do most of the rest, apart from melting the chocolate and lining the tin. The divine flavour of melting chocolate chips, crunchy cookies and soft marsh-mallows blended together is not just kid's stuff.

Makes 16 bars

225g/8oz/1 cup butter
115g/4oz dark (bittersweet) chocolate with more than 60 per cent cocoa solids, roughly broken up
30ml/2 tbsp caster (superfine) sugar
30ml/2 tbsp golden (light corn) syrup
30ml/2 tbsp good quality unsweetened cocoa powder
350g/12oz mixed digestive biscuits (graham crackers) and ginger nuts (ginger snaps)
50g/2oz/1/2 cup mini marshmallows
75g/3oz/1/2 cup mixed white and milk chocolate chips
icing (confectioners') sugar, for dusting (optional)

1 Line a 20cm/8in square cake tin (pan), measuring 2.5cm/1in deep, with baking parchment.

2 Put the butter in a pan with the chocolate, sugar, syrup and cocoa powder. Place over a gentle heat until completely melted.

3 Put the biscuits into a large plastic bag and crush with a rolling pin until broken up into coarse chunks. Stir these into the chocolate mixture. Add the marshmallows, then the chocolate chips, mixing well after each addition.

4 Spoon the mixture into the tin, but don't press down too much – it should look like a rocky road. Chill for at least 1 hour, or until firm. Remove from the tin and cut into 16 bars. Dust the bars with icing sugar before serving.

> **Variation**
> Substitute butter cookies if you don't like ginger.

Chocolate and Prune Bars

Wickedly self-indulgent and very easy to make, these fruity chocolate bars will keep for 2–3 days in the refrigerator – if they don't all get eaten as soon as they are ready. You could try adding different combinations of dried fruit.

Makes 12 bars

250g/9oz good quality milk chocolate
50g/2oz/1/4 cup butter
115g/4oz digestive biscuits (graham crackers)
115g/4oz/1/2 cup ready-to-eat prunes

1 Break the chocolate into small pieces and place in a heatproof bowl. Add the butter and place the bowl over a pan of gently simmering water until the butter and chocolate have melted. Stir to mix and set aside.

2 Put the digestive biscuits in a plastic bag and seal it, then crush them into small pieces with a rolling pin.

3 Coarsely chop the prunes and stir into the melted chocolate with the biscuits.

4 Spoon the chocolate and prune mixture into a 20cm/8in square cake tin (pan) and chill for 1–2 hours until set. Remove the cake from the refrigerator and cut into 12 bars.

> **Cook's Tip**
> Do not cover the bars with cling film (plastic wrap) when chilling, as condensation may spoil their texture.

> **Variations**
> • Other dried fruits are also delicious in these bars. Try dried plums, which are not quite the same as prunes and are usually made from golden rather than red varieties. Apricots would also be a good alternative.
> • For extra flavour, stir 1.5ml/1/4 tsp freshly grated nutmeg or 2.5ml/1/2 tsp ground cinnamon into the chocolate mixture.

Rocky Road Chocolate Bars Energy 296kcal/1237kJ; Protein 2.7g; Carbohydrate 28.6g, of which sugars 15.7g; Fat 19.9g, of which saturates 11.6g; Cholesterol 40mg; Calcium 39mg; Fibre 0.9g; Sodium 245mg. **Chocolate and Prune Bars** Energy 197kcal/826kJ; Protein 2.5g; Carbohydrate 21.7g, of which sugars 16.4g; Fat 11.8g, of which saturates 6.8g; Cholesterol 18mg; Calcium 59mg; Fibre 0.9g; Sodium 102mg.

Gingerbread Brownies

Warm and spicy, ginger liqueur is an inspired addition to this gingerbread cake with its fudge topping.

Serves 10–12
175g/6oz/¾ cup soft dark muscovado (molasses) sugar
175g/6oz/½ cup black treacle (molasses)
50g/2oz/¼ cup clear honey
175g/6oz/¾ cup butter
5ml/1 tsp bicarbonate of soda (baking soda)
275g/10oz/2½ cups plain (all-purpose) flour
pinch of salt
15ml/1 tbsp ground ginger
10ml/2 tsp ground cinnamon
2 eggs, beaten
115g/4oz/1 cup chopped walnuts
50g/2oz/⅓ cup crystallized (candied) ginger, chopped
30ml/2 tbsp ginger liqueur
60ml/4 tbsp milk
extra chopped walnuts and crystallized (candied) ginger, to decorate

For the fudge topping
50g/2oz/4 tbsp butter
45ml/3 tbsp ginger liqueur
225g/8oz/2 cups icing (confectioners') sugar, sifted

1 Preheat the oven to 160°C/325°F/Gas 3. Grease and line a 20cm/8in square cake tin (pan).

2 Put the sugar, treacle, honey and butter into a heavy pan. Stir over a low heat until all the ingredients have melted, then cool. Stir in the bicarbonate of soda.

3 Sift the flour, salt, ginger and ground cinnamon into a bowl. Using a wooden spoon, stir in the melted ingredients.

4 Stir in the eggs, walnuts, crystallized ginger and liqueur, with enough of the milk to make a stiff cake mixture. Turn into the tin and bake for 1¼–1½ hours, until firm. Cool on a wire rack.

5 To make the fudge topping, put the butter, ginger liqueur and icing sugar into a heatproof bowl and set over a pan of barely simmering water. Stir until smooth, remove from the heat and leave to cool. Beat with a wooden spoon until it is thick enough to spread. Swirl over the cake. Cut into slices and decorate with extra walnuts and pieces of crystallized ginger.

Marbled Brownies

These are the perfect brownies – made from a mixture of flavours swirled together before baking.

Makes 24
225g/8oz plain (semisweet) chocolate, chopped
75g/3oz/⅓ cup butter, diced
4 eggs
350g/12oz/1¾ cups caster (superfine) sugar
115g/4oz/1 cup plain (all-purpose) flour
pinch of salt
5ml/1 tsp baking powder
10ml/2 tsp vanilla extract
115g/4oz/1 cup walnuts, chopped

For the plain batter
50g/2oz/¼ cup butter
175g/6oz/¾ cup cream cheese
115g/4oz/generous ½ cup caster (superfine) sugar
2 eggs
30ml/2 tbsp plain (all-purpose) flour
5ml/1 tsp vanilla extract

1 Preheat the oven to 180°C/350°F/Gas 4. Line a 33 × 23cm/ 13 × 9in tin (pan) with baking parchment.

2 Melt the plain chocolate and butter in a small pan over a low heat, stirring occasionally until smooth. Leave to cool slightly.

3 Beat the eggs until light and fluffy. Gradually add the caster sugar and beat well. Sift over the flour, salt and baking powder and fold in with a metal spoon. Fold in the chocolate mixture.

4 Set aside 475ml/16fl oz/2 cups of the chocolate batter. Stir the vanilla extract and walnuts into the rest of the mixture.

5 To make the plain batter, beat the butter and cream cheese with an electric mixer. Add the sugar and continue beating until blended. Beat in the eggs, flour and vanilla extract.

6 Spread the chocolate batter into the tin. Pour over the plain batter. Drop spoonfuls of the reserved chocolate batter on top. Swirl the mixtures to marble. Do not blend completely.

7 Bake for 35–40 minutes, until just set. Unmould when cool and cut into squares for serving.

Marbled Brownies Energy 259kcal/1083kJ; Protein 3.8g; Carbohydrate 28.8g, of which sugars 23.1g; Fat 15.1g, of which saturates 7.1g; Cholesterol 66mg; Calcium 42mg; Fibre 0.6g; Sodium 73mg.
Gingerbread Brownies Energy 387kcal/1632kJ; Protein 5.2g; Carbohydrate 68.3g, of which sugars 50.7g; Fat 11.3g, of which saturates 3.1g; Cholesterol 41mg; Calcium 151mg; Fibre 1.1g; Sodium 70mg.

Nut and Chocolate Chip Brownies

These chunky chocolate brownies are moist, dark and deeply satisfying. They are delicious with a morning cup of coffee and will definitely boost morale on a dreary day.

Makes 16
150g/5oz plain (semisweet) chocolate, chopped
120ml/4fl oz/½ cup sunflower oil
215g/7½oz/scant 1 cup light muscovado (brown) sugar
2 eggs
5ml/1 tsp vanilla extract
65g/2½oz/9 tbsp self-raising (self-rising) flour
60ml/4 tbsp unsweetened cocoa powder
75g/3oz/¾ cup chopped walnuts
60ml/4 tbsp milk chocolate chips

1 Preheat the oven to 180°C/350°F/Gas 4. Lightly grease a shallow 19cm/7½in square cake tin (pan).

2 Melt the plain chocolate in a heatproof bowl over a pan of gently simmering water.

3 Beat together the oil, sugar, eggs and vanilla extract. Stir in the melted chocolate and beat well.

4 Sift the flour and cocoa powder into the bowl and fold in until well combined. Stir in the chopped nuts and milk chocolate chips, then tip the mixture into the prepared tin and spread evenly to the edges.

5 Bake for about 30–35 minutes, until the top is firm and crusty. Cool in the tin before cutting into squares.

Cook's Tip
These brownies freeze well and can be stored in the freezer for 3 months in an airtight container.

Variation
Substitute chopped pecan nuts for the walnuts, if you like.

Raisin Brownies

Adding dried fruit makes brownies a little more substantial, although no less moist and delicious. Try to find Californian or Spanish raisins for the best flavour and texture.

Makes 16
115g/4oz/½ cup butter, diced
50g/2oz/½ cup unsweetened cocoa powder
2 eggs
225g/8oz/generous 1 cup caster (superfine) sugar
5ml/1 tsp vanilla extract
40g/1½ oz/⅓ cup plain (all-purpose) flour
75g/3oz/¾ cup walnuts, chopped
65g/2½oz/½ cup raisins
icing (confectioners') sugar, for dusting

1 Preheat the oven to 180°C/350°F/Gas 4. Line a 20cm/8in square baking tin (pan) with baking parchment and grease the paper lightly.

2 Melt the butter in a small pan over a low heat. Remove from the heat and stir in the cocoa.

3 In a bowl, beat together the eggs, sugar and vanilla extract with an electric mixer until light and fluffy. Add the cocoa mixture and stir to blend.

4 Sift the flour over the cocoa mixture and fold in gently with a metal spoon. Add the walnuts and raisins, mixing them in gently, then scrape the mixture into the prepared tin.

5 Bake for about 30 minutes, until firm to the touch, being careful not to overbake.

6 Leave in the tin on a rack to cool completely. Cut into 5cm/2in squares and remove from the tin. Dust with sifted icing sugar before serving.

Variation
For an adult taste, try substituting rum for the vanilla.

Nut and Chocolate Chip Brownies Energy 235kcal/983kJ; Protein 3.4g; Carbohydrate 25.9g, of which sugars 22.2g; Fat 13.9g, of which saturates 3.8g; Cholesterol 25mg; Calcium 37mg; Fibre 1g; Sodium 49mg. **Raisin Brownies** Energy 181kcal/759kJ; Protein 2.5g; Carbohydrate 20.4g, of which sugars 18.1g; Fat 10.5g, of which saturates 4.6g; Cholesterol 39mg; Calcium 26mg; Fibre 0.7g; Sodium 86mg.

Banana Brownies

Bananas, powerhouses of energy and packed with nutrients, yet very low in fat, make these brownies not only deliciously moist, but also a healthy option.

Makes 9
75ml/5 tbsp unsweetened
  cocoa powder
15ml/1 tbsp caster
  (superfine) sugar
75ml/5 tbsp milk

3 large bananas, mashed
175g/6oz/3/4 cup soft light
  brown sugar
5ml/1 tsp vanilla extract
5 egg whites
75g/3oz/3/4 cup self-raising
  (self-rising) flour
75g/3oz/3/4 cup oat bran
15ml/1 tbsp icing (confectioners')
  sugar, for dusting

1 Preheat the oven to 180°C/350°F/Gas 4. Line a 20cm/8in square cake tin (pan) with baking parchment.

2 Blend the cocoa powder and caster sugar with the milk in a bowl. Add the bananas, soft brown sugar and vanilla extract.

3 In a large bowl, lightly beat the egg whites with a fork. Add the chocolate mixture and continue to beat well.

4 Sift the flour over the mixture and fold in with the oat bran. Pour the mixture into the prepared cake tin.

5 Bake for 40 minutes, or until the top is firm and crusty. Leave to cool completely in the tin before cutting into squares. Lightly dust the brownies with icing sugar before serving.

> **Variation**
> *Adding dried fruit or fresh berries would make these brownies even more of a special treat without dramatically increasing the fat content. Good extras include 50g/2oz/ scant 1/2 cup raisins, 50g/2oz/1/3 cup dried sour cherries or cranberries or 50g/2oz/1/2 cup fresh blueberries or 50g/2oz/ 1/3 cup fresh raspberries.*

Low-fat Brownies

If you ever need proof that you can still enjoy sweet treats even when you are following a low-fat diet, here it is. These brownies are not just tasty, but also very quick and easy to make.

Makes 16
100g/3½oz/scant 1 cup plain
  (all-purpose) flour
2.5ml/½ tsp baking powder

45ml/3 tbsp unsweetened
  cocoa powder
200g/7oz/1 cup caster
  (superfine) sugar
100ml/3½fl oz/scant ½ cup
  natural (plain) low-fat yogurt
2 eggs, beaten
5ml/1 tsp vanilla extract
25ml/1½ tbsp vegetable oil

1 Preheat the oven to 180°C/350°F/Gas 4. Line a 20cm/8in square cake tin (pan) with baking parchment.

2 Sift the flour, baking powder and cocoa powder into a bowl. Stir in the caster sugar, then beat in the yogurt, eggs, vanilla and vegetable oil until thoroughly combined. Put the mixture into the prepared tin.

3 Bake for about 25 minutes, until just firm to the touch. Leave in the tin until cooled completely.

4 Using a sharp knife, cut into 16 squares, then remove from the tin using a spatula.

> **Cook's Tip**
> *Low-fat yogurt is made from concentrated skimmed (low fat) milk, has a fat content of between 0.5 and 2 per cent and contains about 56 calories per 100ml/3½fl oz/scant ½ cup. Very low-fat yogurt, sometimes called low-calorie yogurt, is also available and this has a fat content of less than 0.5 per cent and contains about 41 calories per 100ml/3½fl oz/scant ½ cup. Note that soya yogurt is not a substitute in this recipe. Even though it does not contain milk, it is higher in both fat and calories.*

Banana Brownies Energy 101kcal/426kJ; Protein 4.6g; Carbohydrate 16.6g, of which sugars 10.8g; Fat 2.2g, of which saturates 1.2g; Cholesterol 0mg; Calcium 31mg; Fibre 2.8g; Sodium 167mg.
Low Fat Brownies Energy 53kcal/222kJ; Protein 2.2g; Carbohydrate 5.7g, of which sugars 0.6g; Fat 2.6g, of which saturates 0.7g; Cholesterol 24mg; Calcium 28mg; Fibre 0.5g; Sodium 41mg.

Fudgy-glazed Chocolate Brownies

For a simpler brownie, omit the fudge glaze and dust with icing sugar or cocoa instead.

Makes 8–10
250g/9oz plain (semi-sweet) chocolate, chopped
25g/1oz milk chocolate, chopped
115g/4oz/½ cup unsalted (sweet) butter, diced
100g/3½oz/½ cup light brown sugar
50g/2oz/¼ cup sugar
2 eggs
15ml/1 tbsp vanilla extract
65g/2½oz/9 tbsp plain (all-purpose) flour

115g/4oz/1 cup pecans or walnuts, toasted and chopped
150g/5oz fine quality white chocolate, chopped into 5mm/¼in pieces
pecan halves, to decorate

For the fudgy glaze
170g/6oz plain (semisweet) chocolate, chopped
50g/2oz/4 tbsp unsalted butter, diced
30ml/2 tbsp golden (light corn) syrup
10ml/2 tsp vanilla extract
5ml/1 tsp instant coffee powder

1 Preheat the oven to 180°C/350°F/Gas 4. Line a 20cm/8in cake tin (pan) with foil. Lightly grease the foil.

2 In a large pan, melt the plain and milk chocolate with the butter, until smooth, stirring frequently. Remove from the heat.

3 Stir in the sugars until dissolved. Beat in the eggs and vanilla. Stir in the flour until just blended. Stir in the chopped pecans and white chocolate. Pour the batter into the prepared tin.

4 Bake for 20–25 minutes, until a skewer inserted into the centre comes out clean. Remove to a wire rack for 30 minutes, then use the foil to lift the brownies and leave to cool for 2 hours.

5 To make the glaze, in a medium pan over a medium heat, melt the glaze ingredients, stirring frequently. Remove from the heat, chill for 1 hour. Spread a layer of the glaze over the brownies. Cut into bars with a sharp knife and decorate each bar with a pecan half. Chill until set.

Chocolate and Date Brownies

Dark and full of flavour, these brownies are irresistible. They make a good teatime treat, or are perfect for accompanying a cup of coffee with friends.

Makes 20
150g/5oz/⅔ cup butter
150g/5oz/scant 1 cup stoned (pitted) dates, softened in boiling water, then drained and finely chopped

150g/5oz/1¼ cups self-raising (self-rising) wholemeal (whole-wheat) flour
10ml/2 tsp baking powder
60ml/4 tbsp unsweetened cocoa powder dissolved in 30ml/2 tbsp hot water
60ml/4 tbsp apple and pear spread
90ml/6 tbsp unsweetened coconut milk
50g/2oz/½ cup walnuts or pecan nuts, coarsely broken

1 Preheat the oven to 160°C/325°F/Gas 3. Lightly grease a 28 × 18cm/11 × 7in shallow baking tin.

2 Beat the butter and dates together in a bowl. Sift together the flour and baking powder into another bowl, then, using a flexible spatula, gradually fold the dry ingredients into the butter mixture in batches, alternating with the cocoa, apple and pear spread and coconut milk. Stir in the nuts.

3 Spoon the mixture into the prepared tin and smooth the surface with the back of the spoon.

4 Bake for about 45 minutes, or until a fine skewer inserted in the centre comes out clean. Cool for a few minutes in the tin, then cut into bars or squares. Using a metal spatula, transfer to a wire rack to cool completely.

> **Cook's Tip**
> You can use dried dates straight from the packet but they are better softened first. Put them in a small pan and add water to cover. Bring to the boil, then lower the heat and simmer gently for about 5 minutes. Drain well and pat dry with kitchen paper before chopping.

Fudge-glazed Chocolate Brownies Energy 574kcal/2393kJ; Protein 6.5g; Carbohydrate 50.3g, of which sugars 44.8g; Fat 40g, of which saturates 19.9g; Cholesterol 76mg; Calcium 88mg; Fibre 1.8g; Sodium 144mg. **Chocolate and Date Brownies** Energy 285kcal/1189kJ; Protein 4.3g; Carbohydrate 26.3g, of which sugars 13.3g; Fat 9.8g, of which saturates 5.3g; Cholesterol 56mg; Calcium 38mg; Fibre 1.3g; Sodium 62mg.

Chocolate Cheesecake Brownies

A very dense chocolate brownie mixture is swirled with creamy cheese to give a marbled effect. Cut into squares for little mouthfuls of absolute heaven.

Makes 16

1 egg
225g/8oz/1 cup full-fat
   cream cheese
50g/2oz/1/4 cup caster
   (superfine) sugar
5ml/1 tsp vanilla extract

For the brownie mixture

115g/4oz dark (bittersweet)
   chocolate (minimum
   70 per cent cocoa solids)
115g/4oz/1/2 cup unsalted butter
150g/5oz/3/4 cup light muscovado
   (brown) sugar
2 eggs, beaten
50g/2oz/1/2 cup plain
   (all-purpose) flour

1 Preheat the oven to 160°C/325°F/Gas 3. Line the base and sides of a 20cm/8in cake tin (pan) with baking parchment.

2 To make the cheesecake mixture, beat the egg in a mixing bowl, then add the cream cheese, caster sugar and vanilla extract. Beat together until smooth and creamy.

3 To make the brownie mixture, put the chocolate and butter in a heatproof bowl set over a pan of gently simmering water and heat, stirring occasionally, until melted. Remove from the heat and leave to cool slightly.

4 Stir the sugar into the chocolate mixture until dissolved, then gradually add the beaten eggs, beating well after each addition. Gently fold in the flour with a flexible spatula.

5 Spread two-thirds of the brownie mixture over the base of the tin. Spread the cheesecake mixture on top, then spoon on the remaining brownie mixture in heaps. Using a skewer, swirl the mixtures together.

6 Bake for 30–35 minutes, or until just set in the centre. Leave to cool in the tin, then cut into squares. Store for up to one week in an airtight container.

White Chocolate Brownies

These irresistible brownies are packed full of creamy white chocolate and juicy dried fruit. They are best served cut into very small portions as they are incredibly rich.

Makes 18

75g/3oz/6 tbsp unsalted
   butter, diced
400g/14oz white chocolate,
   coarsely chopped
3 eggs
90g/3½oz/½ cup golden caster
   (superfine) sugar
10ml/2 tsp vanilla extract
90g/3½oz/¾ cup sultanas
   (golden raisins)
coarsely grated rind of 1 lemon,
   plus 15ml/1 tbsp juice
200g/7oz/1¾ cups plain
   (all-purpose) flour

1 Preheat the oven to 190°C/375°F/Gas 5. Grease and line a 28 × 20cm/11 × 8in shallow, rectangular baking tin (pan) with baking parchment.

2 Put the butter and 300g/11oz of the chocolate in a heatproof bowl and set over a pan of gently simmering water, stirring frequently until melted.

3 Remove the bowl from the heat and beat in the eggs and sugar, then add the vanilla extract, sultanas, lemon rind and juice, flour and the remaining chocolate. Pour the mixture into the tin and spread into the corners.

4 Bake for about 20 minutes, until slightly risen and the surface is only just turning golden. The centre should still be slightly soft. Leave to cool in the tin.

5 Cut the brownies into small squares and remove from the tin.

Variation
White chocolate is very sweet so, to compromise, make the brownie mixture with white chocolate as described, then stir in 100g/3½oz chopped milk chocolate with the flour.

Chocolate Cheesecake Brownies Energy 226kcal/940kJ; Protein 2.4g; Carbohydrate 20.1g, of which sugars 17.7g; Fat 15.7g, of which saturates 9.4g; Cholesterol 65mg; Calcium 34mg; Fibre 0.3g; Sodium 100mg. **White Chocolate Brownies** Energy 232kcal/973kJ; Protein 4g; Carbohydrate 30.3g, of which sugars 21.8g; Fat 11.4g, of which saturates 6.5g; Cholesterol 41mg; Calcium 86mg; Fibre 0.4g; Sodium 65mg.

Butterscotch Brownies

These gorgeous treats are made with brown sugar, white chocolate chips and walnuts. Who could possibly have the will power to resist? You might want to make two batches at a time.

Makes 12

450g/1lb white chocolate chips
75g/3oz/6 tbsp unsalted butter
3 eggs
175g/6oz/¾ cup light muscovado (brown) sugar
175g/6oz/1½ cups self-raising (self-rising) flour
175g/6oz/1½ cups walnuts, chopped
5ml/1 tsp vanilla extract

1 Preheat the oven to 190°C/375°F/Gas 5. Line the base of a 28 × 18cm/11 × 7in shallow tin (pan) with baking parchment. Lightly grease the sides.

2 Put 90g/3½oz/generous ½ cup of the chocolate chips and the butter into a heatproof bowl set over a pan of barely simmering water and heat gently, stirring occasionally, until melted and smooth. Remove the bowl from the heat and leave to cool slightly.

3 Put the eggs and light muscovado sugar into a large bowl and whisk well, then whisk in the melted chocolate mixture.

4 Sift the flour into the bowl and, using a flexible spatula, gently fold it into the mixture together with the chopped walnuts, vanilla extract and the remaining chocolate chips until thoroughly combined.

5 Spoon the mixture into the prepared tin and spread it out evenly with the back of the spoon. Bake for about 30 minutes, or until risen and light golden brown. The centre should be firm but will still be slightly soft until it cools. Leave to cool completely in the tin.

6 Cut into 12 bars when the brownie is completely cold. Store in an airtight container.

Chunky White Chocolate and Coffee Brownies

Brownies should have a gooey texture, so take care not to overcook them – when ready, the mixture will still be slightly soft under the crust, but will firm as it cools.

Makes 12
25ml/1½ tbsp ground coffee
45ml/3 tbsp near-boiling water

300g/11oz plain (semisweet) chocolate, broken into pieces
225g/8oz/1 cup butter
225g/8oz/generous 1 cup caster (superfine) sugar
3 eggs
75g/3oz/¾ cup self-raising (self-rising) flour, sifted
225g/8oz white chocolate, coarsely chopped

1 Preheat the oven to 190°C/375°F/Gas 5. Grease and line the base of an 18 × 28cm/7 × 11in shallow tin with baking parchment.

2 Put the coffee in a bowl and pour the water over. Leave to infuse (steep) for 4 minutes, then strain through a sieve (strainer).

3 Put the plain chocolate and butter in a bowl over a pan of hot water and stir occasionally until melted. Remove from the heat and leave to cool for 5 minutes.

4 In a large bowl, beat the sugar and eggs together. Stir in the chocolate and butter mixture and the coffee. Stir in the sifted flour.

5 Fold in the white chocolate pieces. Pour into the prepared tin.

6 Bake for 45–50 minutes, or until firm and the top is crusty. Leave to cool in the tin. When completely cold, cut into squares and remove from the tin.

> **Cook's Tip**
> If it's easier, make 45ml/3 tbsp strong instant coffee.

Butterscotch Brownies Energy 469kcal/1961kJ; Protein 8.1g; Carbohydrate 48.7g, of which sugars 37.7g; Fat 28.3g, of which saturates 11.4g; Cholesterol 61mg; Calcium 182mg; Fibre 1g; Sodium 151mg.
Chunky White Chocolate and Coffee Brownies Energy 480kcal/2005kJ; Protein 5.1g; Carbohydrate 51.4g, of which sugars 46.4g; Fat 29.7g, of which saturates 17.8g; Cholesterol 89mg; Calcium 88mg; Fibre 0.8g; Sodium 155mg.

Date and Walnut Brownies

These rich brownies are great for afternoon tea, but they also make a fantastic dessert. Reheat slices briefly in the microwave oven and serve with crème fraîche.

Makes 12
350g/12oz plain (semisweet) chocolate, broken into squares
225g/8oz/1 cup butter, diced
3 large (US extra large) eggs

115g/4oz/generous ½ cup caster (superfine) sugar
5ml/1 tsp vanilla extract
75g/3oz/¾ cup plain (all-purpose) flour, sifted
225g/8oz/1½ cups fresh dates, peeled, stoned (pitted) and chopped
200g/7oz/1¾ cups walnut pieces
icing (confectioners') sugar, for dusting

1 Preheat the oven to 190°C/375°F/Gas 5. Generously grease a 30 × 20cm/12 × 8in rectangular baking tin (pan) and line with baking parchment.

2 Put the chocolate squares and diced butter into a large heatproof bowl. Set the bowl over a pan of gently simmering water and heat gently until melted. Stir until smooth, then remove the bowl from the heat and leave to cool slightly.

3 In a separate bowl, beat together the eggs, sugar and vanilla. Beat into the chocolate mixture, then fold in the flour, dates and nuts. Pour into the tin.

4 Bake for 30–40 minutes, until firm and the mixture comes away from the sides of the tin. Cool in the tin, then turn out, remove the parchment and dust with icing sugar. Cut the brownies into bars or squares.

> **Cook's Tip**
> When melting the chocolate and butter, keep the water in the pan beneath simmering gently, but do not let it approach boiling point. Chocolate is notoriously sensitive to heat; it is vital not to let it get too hot or it may stiffen into an unmanageable mass.

Chocolate Chip Brownies

These easy-to-make classic brownies never fail to please, and make great snacks and lunchtime treats for children and adults alike.

Makes 24
115g/4oz plain (semisweet) chocolate
115g/4oz/½ cup butter
3 eggs

200g/7oz/1 cup caster (superfine) sugar
2.5ml/½ tsp vanilla extract
pinch of salt
150g/5oz/1¼ cups plain (all-purpose) flour
175g/6oz/1 cup chocolate chips

1 Preheat the oven to 180°C/350°F/Gas 4. Lightly grease and line a 33 × 23cm/13 × 9in rectangular cake tin (pan) with baking parchment.

2 Break the chocolate into pieces and put into a heatproof bowl with the butter, then set the bowl over a pan of barely simmering water and heat gently, stirring occasionally, until melted and smooth. Remove the bowl from the heat and leave to cool slightly.

3 Beat together the eggs, caster sugar, vanilla extract and salt in a bowl until creamy. Stir in the cooled chocolate mixture. Sift the flour over the mixture and gently fold in with a flexible spatula, then add the chocolate chips and gently stir in.

4 Pour the mixture into the prepared tin and spread evenly with a metal spatula. Bake in the oven for about 30 minutes, until just set. Be careful not to overbake; the brownies should still be slightly moist inside. Remove the tin from the oven and leave to cool completely.

5 To turn out, run a round-bladed knife all around the edge of the tin and invert on to a baking sheet. Remove and discard the baking parchment. Place another baking sheet on top of the brownies and invert again so that they are the right side up. Cut into bars or squares for serving. Store in an airtight container for up to 1 week.

Date and Walnut Brownies Energy 504kcal/2097kJ; Protein 6.5g; Carbohydrate 39.9g, of which sugars 34.8g; Fat 36.5g, of which saturates 16g; Cholesterol 89mg; Calcium 54mg; Fibre 1.8g; Sodium 136mg. **Chocolate Chip Brownies** Energy 161kcal/674kJ; Protein 2g; Carbohydrate 21.3g, of which sugars 16.4g; Fat 8.1g, of which saturates 4.7g; Cholesterol 35mg; Calcium 22mg; Fibre 0.5g; Sodium 39mg.

Cranberry and Chocolate Cakes

There is no doubt that the contrasting flavours of tangy, sharp cranberries and sweet chocolate were made for each other – and make simply fabulous cream-topped squares.

Makes 12
115g/4oz/½ cup unsalted (sweet) butter
60ml/4 tbsp unsweetened cocoa powder
215g/7½oz/scant 1 cup light muscovado (brown) sugar
150g/5oz/1¼ cups self-raising (self-rising) flour, plus extra for dusting

2 eggs, beaten
115g/4oz/1 cup fresh or thawed frozen cranberries

For the topping
150ml/¼ pint/⅔ cup sour cream
75g/3oz/scant ½ cup caster (superfine) sugar
30ml/2 tbsp self-raising (self-rising) flour
50g/2oz/4 tbsp soft butter
1 egg, beaten
2.5ml/½ tsp vanilla extract
75ml/5 tbsp coarsely grated plain (semisweet) chocolate, for sprinkling

1 Preheat the oven to 180°C/350°F/Gas 4. Lightly grease an 18 × 25cm/7 × 10in cake tin (pan) and dust lightly with flour, shaking out any excess.

2 Combine the butter, cocoa powder and sugar in a pan and stir over a low heat until melted and smooth.

3 Remove the pan from the heat and stir in the flour and beaten eggs. Stir in the cranberries, then spread the mixture evenly in the prepared cake tin.

4 To make the topping, put the sour cream, sugar, flour, butter, beaten egg and vanilla extract into a bowl and beat well until smooth and thoroughly combined. Spoon the mixture into the tin and gently spread it evenly over the chocolate and cranberry base.

5 Sprinkle evenly with the coarsely grated chocolate and bake for about 40 minutes, or until risen and firm. Leave to cool completely in the tin, then cut into 12 squares.

Rainbow Gingerbread Cakes

These gingerbread squares have a more spongy texture than traditional gingerbread cookies and look stunning decorated with vibrantly coloured sprinkles. Ground and preserved stem ginger gives a really spicy flavour, but can easily be left out for younger children.

Makes 16
225g/8oz/2 cups plain (all-purpose) flour
5ml/1 tsp baking powder
10ml/2 tsp ground ginger
2 pieces preserved stem ginger, finely chopped
90g/3½oz/¾ cup raisins

50g/2oz/¼ cup glacé (candied) cherries, chopped
115g/4oz/½ cup unsalted (sweet) butter, diced
115g/4oz/⅓ cup golden (light corn) syrup
30ml/2 tbsp black treacle (molasses)
75g/3oz/⅓ cup dark muscovado (molasses) sugar
2 eggs, beaten

For the topping
200g/7oz/1¾ cups icing (confectioners') sugar
50g/2oz/¼ cup unsalted (sweet) butter, at room temperature, diced
multi-coloured sprinkles

1 Preheat the oven to 160°C/325°F/Gas 3. Lightly grease and line a 20cm/8in square baking tin (pan) with baking parchment.

2 Sift the flour, baking powder and ground ginger into a bowl. Add the stem ginger, raisins and cherries and stir together.

3 Put the butter, syrup, treacle and muscovado sugar in a small pan and heat gently until the butter melts. Pour the mixture into the dry ingredients. Add the eggs and stir until combined.

4 Pour into the baking tin and spread in an even layer. Bake for 55 minutes, or until risen and firm in the centre. Leave to cool.

5 To make the topping, put the icing sugar and butter in a bowl with 20ml/4 tsp hot water and beat until smooth.

6 Turn the gingerbread on to a board. Cut into 16 squares. Drizzle a thick line of icing around the top edge of each square. Scatter the coloured sprinkles over the icing.

Cranberry and Chocolate Squares Energy 343kcal/1439kJ; Protein 4.8g; Carbohydrate 42.9g, of which sugars 30.8g; Fat 18.2g, of which saturates 8.7g; Cholesterol 76mg; Calcium 63mg; Fibre 1.4g; Sodium 164mg. **Rainbow Gingerbread Cakes** Energy 251kcal/1057kJ; Protein 2.4g; Carbohydrate 41.9g, of which sugars 31.1g; Fat 9.4g, of which saturates 5.6g; Cholesterol 46mg; Calcium 50mg; Fibre 0.6g; Sodium 100mg.

Almond Cakes

This firm cookie-like cake has the flavour of macaroons and marzipan. It is easy to make and tastes delicious served with a cup of tea or coffee. If you can wait, the texture and flavour of the cake are improved by a few days of storage.

Serves 16
350g/12oz/3 cups ground
  almonds
50g/2oz/½ cup matzo meal
pinch of salt
30ml/2 tbsp vegetable oil
250g/9oz/generous 1 cup sugar
300g/11oz/1⅓ cups brown sugar
3 eggs, separated
7.5ml/1½ tsp almond extract
5ml/1 tsp vanilla extract
150ml/¼ pint/⅔ cup
  orange juice
75ml/5 tbsp brandy

For the topping
75ml/5 tbsp brandy
200g/7oz/1¾ cups icing
  (confectioners') sugar
90g/3½oz/scant 1 cup flaked
  (sliced) almonds

1 Preheat the oven to 180°C/350°F/Gas 4. Lightly grease a 30–38cm/12–15in square cake tin (pan).

2 Put the ground almonds, matzo meal and salt in a bowl and mix together.

3 Put the oil, sugars, egg yolks, almond extract, vanilla extract, orange juice and half the brandy in a separate bowl. Stir, then add the almond mixture to form a thick lumpy batter.

4 Whisk the egg whites until stiff. Fold one-third of the egg whites into the mixture to lighten it, then fold in the rest. Pour the mixture into the prepared tin and bake for 25–30 minutes.

5 To make the icing, mix the brandy with the icing sugar. If necessary, add a little water to make an icing (frosting) with the consistency of single (light) cream.

6 Remove from the oven and prick the top all over with a skewer. Pour the icing evenly over the top of the cake, then return the cake to the oven for 10 minutes, or until the top is crusty. Leave the cake to cool in the tin, then cut into squares.

Apricot and Almond Cakes

What an utterly perfect combination. If they aren't eaten immediately, these fruity cakes will stay moist for several days if stored in an airtight container.

Makes 18
225g/8oz/2 cups self-raising
  (self-rising) flour
115g/4oz/½ cup light muscovado
  (brown) sugar
50g/2oz/⅓ cup semolina
175g/6oz/¾ cup ready-to-eat
  dried apricots, chopped
2 eggs
30ml/2 tbsp malt extract
30ml/2 tbsp clear honey
60ml/4 tbsp skimmed milk
60ml/4 tbsp sunflower oil
a few drops of almond extract
30ml/2 tbsp flaked
  (sliced) almonds

1 Preheat the oven to 160°C/325°F/Gas 3. Lightly grease a 28 × 18cm/11 × 7in shallow cake tin (pan) and line with baking parchment.

2 Sift the flour into a bowl and add the muscovado sugar, semolina, dried apricots and eggs. Add the malt extract, clear honey, milk, sunflower oil and almond extract. Mix well until smooth.

3 Turn the mixture into the prepared cake tin and spread to the edges. Smooth the top. Sprinkle the flaked almonds all over the surface in as even a layer as possible.

4 Bake for 30–35 minutes, until the centre of the cake springs back when lightly pressed.

5 Transfer the tin to a wire rack and leave to cool, then turn out the cake. Remove and discard the lining paper, place the cake on a board and cut it into 18 slices with a sharp knife, to serve.

> **Variation**
> *You can substitute dried peaches or nectarines for the apricots; they both have an affinity with almonds.*

Almond Cakes Energy 415kcal/1742kJ; Protein 7.6g; Carbohydrate 54g, of which sugars 51g; Fat 17.9g, of which saturates 1.7g; Cholesterol 36mg; Calcium 97mg; Fibre 2.1g; Sodium 21mg.
Apricot and Almond Fingers Energy 140kcal/589kJ; Protein 3.1g; Carbohydrate 23.6g, of which sugars 11.9g; Fat 4.3g, of which saturates 0.6g; Cholesterol 21mg; Calcium 40mg; Fibre 1.2g; Sodium 13mg.

Chocolate Orange Sponge Drops

Light as air with a melt-in-the-mouth mixture of flavours, these drops are sure to be popular.

Makes about 14
2 eggs
50g/2oz/¼ cup caster (superfine) sugar
2.5ml/½ tsp grated orange rind
50g/2oz/½ cup plain (all-purpose) flour
60ml/4 tbsp finely shredded orange marmalade
40g/1½oz plain (semisweet) chocolate, chopped into small pieces

1 Preheat the oven to 200°C/400°F/Gas 6. Line three baking sheets with baking parchment.

2 Put the eggs and sugar in a large heatproof bowl and whisk over a pan of simmering water until the mixture is thick and pale, and leaves a ribbon trail when the whisk is lifted. Remove the bowl from the pan of water and continue whisking until the mixture is cool.

3 Whisk in the grated orange rind. Sift the flour over the whisked mixture and fold it in gently.

4 Put spoonfuls of the mixture on the baking sheets, spacing them well apart to allow for spreading. The mixture will make 28–30 drops.

5 Bake for about 8 minutes, or until the cookies are golden. Leave them to cool on the baking sheets for a few minutes, then use a metal spatula to transfer them to a wire rack to cool completely.

6 Spread the flat sides of half the cookies with the orange marmalade, then gently press the remaining cookies on top to sandwich the drops together.

7 Melt the chocolate in a heatproof bowl set over a pan of barely simmering water. Drizzle or pipe zig-zag lines of the chocolate over the tops of the sponge drops. Leave to set completely before serving.

Coffee Sponge Drops

These are delicious on their own, but taste even better with a filling of low-fat soft cheese and chopped preserved stem ginger.

Makes 12
50g/2oz/½ cup plain (all-purpose) flour
15ml/1 tbsp instant coffee powder
2 eggs
75g/3oz/scant ½ cup caster (superfine) sugar

For the filling
115g/4oz/½ cup low-fat soft cheese
40g/1½oz/¼ cup chopped preserved stem ginger

1 Preheat the oven to 190°C/375°F/Gas 5. Line two or three baking sheets with baking parchment.

2 To make the filling, beat together the soft cheese and preserved stem ginger. Chill until required.

3 Sift the flour and instant coffee powder together into a bowl and set aside.

4 In a large bowl, combine the eggs and caster sugar. Beat with an electric whisk until thick and mousse-like.

5 Add the sifted flour and coffee to the egg mixture and gently fold in with a metal spoon, being careful not to knock out any air.

6 Spoon the mixture into a piping (pastry) bag fitted with a 1cm/½in plain nozzle. Pipe 4cm/1½in rounds on the prepared baking sheets, spaced well apart.

7 Bake for 12 minutes. Cool on a wire rack. Sandwich together with the filling.

Variation
For a richer, creamier filling, use mascarpone.

Chocolate Orange Sponge Drops Energy 58kcal/247kJ; Protein 1.3g; Carbohydrate 10.6g, of which sugars 8g; Fat 1.5g, of which saturates 0.7g; Cholesterol 26mg; Calcium 12mg; Fibre 0.2g; Sodium 12mg. **Coffee Sponge Drops** Energy 33kcal/138kJ; Protein 1.5g; Carbohydrate 5.2g, of which sugars 3.6g; Fat 0.9g, of which saturates 0.4g; Cholesterol 17mg; Calcium 13mg; Fibre 0.1g; Sodium 27mg.

Lady Fingers

These long, delicate cookies are named after the pale, slim fingers of highborn gentlewomen. They are also known, much more mundanely, as sponge fingers.

Makes 18
90g/3½oz/generous ¾ cup plain (all-purpose) flour, plus extra for dusting
pinch of salt
4 eggs, separated
115g/4oz/generous ½ cup caster (superfine) sugar
2.5ml/½ tsp vanilla extract
icing (confectioners') sugar, for sprinkling

1 Preheat the oven to 150°C/300°F/Gas 2. Lightly grease two large baking sheets, then dust lightly with flour and shake off the excess.

2 Sift the flour and salt together twice on to baking parchment and set aside.

3 With an electric mixer, beat the egg yolks with half of the sugar until thick enough to leave a ribbon trail when the beaters are lifted.

4 In another grease-free bowl, whisk the egg whites until they form stiff peaks. Gradually whisk in the remaining sugar until the mixture is very glossy.

5 Sift the flour mixture over the yolks and spoon about a quarter of the egg whites over the flour. Carefully fold in with a large metal spoon to slacken, adding the vanilla extract. Then gently fold in the remaining egg whites.

6 Spoon the mixture into a piping (pastry) bag fitted with a large plain nozzle. Pipe 10cm/4in long lines on the prepared baking sheets. Sift over a layer of icing sugar. Tap off any excess sugar.

7 Bake for 20 minutes, until crusty on the outside with soft centres. Cool slightly on the baking sheets before transferring to a wire rack.

Lemon Sponge Fingers

These sponge fingers are perfect for serving with fruit salads or light, creamy desserts and mousses.

Makes about 20
2 eggs
75g/3oz/scant ½ cup caster (superfine) sugar
grated rind of 1 lemon
50g/2oz/½ cup plain (all-purpose) flour, sifted
caster (superfine) sugar, for sprinkling

1 Preheat the oven to 190°C/375°F/Gas 5. Line two baking sheets with baking parchment.

2 Whisk the eggs, sugar and lemon rind together with a hand-held electric whisk until thick and mousse-like (when the whisk is lifted, a trail should remain on the surface of the mixture for at least 15 seconds).

3 Gently fold in the flour with a large metal spoon using a figure-of-eight action.

4 Place the mixture in a large piping (pastry) bag fitted with a 1cm/½in plain nozzle. Pipe the mixture into finger lengths on the prepared baking sheets. Sprinkle the fingers with caster sugar.

5 Bake for about 6–8 minutes, until golden brown, then transfer the sponge fingers to a wire rack to cool.

Cook's Tip
Use an unwaxed lemon, if possible. Otherwise, wash the lemon well under hot water and pat dry before grating.

Variation
To make Spicy Orange Fingers, substitute grated orange rind for the lemon rind and add 5ml/1 tsp ground cinnamon with the flour.

Lady Fingers Energy 59kcal/248kJ; Protein 1.9g; Carbohydrate 10.6g, of which sugars 6.8g; Fat 1.3g, of which saturates 0.4g; Cholesterol 42mg; Calcium 17mg; Fibre 0.2g; Sodium 16mg.
Lemon Sponge Fingers Energy 33Kcals/137KJ; Fat 0.57g Saturated Fat 0.16g; Cholesterol 19.30mg; Fibre 0.08g.

Madeleines

These little tea cakes, baked in a special tin with shell-shaped cups, were made famous by Marcel Proust, who referred to them in his memoirs. They are best eaten on the day that they are made.

Makes 12
100g/4oz/1¼ cups self-raising (self-rising) flour
5ml/1 tsp baking powder

2 eggs
75g/3oz/¾ cup icing (confectioners') sugar, plus extra for dusting
grated rind of 1 lemon or orange
15ml/1 tbsp lemon or orange juice
75g/3oz/6 tbsp unsalted butter, melted and slightly cooled

1 Preheat the oven to 190°C/375°F/Gas 5. Generously grease a 12-cup madeleine tin (pan).

2 Sift together the flour and baking powder into a bowl and set aside.

3 Put the eggs and icing sugar into another bowl. Using a hand-held electric mixer, beat together for 5–7 minutes, until thick and creamy and the mixture leaves a ribbon trail when the beaters are lifted.

4 Gently fold in the lemon or orange rind and the lemon or orange juice. Fold in the flour and the melted butter in four batches, beginning with the flour.

5 Let the mixture stand for 10 minutes, then carefully spoon into the tin, dividing it equally among the cups. Tap gently to release any air bubbles.

6 Bake for 12–15 minutes, rotating the pan halfway through cooking, until a skewer inserted into the centre of a cake comes out clean.

7 Turn out on to a wire rack to cool completely and dust with icing sugar.

Fat Rascals

These delicious teacakes are a cross between a scone and a rock cake and are really simple to make. They would originally have been baked in a small pot oven standing over an open fire. Serve them warm or cold, just as they are or with butter.

Makes 10
350g/12oz/3 cups self-raising (self rising) flour, plus extra for dusting
175g/6oz/¾ cup butter, diced

115g/4oz/generous ½ cup caster (superfine) sugar
75g/3oz/⅓ cup mixed currants, raisins and sultanas (golden raisins)
25g/1oz/1½ tbsp chopped mixed peel
50g/2oz/⅓ cup glacé (candied) cherries
50g/2oz/½ cup blanched almonds, coarsely chopped
1 egg
about 75ml/5 tbsp milk

1 Preheat the oven to 200°C/400°F/Gas 6. Line one or two baking sheets with baking parchment.

2 Sift the flour into a large bowl. Add the butter and, with your fingertips, rub it into the flour until the mixture resembles fine breadcrumbs, alternatively, process the ingredients briefly in a food processor.

3 Stir in the sugar, dried fruit, mixed peel, glacé cherries and almonds until well mixed.

4 Lightly beat the egg and stir into the flour mixture with sufficient milk to gather the mixture into a ball of soft but not sticky dough.

5 With lightly floured hands, divide the dough into 10 balls, press them into rounds about 2cm/¾in thick and arrange them on the prepared baking sheets, spaced well apart to allow room for spreading.

6 Cook for 15–20 minutes, until risen and golden brown. Transfer to a wire rack to cool.

Madeleines Energy 132kcal/557kJ; Protein 2.3g; Carbohydrate 21.1g, of which sugars 5.8g; Fat 4.9g, of which saturates 2.4g; Cholesterol 8mg; Calcium 42mg; Fibre 0.7g; Sodium 118mg.
Fat Rascals Energy 191kcal/803kJ; Protein 2.9g; Carbohydrate 28.4g, of which sugars 11.3g; Fat 8.1g, of which saturates 4.8g; Cholesterol 38mg; Calcium 45mg; Fibre 0.7g; Sodium 62mg.

Singing Hinnies

These sweet and moreish scone-like little cakes "sing" as they cook on the hot buttered griddle. Serve them warm, split and spread with butter.

Makes about 20

400g/14 oz/3½ cups self-raising (self-rising) flour, plus extra for dusting
7.5ml/1½ tsp baking powder
pinch of salt
50g/2oz/¼ cup butter, diced
50g/2oz/⅓ cup lard, diced
50g/2oz/¼ cup caster (superfine) sugar
75g/3oz/⅓ cup currants, raisins or sultanas (golden raisins)
about 150ml/¼ pint/⅔ cup milk

1 Sift the flour, baking powder and salt into a large bowl. Add the butter and lard and, with your fingertips, rub them into the flour until the mixture resembles fine breadcrumbs.

2 Stir the sugar and dried fruit into the fat and flour mixture.

3 Add the milk in batches and, with a flat-ended knife, stir the mixture until it can be gathered into a ball of soft dough. The mixture should form a dry dough. It should not be at all wet to the touch.

4 Transfer to a lightly floured surface and roll out to about 5mm/¼in thick. With a 7.5cm/3in cookie cutter, stamp out rounds, gathering up the offcuts (scraps) and re-rolling to make more rounds.

5 Heat a heavy frying pan or griddle. Rub with butter and cook the scones in batches for 3–4 minutes on each side, until well browned. Lift off and keep warm until all are cooked. Serve while warm.

> **Variation**
> Instead of making small cakes, try cooking the dough in a large, pan-sized round, cutting it into wedges first to facilitate easy turning.

Soul Cakes

These soul cakes have a texture between a biscuit and a cake-like crumb. They are full of fruit and spices and are deliciously sweet.

Makes about 20

450g/1lb/4 cups self-raising (self-rising) flour, plus extra for dusting
5ml/1 tsp mixed spice (apple pie spice)
2.5ml/½ tsp ground ginger
175g/6oz/¾ cup butter, softened
175g/6oz/scant 1 cup caster (superfine) sugar, plus extra for sprinkling
2 eggs, lightly beaten
50g/2oz/¼ cup currants, raisins or sultanas (golden raisins)
about 30ml/2 tbsp warm milk

1 Preheat the oven to 180°C/350°F/Gas 4. Lightly grease two baking sheets or line with baking parchment.

2 Sift the flour and spices into a bowl and set aside. Beat the butter with the sugar until the mixture is pale and fluffy.

3 Gradually beat the eggs into the mixture. Fold in the flour mixture and the dried fruit, then add sufficient warm milk to bind the mixture and gather it up into a ball of soft dough.

4 Transfer to a lightly floured surface and roll out to about 5mm/¼in thick. With a floured 7.5cm/3in cutter, cut into rounds, gathering up the offcuts (scraps) and re-rolling to make more rounds.

5 Arrange the cakes on the prepared baking sheets. Prick the surface of the cakes lightly with a fork then, with the back of a knife, mark a deep cross on top of each.

6 Put the cakes into the hot oven and cook for about 15 minutes, until risen and golden brown.

7 Sprinkle the cooked cakes with a little caster sugar and then transfer to a wire rack to cool.

Singing Hinnies Energy 132kcal/557kJ; Protein 2.3g; Carbohydrate 21.1g, of which sugars 5.8g; Fat 4.9g, of which saturates 2.4g; Cholesterol 8mg; Calcium 42mg; Fibre 0.7g; Sodium 118mg.
Soul Cakes Energy 191kcal/803kJ; Protein 2.9g; Carbohydrate 28.4g, of which sugars 11.3g; Fat 8.1g, of which saturates 4.8g; Cholesterol 38mg; Calcium 45mg; Fibre 0.7g; Sodium 62mg.

Caraway Buns

Caraway seeds were once a popular ingredient of breads and cakes.

Makes about 12

350g/12oz/3 cups plain (all-purpose) flour, plus extra for dusting
115g/4oz/⅔ cup ground rice or semolina
10ml/2 tsp baking powder
115g/4oz/½ cup butter
75g/3oz/scant ½ cup caster (superfine) sugar, plus extra for sprinkling
30ml/2 tbsp caraway seeds
2 eggs
about 75ml/5 tbsp milk

1 Preheat the oven to 200°C/400°F/Gas 6. Line a baking sheet with baking parchment.

2 Sift the flour, ground rice and baking powder together into a large mixing bowl. Add the butter and, with your fingertips, rub it into the flour until the mixture resembles fine breadcrumbs. Stir the sugar and caraway seeds into the flour mixture.

3 Lightly beat the eggs and stir them into the flour mixture, together with sufficient milk to enable you to gather the mixture into a ball of dough. Transfer to a lightly floured surface.

4 Roll out to about 2.5cm/1in thick. Using a 5cm/2in cookie cutter, cut into rounds, gathering up the scraps and re-rolling to make more.

5 Arrange the rounds on the lined baking sheet, setting them quite close together so they support each other as they rise.

6 Put into the hot oven and cook for 15–20 minutes, until risen and golden brown. Transfer to a wire rack and sprinkle with caster sugar. Leave to cool.

Cook's Tip
Replace the caraway seeds with 50g/2oz dried fruit, such as raisins or finely chopped apricots.

Oat and Raisin Drop Scones

Serve these scones at tea time or as a dessert with real maple syrup or honey. If you are feeling indulgent, add a spoonful of sour cream or crème fraîche.

Makes about 16

75g/3oz/¾ cup self-raising (self-rising) flour
pinch of salt
2.5ml/½ tsp baking powder
50g/2oz/scant ½ cup raisins
25g/1oz/¼ cup fine oatmeal
25g/1oz/2 tbsp caster (superfine) sugar
grated rind of 1 orange
2 egg yolks
7.5ml/1½ tsp unsalted (sweet) butter, melted
100ml/3½fl oz single (light) cream
100ml/3½fl oz/scant ½ cup water

1 Sift together the flour, salt and baking powder into a large mixing bowl.

2 Add the raisins, oatmeal, caster sugar and grated orange rind and stir well to mix. Gradually beat in the egg yolks, melted butter, cream and measured water until thoroughly combined into a creamy batter.

3 Lightly grease and heat a large frying pan or griddle and drop about 30ml/2 tbsp of batter at a time on to the pan or griddle to make six or seven small pancakes.

4 Cook over a medium heat until bubbles show on the scones' surface, then turn them over and cook for another 2 minutes until golden.

5 Transfer the scones to a plate and keep warm while cooking the remaining mixture. Serve warm.

Cook's Tip
There are two secrets to making light-as-air drop scones. Firstly, do not leave the batter to stand once it has been mixed. The second is to heat the frying pan or griddle slowly until it is very hot before adding the batter.

Suffolk Buns Energy 244kcal/1026kJ; Protein 5.1g; Carbohydrate 36.9g, of which sugars 7.3g; Fat 9.5g, of which saturates 5.4g; Cholesterol 53mg; Calcium 60mg; Fibre 1.1g; Sodium 75mg.
Oat and Raisin Drop Scones Energy 375kcal/1574kJ; Protein 5.6g; Carbohydrate 50g, of which sugars 23.2g; Fat 18.4g, of which saturates 9.6g; Cholesterol 57mg; Calcium 93mg; Fibre 1.8g; Sodium 129mg.

Individual Apple Cakes

These delicate little cakes can be rustled up in next to no time for eating hot when visitors call. The quantities have been kept small because they really must be eaten while still fresh. To make more, simply double up on the measures.

Makes 8–10
125g/4¹/₂oz/generous 1 cup self-raising (self-rising) flour, plus extra for dusting
pinch of salt
65g/2¹/₂oz/5 tbsp butter, diced
50g/2oz/4 tbsp demerara (raw) or light muscovado (brown) sugar
1 small cooking apple, weighing about 150g/5oz
about 30ml/2 tbsp milk
caster (superfine) sugar, for dusting

1 Sift the flour and salt into a mixing bowl. Add the butter and, with your fingertips, rub it into the flour until the mixture resembles fine breadcrumbs. Stir in the sugar.

2 Peel and grate the apple, discarding the core, and stir the apple into the flour mixture with enough milk to make a mixture that can be gathered into a ball of soft, moist dough. Work it slightly to make sure the flour is mixed in well.

3 Transfer to a lightly floured surface and roll out the dough to about 5mm/¼in thick. With a 6–7.5cm/2½–3in cookie cutter, stamp out rounds, gathering up the scraps and re-rolling them to make more rounds.

4 Heat a heavy frying pan over low to medium heat. Smear a little butter on the pan and cook in batches, for about 4–5 minutes on each side, or until golden and cooked through.

5 Lift on to a wire rack and dust with caster sugar. Serve warm.

> **Cook's Tip**
> Add a pinch of ground cinnamon or nutmeg to the flour.

Hot Currant Cakes

Traditionally many cooks use half lard and half butter in this recipe. Serve the hot currant cakes warm or cold, as they are, or buttered.

Makes about 16
250g/9oz/2¹/₄ cups plain (all-purpose) flour, plus extra for dusting
pinch of salt
7.5ml/1¹/₄ tsp baking powder
125g/4¹/₂oz/¹/₂ cup butter, diced
100g/3¹/₂oz/¹/₂ cup caster (superfine) sugar, plus extra for dusting
75g/3oz/¹/₃ cup currants
1 egg
45ml/3 tbsp milk

1 Sift the flour, salt and baking powder into a large mixing bowl. Add the butter and, with your fingertips, rub it into the flour until it resembles fine breadcrumbs. Stir in the sugar and currants.

2 Lightly beat the egg and with a round-end knife and with a cutting action, stir it into the flour mixture with enough milk to gather the mixture into a ball of soft dough.

3 Transfer to a lightly floured surface and roll out to about 5mm/¼in thick. With a 6–7.5cm/2½–3in cookie cutter, stamp out rounds, gathering up the scraps and re-rolling to make more rounds.

4 Heat a heavy frying pan over medium to low heat. Smear a little butter or oil over the pan and cook the cakes, in small batches, for about 4–5 minutes on each side, or until they are slightly risen, golden brown and cooked through.

5 Transfer to a wire rack, dust with caster sugar on both sides and leave to cool.

> **Variation**
> For a change, add a large pinch of mixed spice (apple pie spice) in step 1, or a little vanilla extract in step 2.

Hot Currant Cakes Energy 128kcal/540kJ; Protein 4.1g; Carbohydrate 22.8g, of which sugars 1.3g; Fat 2.9g, of which saturates 1.4g; Cholesterol 29mg; Calcium 66mg; Fibre 0.9g; Sodium 29mg.
Individual Apple Cakes Energy 121kcal/508kJ; Protein 1.4g; Carbohydrate 16.5g, of which sugars 6.9g; Fat 6g, of which saturates 3.7g; Cholesterol 15mg; Calcium 26mg; Fibre 0.6g; Sodium 45mg.

Pineapple and Cinnamon Drop Scones

Making the batter with pineapple juice instead of milk cuts down on the amount of fat and adds a delicious piquancy to the flavour of these delicious drop scones.

Makes 24
115g/4oz/1 cup self-raising (self-rising) wholemeal (whole-wheat) flour
115g/4oz/1 cup self-raising (self-rising) white flour
5ml/1 tsp ground cinnamon
15ml/1 tbsp caster (superfine) sugar
1 egg
300ml/½ pint/1¼ cups pineapple juice
75g/3oz/½ cup semi-dried pineapple, chopped

1 Put the wholemeal flour in a mixing bowl. Sift in the white flour, add the cinnamon and caster sugar and mix together. Make a well in the centre. Add the egg with half of the pineapple juice to the well.

2 Gradually incorporate the flour to make a smooth batter, then beat in the remaining pineapple juice and stir in the chopped pineapple.

3 Heat a griddle, then lightly grease it. Drop tablespoons of the batter on to the surface, spacing them apart, and leave them until they bubble and the bubbles begin to burst.

4 Turn over the drop scones with a metal spatula and cook until the underside is golden brown. Continue to cook in successive batches.

> **Cook's Tips**
> • Drop scones do not keep well and are best eaten freshly cooked. In any case, they are especially delicious served hot.
> • If self-raising (self-rising) wholemeal (whole-wheat) flour is not readily available, use white self-raising flour instead.

Drop Scones

These little scones are delicious, spread with jam.

Makes 18
225g/8oz/2 cups self-raising (self-rising) flour
pinch of salt
15ml/1 tbsp caster (superfine) sugar
1 egg, beaten
300ml/½ pint/1¼ cups skimmed (low fat) milk

1 Preheat a griddle or heavy frying pan.

2 Sift the flour and salt into a mixing bowl. Stir in the sugar and make a well in the centre.

3 Add the egg and half the milk, then gradually incorporate the surrounding flour to make a smooth batter. Beat in the remaining milk.

4 Lightly grease the griddle or pan. Drop tablespoons of the batter on to the surface, leaving them until they bubble and the bubbles begin to burst.

5 Turn the drop scones over with a metal spatula and cook until the underside is golden brown. Keep the cooked drop scones warm and moist by wrapping them in a clean napkin while cooking successive batches.

> **Variation**
> For savoury scones, omit the sugar and add 2 chopped spring onions (scallions) and 15ml/1 tbsp freshly grated Parmesan cheese to the batter. Serve with cottage cheese.

Scotch Pancakes

Serve these pancakes while they're still warm, with butter and jam.

Makes 24
225g/8oz/2 cups self-raising (self-rising) flour
50g/2oz/4 tbsp caster (superfine) sugar
50g/2oz/4 tbsp butter, melted
1 egg
300ml/½ pint/1¼ cups milk
15g/½oz/1 tbsp lard

1 Mix the flour and sugar together in a bowl.

2 Add the melted butter and egg and two-thirds of the milk. Mix to a smooth batter, adding more milk, if necessary — it should be thin enough to find its own level.

3 Heat a griddle or heavy frying pan and wipe it with a little lard. When hot, drop spoonfuls of the mixture on to the hot griddle or pan. When bubbles come to the surface of the pancakes, flip them over to cook until golden on the other side. Keep the pancakes warm wrapped in a dish towel while cooking the rest of the mixture.

Drop Scones Energy 64 Kcals/270 KJ; Fat 1.09 g; Saturated Fat 0.20 g; Cholesterol 11.03 mg; Fibre 0.43 g. Scotch Pancakes Energy 67kcal/282kJ; Protein 1.6g; Carbohydrate 10.1g, of which sugars 2.9g; Fat 2.6g, of which saturates 1.3g; Cholesterol 13mg; Calcium 31mg; Fibre 0.3g; Sodium 19mg. Pineapple and Cinnamon Drop Scones Energy 64 Kcals/270 KJ; Fat 1.09 g; Saturated Fat 0.20 g; Cholesterol 11.03 mg; Fibre 0.43 g.

Lavender Scones

Lend an unusual but delicious lavender perfume to your scones – its fragrance marries well with the sweetness of summer soft fruit and makes for an elegant, romantic teatime treat. Nowadays, the flavour can seem quite surprising, because the scented quality of the lavender permeates through the well-known tea scone.

Makes 12
225g/8oz/2 cups plain
   (all-purpose) flour
15ml/1 tbsp baking powder
50g/2oz/¼ cup butter
50g/2oz/¼ cup sugar
10ml/2 tsp fresh lavender florets
   or 5ml/1 tsp dried culinary
   lavender, coarsely chopped
about 150ml/¼ pint/⅔ cup milk
plum jam and clotted or whipped
   double (heavy) cream, to serve

1 Preheat the oven to 220°C/425°F/Gas 7. Lightly grease a baking sheet.

2 Sift the flour and baking powder together. Rub the butter into the flour mixture until it resembles breadcrumbs.

3 Stir in the sugar and lavender, reserving a pinch to sprinkle on the top of the scones before baking them. Add enough milk to make a soft, sticky dough. Bind the dough together and then turn it out on to a well-floured surface.

4 Shape the dough into a round, gently patting down the top to give a 2.5cm/1in depth. Using a floured cookie cutter, stamp out 12 scones. Place on the baking sheet. Brush the tops with a little milk and sprinkle over the reserved lavender.

5 Bake for 10–12 minutes, until golden. Transfer to a wire rack to cool. Serve warm, split in half and spread with plum jam and clotted or whipped cream.

> **Variation**
> *Other fragrant flowers can also be used to make these scones.*
> *Try rosemary flowers, mimosa or rose petals.*

Scones with Jam and Cream

Scones, often known as biscuits in the US, are thought to originate from Scotland, where they are still a popular part of afternoon tea served with jams, jellies and thick whipped cream.

Makes about 12
450g/1lb/4 cups self-raising
   (self-rising) flour, plus extra
   for dusting
pinch of salt
50g/2oz/¼ cup butter, chilled
   and diced
15ml/1 tbsp lemon juice
about 400ml/14fl oz/1⅔ cups
   milk, plus extra to glaze
fruit jam and clotted cream or
   whipped double (heavy)
   cream, to serve

1 Preheat the oven to 230°C/450°F/Gas 8. Sift flour over a baking sheet.

2 Sift the flour and salt into a mixing bowl. Add the butter and rub it into the flour with your fingertips until the mixture resembles fine breadcrumbs.

3 Whisk the lemon juice into the milk and leave for about 1 minute to thicken slightly, then pour into the flour mixture and mix quickly to form a soft but pliable dough. The wetter the mixture, the lighter the resulting scone will be, but if they are too wet they will spread during baking and lose their shape.

4 Knead the dough lightly to form a ball, then roll it out on a floured surface to a thickness of at least 2.5cm/1in. Using a 5cm/2in cookie cutter, and dipping it into flour each time, stamp out 12 scones. Place on the baking sheet. Re-roll any trimmings and cut out more scones if you can.

5 Brush the tops of the scones lightly with a little milk, then bake for about 20 minutes, or until risen and golden brown.

6 Wrap the scones in a clean dish towel to keep them warm and soft until ready to serve. Split the scones in half and spread with fruit jam and a generous spoonful of cream.

Lavender Scones Energy 115kcal/484kJ; Protein 2.3g; Carbohydrate 18.8g, of which sugars 4.5g; Fat 3.9g, of which saturates 2.4g; Cholesterol 10mg; Calcium 46mg; Fibre 0.6g; Sodium 32mg.
Scones with Jam and Cream Energy 177kcal/749kJ; Protein 4.7g; Carbohydrate 30.7g, of which sugars 2.2g; Fat 4.8g, of which saturates 2.8g; Cholesterol 12mg; Calcium 93mg; Fibre 1.2g; Sodium 43mg.

Sunflower Sultana Scones

Traditional fruit scones are given a delightful new twist with a crunchy topping of sunflower seeds.

Makes 10–12
225g/8oz/2 cups self-raising (self-rising) flour, plus extra for dusting
5ml/1 tsp baking powder
25g/1oz/2 tbsp butter
30ml/2 tbsp golden caster (superfine) sugar
50g/2oz/⅓ cup sultanas (golden raisins)
30ml/2 tbsp sunflower seeds
150g/5oz/⅔ cup natural (plain) yogurt
about 30–45ml/2–3 tbsp milk
butter and jam, to serve

1 Preheat the oven to 230°C/450°F/Gas 8. Lightly grease a baking sheet.

2 Sift together the flour and baking powder into a bowl. Add the butter and rub it in with your fingertips until the mixture resembles fine breadcrumbs. Add the sugar, sultanas and half the sunflower seeds and stir well to mix.

3 Stir in the yogurt, then add just enough milk to mix to a soft but not wet dough.

4 Roll out on a lightly floured surface to about 2cm/¾in thick. Stamp out 6cm/2½in rounds with a floured cookie cutter and lift on to the baking sheet.

5 Brush the tops of the scones with milk and sprinkle with the reserved sunflower seeds.

6 Bake for 10–12 minutes, until well risen and golden brown. Transfer to a wire rack. Serve while still warm, split in half and spread with butter and jam.

> **Variation**
> *You could substitute pumpkin seeds for the sunflower ones. Both are high in nutrients and have the essential crunch factor.*

Traditional Sweet Scones

These traditional breakfast or teatime treats have a golden crust and a lovely, light soft inside.

Makes 8
170g/6oz/1½ cups self-raising (self-rising) flour, plus extra for dusting
30ml/2 tbsp sugar
15ml/1 tbsp baking powder
pinch of salt
50g/2oz/4 tbsp butter, chilled and diced
120ml4fl oz/½ cup milk
butter and jam, to serve

1 Preheat the oven to 425°F/220°C/Gas 7. Lightly grease a baking sheet.

2 Sift the flour, sugar, baking powder and salt into a bowl.

3 Add the butter and rub in with your fingertips until the mixture resembles fine breadcrumbs.

4 Pour in the milk and stir with a fork to form a soft dough.

5 Roll out the dough on a lightly floured surface to 3cm/1¼in thick. Stamp out rounds using a floured 5cm/2in cookie cutter.

6 Place on the baking sheet and bake for about 12 minutes, until golden. Serve hot or warm, split in half and spread with butter and jam.

Buttermilk Scones

At one time, buttermilk was thought to be a good food for children – it certainly makes scones they'll find irresistible.

Makes 15
200g/7oz/1¾ cups plain (all-purpose) flour, plus extra for dusting
pinch of salt
5ml/1 tsp baking powder
2.5ml/½ tsp bicarbonate of soda (baking soda)
50g/2oz/¼ cup cold butter
175ml/6fl oz/¾ cup buttermilk

1 Preheat the oven to 220°C/425°F/Gas 7. Lightly grease and dust a baking sheet with flour.

2 Sift the flour, salt, baking powder and bicarbonate of soda into a bowl. Rub in the butter with your fingertips until the mixture resembles breadcrumbs.

3 Gradually pour in the buttermilk, stirring with a fork to form a soft dough.

4 Roll out the dough on a lightly floured surface to about 3cm/1¼in thick. Stamp out rounds with a 5cm/2in cookie cutter.

5 Place on the prepared baking sheet and bake for 12–15 minutes, until golden. Serve the scones warm, split in half and spread with butter.

Sunflower Sultana Scones Energy 121kcal/513kJ; Protein 3g; Carbohydrate 21.2g, of which sugars 6.9g; Fat 3.3g, of which saturates 0.6g; Cholesterol 0mg; Calcium 99mg; Fibre 0.8g; Sodium 97mg.
Traditional Sweet Scones Energy 89kcal/379kJ; Protein 2.6g; Carbohydrate 19.7g, of which sugars 3g; Fat 0.6g, of which saturates 0.2g; Cholesterol 1mg; Calcium 50mg; Fibre 0.7g; Sodium 8mg.
Buttermilk Scones Energy 74kcal/311kJ; Protein 1.7g; Carbohydrate 10.9g, of which sugars 0.7g; Fat 2.9g, of which saturates 1.8g; Cholesterol 8mg; Calcium 34mg; Fibre 0.4g; Sodium 26mg.

Orange and Raisin Scones

These sweet, tangy scones are really at their best served warm, in the traditional Cornish way, with thick cream and homemade jam.

Makes 16

225g/8oz/2 cups plain (all-purpose) flour, plus extra for dusting
25ml/1½ tbsp baking powder
75g/3oz/scant ½ cup caster (superfine) sugar
pinch of salt
65g/2½oz/5 tbsp butter, chopped
grated rind of 1 large orange
50g/2oz/⅓ cup raisins
115g/4oz/½ cup buttermilk
milk, for glazing

1 Preheat the oven to 220°C/425°F/Gas 7. Lightly grease and flour a large baking sheet.

2 Sift the flour, baking powder, caster sugar and salt into a large bowl. Rub in the butter with your fingertips until the mixture resembles fine breadcrumbs.

3 Add the orange rind and raisins and mix well. Gradually stir in the buttermilk to form a soft dough.

4 Roll out the dough on a lightly floured surface to about 2cm/¾in thick. Stamp out rounds with a floured 5cm/2in cookie cutter.

5 Place on the baking sheet and brush the tops with milk to glaze. Bake for 12–15 minutes, until golden brown. Serve hot or warm, split in half and spread with butter or whipped cream and jam.

> **Cook's Tips**
> • To be sure that the scones are light and delicate, handle the dough as little as possible and bake them as soon as they are ready to go in the oven.
> • If you wish, split the scones when cool and toast them under a preheated grill (broiler). Butter them while they are still hot.

Wholemeal Scones

These scones make a delicious and healthy option. As you would expect, they taste great spread with jam, but they are also surprisingly good with cheese – either soft or hard.

Makes 16

225g/8oz/2 cups wholemeal (whole-wheat) flour
115g/4oz/1 cup plain (all-purpose) flour, plus extra for dusting
30ml/2 tbsp caster (superfine) sugar
pinch of salt
12.5ml/2½ tsp bicarbonate of soda (baking soda)
175g/6oz/¾ cup butter, chilled and diced
2 eggs
175ml/6fl oz/¾ cup buttermilk
40g/1½oz/⅓ cup raisins

1 Preheat the oven to 200°C/400°F/Gas 6. Lightly grease and flour a large baking sheet.

2 Sift together the flours, caster sugar, salt and bicarbonate of soda into a large bowl. Add the diced butter and rub it in with your fingertips until the mixture resembles fine breadcrumbs. Set aside.

3 In another bowl, whisk together the eggs and buttermilk. Set aside 30ml/2 tbsp for glazing.

4 Add the remaining egg mixture to the dry ingredients and stir to mix to a soft but not wet dough. Add the raisins and knead lightly until they are incorporated.

5 Roll out the dough on a lightly floured surface to about 2cm/¾in thick. Stamp out rounds with a floured cookie cutter. Place on the prepared baking sheet and brush the tops with the reserved egg mixture.

6 Bake for 12–15 minutes until golden brown. Leave to cool slightly before serving. Split the scones in half while they are still warm and spread with butter. Eat within a day of baking, or freeze for later use.

Wholemeal Scones Energy 207kcal/869kJ; Protein 4.9g; Carbohydrate 25.3g, of which sugars 4.6g; Fat 10.3g, of which saturates 6g; Cholesterol 48mg; Calcium 42mg; Fibre 2.3g; Sodium 82mg.
Orange and Raisin Scones Energy 145kcal/606kJ; Protein 2g; Carbohydrate 19.8g, of which sugars 6.7g; Fat 6.9g, of which saturates 2.2g; Cholesterol 9mg; Calcium 38mg; Fibre 0.6g; Sodium 63mg.

Microwave Iced Cup Cakes

Make these ever-popular little cakes in just minutes and with no fuss at all.

Makes about 24
115g/4oz/1 cup self-raising (self-rising) flour
pinch of salt

50g/2oz/4 tbsp butter
50g/2oz/4 tbsp soft light brown sugar
1 egg, beaten
milk, to mix
glacé icing, to top
glacé (candied) cherries, to decorate

1 Sift the flour with the salt into a bowl, rub in the butter until the mixture resembles fine breadcrumbs, then stir in the sugar.

2 Mix in the egg and enough milk to form a mixture with a soft dropping (pourable) consistency.

3 Place six paper cases in a six-hole microwave-proof muffin pan and place spoonfuls of the prepared cake mixture into each, filling them each about two-thirds full.

4 Microwave on 100 per cent power for 2 minutes, giving the dish a half-turn after 1 minute. Transfer to a wire rack to cool. Repeat with the remaining mixture, cooking in batches of six. Leave to cool completely before decorating.

5 To finish, coat the tops of the cakes with soft glacé icing. Decorate with a cherry.

> **Cook's Tip**
> Make and eat microwave-cooked cup cakes on the same day. Alternatively, freeze them before adding any toppings.

> **Variation**
> For Chocolate Cup Cakes prepare as above but add 15ml/ 1 tbsp sifted unsweetened cocoa powder to the flour mixture. For Fairy Currant Cakes prepare the mixture as above but add 25g/1oz/2 tbsp currants to the mixture with the eggs and milk.

Fairy Cakes with Blueberries

This luxurious way to make fairy cakes means you can serve them to adults and guests as well as kids.

Makes 12–14 cakes
115g/4oz/½ cup butter
115g/4oz/generous ½ cup caster (superfine) sugar
5ml/1 tsp grated lemon rind
pinch of salt
2 eggs, beaten

115g/4oz/1 cup self-raising (self-rising) flour
120ml/4fl oz/½ cup whipping cream
75–115g/3–4oz/¾–1 cup blueberries
icing sugar (confectioners') sugar, for dusting

1 Preheat the oven to 190°C/375°F/Gas 5. Arrange 12–14 paper cases in a small muffin tin (pan).

2 In a large bowl, beat the butter, sugar, lemon rind and salt until pale and fluffy.

3 Gradually beat in the eggs, then gradually sift over the flour and fold in until well mixed.

4 Spoon the mixture into the paper cake cases, and bake for 15–20 minutes, until just golden. Leave the cakes to cool.

5 Scoop out a circle of sponge from the top of each cake using the point of a small sharp knife, and set them aside.

6 Whip the cream until stiff peaks form. Place a spoonful of cream in each sponge, plus 2–3 blueberries. Replace the lids at an angle and dust with sifted icing sugar.

> **Variation**
> You can substitute other fruit, such as small strawberries, for the blueberries, but do not prepare the cakes too far in advance of serving them or the cream will discolour with the juices from the fruit.

Microwave Iced Cup Cakes Energy 43kcal/181kJ; Protein 0.7g; Carbohydrate 5.9g, of which sugars 2.3g; Fat 2g, of which saturates 1.2g; Cholesterol 12mg; Calcium 9mg; Fibre 0.2g; Sodium 16mg.
Fairy Cakes with Blueberries Energy 231kcal/962kJ; Protein 2.7g; Carbohydrate 21.5g, of which sugars 13g; Fat 15.5g, of which saturates 3.4g; Cholesterol 51mg; Calcium 63mg; Fibre 0.6g; Sodium 151mg.

Daisy Cakes

What could be prettier for afternoon tea or a children's birthday party than these scrumptious little cakes decorated with daisy petals? The daisy centre is made from coloured icing.

Makes 15–20
115g/4oz/½ cup butter, softened
115g/4oz/generous ½ cup caster (superfine) sugar
2 eggs
115g/4oz/1 cup self-raising (self-rising) flour
2.5ml/½ tsp baking powder
10ml/2 tsp lemon juice

To decorate
115g/4oz/1 cup icing (confectioners') sugar
15ml/1 tbsp water
dash of yellow food colouring
2–3 daisies

1 Preheat the oven to 180°C/350°F/Gas 4. Arrange 15–20 paper cases in a small muffin tin (pan).

2 Put the butter in a bowl with the sugar and eggs. Sift the flour and baking powder into the bowl. Add the lemon juice and beat until pale and creamy.

3 Spoon the mixture into the cases and bake for about 15 minutes, until risen and golden. Transfer to a wire rack and leave to cool.

4 To decorate, beat the icing sugar with the water until the glaze thinly coats the back of the spoon. Add a dash of yellow food colouring to match the centre of the real daisy flowers.

5 Spoon a little icing on to each cake. Gently pull the petals from a daisy and use to decorate. Repeat with the remainder of the cakes.

> **Cook's Tip**
> When using fresh flowers, make sure that they are clean and not polluted with pesticides or traffic fumes.

Iced Fancies

Everyone loves these pretty cakes. Utilize your artistic skills to make them look as tempting as possible.

Makes 16
115g/4oz/½ cup butter, at room temperature
225g/8oz/generous 1 cup caster (superfine) sugar
2 eggs, at room temperature
175g/6oz/1½ cups plain (all-purpose) flour
pinch of salt
7.5ml/1½ tsp baking powder
120ml/4fl oz/½ cup plus 15ml/1 tbsp milk
5ml/1 tsp vanilla extract

For icing and decorating
2 large (US extra large) egg whites
400g/14oz/3½ cups sifted icing (confectioners') sugar
1–2 drops glycerine
juice of 1 lemon
food colourings, hundreds and thousands, crystallized (candied) lemon and orange slices, to decorate

1 Preheat the oven to 190°C/375°F/Gas 5. Arrange 16 paper cases in a muffin tin (pan).

2 In a large bowl, beat the butter and sugar until light and fluffy. Add the eggs, one at a time, beating well after each addition.

3 Sift together the flour, salt and baking powder into the butter mixture in batches, alternating with the milk. Stir in the vanilla. Beat well to combine.

4 Fill the paper cups half-full and bake for about 20 minutes until the tops spring back when touched lightly. Let the cakes stand in the tray for 5 minutes, then turn out and transfer to a rack to cool completely.

5 For the icing, beat the egg whites until stiff but not dry. Gradually add the sugar, glycerine and lemon juice, and continue beating for 1 minute. The consistency should be spreadable. If necessary, thin with a little water or add more sifted icing sugar to thicken. Divide among several bowls and tint with food colourings. Spread different coloured icings over the cakes and decorate as desired.

Iced Fancies Energy 259kcal/1094kJ; Protein 2.7g; Carbohydrate 49.7g, of which sugars 41.4g; Fat 6.9g, of which saturates 4g; Cholesterol 40mg; Calcium 50mg; Fibre 0.3g; Sodium 66mg.
Daisy Cakes Energy 115kcal/483kJ; Protein 1.3g; Carbohydrate 16.5g, of which sugars 12.1g; Fat 5.4g, of which saturates 3.2g; Cholesterol 31mg; Calcium 18mg; Fibre 0.2g; Sodium 43mg.

Blueberry Muffins

Light and fruity, these well-known American muffins are delicious at any time of day. Serve them warm for breakfast or brunch, or as a tea-time treat.

Makes 12
2 eggs
50g/2oz/4 tbsp butter, melted
175ml/6fl oz/³/₄ cup milk
5ml/1 tsp vanilla extract

5ml/1 tsp grated lemon rind
180g/6¹/₄oz/generous 1¹/₂ cups
    plain (all-purpose) flour
60g/2¹/₄oz/generous ¹/₄ cup sugar
10ml/2 tsp baking powder
pinch of salt
175g/6oz/1¹/₂ cups fresh
    blueberries

1 Preheat the oven to 200°C/400°F/Gas 6. Arrange 12 paper cases in a muffin tin (pan) or grease the tin.

2 In a bowl, whisk the eggs until blended. Add the melted butter, milk, vanilla and lemon rind, and stir to combine.

3 Sift the flour, sugar, baking powder and salt into a large bowl. Make a well in the centre and pour in the egg mixture. With a metal spoon, stir until the flour is just moistened.

4 Add the blueberries to the muffin mixture and gently fold in.

5 Spoon the batter into the muffin tin or paper cases, leaving enough room for the muffins to rise.

6 Bake for 20–25 minutes, until the tops spring back when touched lightly. Leave the muffins in the tin, if using, for 5 minutes before turning out on to a wire rack to cool.

> **Variation**
> *Muffins are delicious with all kinds of different fruits. Try out some variations using this basic muffin recipe. Replace the blueberries with the same weight of bilberries, blackcurrants, pitted cherries or raspberries.*

Wholemeal Banana Muffins

Wholemeal muffins, with banana for added fibre, make a great treat at any time of the day. If you like, slice off the tops and fill with a teaspoon of jam or marmalade, then replace the tops before serving.

Makes 12
75g/3oz/³/₄ cup plain
    (all-purpose) wholemeal
    (whole-wheat) flour
50g/2oz/¹/₂ cup plain
    (all-purpose) white flour

10ml/2 tsp baking powder
pinch of salt
5ml/1 tsp mixed spice (apple
    pie spice)
40g/1¹/₂oz/scant ¹/₄ cup soft light
    brown sugar
50g/2oz/¹/₄ cup butter
1 egg, beaten
150ml/¹/₄ pint/²/₃ cup semi-
    skimmed (low-fat) milk
grated rind of 1 orange
1 ripe banana
20g/³/₄oz/¹/₄ cup rolled oats
20g/³/₄oz/scant ¹/₄ cup chopped
    hazelnuts

1 Preheat the oven to 200°C/400°F/Gas 6. Arrange 12 paper cases in a muffin tin (pan)

2 Sift together both flours, the baking powder, salt and mixed spice into a bowl, then add the bran remaining in the sieve (strainer) to the bowl. Stir in the sugar.

3 Melt the butter in a pan over a very low heat. Remove from the heat and leave to cool slightly, then beat in the egg, milk and grated orange rind. Make a well in the centre of the flour mixture, pour in the butter mixture and beat well to incorporate the dry ingredients.

4 Mash the banana with a fork, then stir it gently into the mixture, being careful not to overmix. Spoon the mixture into the paper cases.

5 Combine the oats and hazelnuts and sprinkle a little of the mixture over each muffin.

6 Bake for 20 minutes until the muffins are well risen and golden, and a skewer inserted in the centre comes out clean. Transfer to a wire rack and serve warm or cold.

Blueberry Muffins Energy 236kcal/992kJ; Protein 4.9g; Carbohydrate 34.7g, of which sugars 12.4g; Fat 9.6g, of which saturates 5.6g; Cholesterol 54mg; Calcium 88mg; Fibre 1.4g; Sodium 82mg.
Wholemeal Banana Muffins Energy 110Kcals/465KJ; Fat 5g Saturated Fat 1g; Cholesterol 17.5mg.

Banana Muffins

Make sure that you use really ripe bananas for these muffins, not just because those are the sweetest, but also because they are easy to mash to the proper smooth consistency.

Makes 12
225g/8oz/2 cups plain (all-purpose) flour
5ml/1 tsp baking powder
5ml/1 tsp bicarbonate of soda (baking soda)
pinch of salt
2.5ml/½ tsp ground cinnamon
1.5ml/¼ tsp grated nutmeg
3 large ripe bananas
1 egg
50g/2oz/¼ cup soft dark brown sugar
50ml/2fl oz/¼ cup vegetable oil
40g/1½oz/⅓ cup raisins

1 Preheat the oven to 190°C/375°F/Gas 5. Arrange 12 paper cases in a muffin tin (pan).

2 Sift together the flour, baking powder, bicarbonate of soda, salt, cinnamon and nutmeg. Set aside.

3 Using a fork, mash the peeled bananas to a smooth consistency in a large bowl.

4 Beat the egg, sugar and oil into the mashed bananas until fully combined.

5 Add the dry ingredients and beat in gradually, using an electric whisk set at low speed. Mix until just blended. With a wooden spoon, stir in the raisins until just combined. Spoon the mixture into the muffin tins, filling them two-thirds full.

6 Bake for 20–25 minutes, until the tops spring back when touched lightly with your finger. Transfer the muffins to a wire rack to cool completely before serving.

Variation
For Banana and Chocolate Muffins, substitute 50g/2oz/⅓ cup plain (semisweet) chocolate chips for the raisins.

Honey and Spice Muffins

These little golden muffins are fragrant with honey and cinnamon. Although their appearance is traditional when cooked directly in a bun tin, they tend to rise higher and are therefore lighter when baked in paper cases.

Makes 18
250g/9oz/2¼ cups plain (all-purpose) flour
5ml/1 tsp ground cinnamon
5ml/1 tsp bicarbonate of soda (baking soda)
125g/4½oz/generous ½ cup butter
125g/4½oz/generous ½ cup brown sugar
1 large (US extra large) egg, separated
125g/4½oz/generous ½ cup clear honey
caster (superfine) sugar, for sprinkling

1 Preheat the oven to 200°C/400°F/Gas 6. Line a bun tin (muffin pan) with paper cases.

2 Sift together the flour, cinnamon and the bicarbonate of soda into a large bowl.

3 In another bowl, beat the butter with the sugar until light and fluffy. Beat in the egg yolk, then gradually add the honey and beat well until fully incorporated.

4 With a large metal spoon and a cutting action, fold in the flour mixture plus sufficient milk to make a soft mixture that will just drop off the spoon.

5 In a separate grease-free bowl, whisk the egg white until stiff peaks form. Using a large metal spoon, fold the egg white into the cake mixture.

6 Divide the mixture among the paper cases in the prepared tin. Bake for 15–20 minutes, or until risen, firm to the touch and golden brown.

7 Sprinkle the tops lightly with caster sugar and leave to cool completely on a wire rack.

Banana Muffins Energy 152kcal/642kJ; Protein 2.8g; Carbohydrate 29g, of which sugars 13.9g; Fat 3.6g, of which saturates 0.5g; Cholesterol 16mg; Calcium 34mg; Fibre 1g; Sodium 9mg.
Honey and Spice Muffins Energy 152kcal/639kJ; Protein 1.9g; Carbohydrate 23.6g, of which sugars 13g; Fat 6.3g, of which saturates 3.8g; Cholesterol 26mg; Calcium 30mg; Fibre 0.4g; Sodium 49mg.

Apricot and Orange Muffins

Serve these fruity muffins freshly baked and warm.

Makes 8 large or 12 medium muffins
115g/4oz/1 cup cornmeal
75g/3oz/¾ cup rice flour
15ml/1 tbsp baking powder
pinch of salt

50g/2oz/4 tbsp butter, melted
50g/2oz/¼ cup light soft
    brown sugar
1 egg, beaten
200ml/7fl oz/scant 1 cup semi-
    skimmed (low-fat) milk
finely grated rind of 1 orange
115g/4oz/½ cup ready-to-eat
    dried apricots, chopped

1 Preheat the oven to 200°C/400°F/Gas 6. Arrange 12 paper cases in a muffin tin (pan).

2 Place the cornmeal, rice flour, baking powder and salt in a bowl and mix together.

3 Stir together the melted butter, sugar, egg, milk and orange rind, then pour the mixture over the dry ingredients. Fold the ingredients gently together. The mixture will look quite lumpy, which is correct, as over-mixing will result in heavy muffins.

4 Fold in the chopped dried apricots, then spoon the mixture into the prepared paper cases, dividing it equally among them.

5 Bake for 15–20 minutes, until the muffins have risen and are golden brown and springy to the touch. Turn them out on to a wire rack to cool.

6 Serve the muffins warm or cold, on their own or cut in half and spread with a little butter or low-fat spread. Store in an airtight container for up to 1 week or seal in plastic bags and freeze for up to 3 months.

Variation
Try substituting grapefruit rind for the orange and the same quantity of chopped dried mango for the apricots.

Lemon Meringue Muffins

This recipe is a delightful variation on the classic fairy cake – soft lemon sponge cake is topped with crisp meringue.

Makes 18
115g/4oz/½ cup butter
200g/7oz/scant 1 cup caster
    (superfine) sugar

2 eggs
115g/4oz/1 cup self-raising
    (self-rising) flour
5ml/1 tsp baking powder
grated rind of 2 lemons
30ml/2 tbsp lemon juice
2 egg whites

1 Preheat the oven to 190°C/375°F/Gas 5. Arrange 18 paper cases in a muffin tin (pan).

2 Put the butter in a bowl and beat until soft. Add 115g/4oz/ generous ½ cup of the caster sugar and continue to beat until the mixture is smooth and creamy.

3 Beat in the eggs. Sift together the flour and baking powder over the mixture, add half the lemon rind and all the lemon juice and beat well until thoroughly combined.

4 Divide the mixture among the paper cases.

5 To make the meringue, whisk the egg whites in a clean grease-free bowl until they stand in soft peaks. Stir in the remaining caster sugar and lemon rind. Put a spoonful of the meringue mixture on each cake.

6 Cook for 20–25 minutes, until the meringue is crisp and brown. Serve hot or cold.

Cook's Tip
Make sure that you whisk the egg whites enough before adding the sugar – when you lift out the whisk they should stand in peaks that just flop over slightly at the top.

Apricot and Orange Muffins Energy136kcals/572kJ; Fat, total 4.6g; saturated fat 1g; Protein2.9g; Carbohydrate 21g; sugar, total 8.5g; Fibre 0.9g; Sodium195mg.
Lemon Meringue Muffins Energy 123kcal/514kJ; Protein 1.7g; Carbohydrate 16.6g, of which sugars 11.7g; Fat 6g, of which saturates 3.5g; Cholesterol 35mg; Calcium 19mg; Fibre 0.2g; Sodium 54mg.

Raspberry Crumble Muffins

Make these stylish muffins for a special occasion in the summer when raspberries are bursting with flavour. For total luxury, serve like scones, with raspberry jam and cream.

Makes 12
175g/6oz/1½ cups plain
  (all-purpose) flour
10ml/2 tsp baking powder
pinch of salt
5ml/1 tsp ground cinnamon
50g/2oz/¼ cup sugar
50g/2oz/¼ cup soft light
  brown sugar

115g/4oz/½ cup butter, melted
1 egg
120ml/4fl oz/½ cup milk
225g/8oz/1⅓ cups fresh
  raspberries
grated rind of 1 lemon

For the crumble topping
50g/2oz/½ cup pecan nuts,
  finely chopped
50g/2oz/¼ cup soft dark
  brown sugar
45ml/3 tbsp plain
  (all-purpose) flour
5ml/1 tsp ground cinnamon
40g/1½oz/3 tbsp butter, melted

1 Preheat the oven to 180°C/350°F/Gas 4. Arrange 12 paper cases in a muffin tin (pan).

2 Sift the flour, baking powder, salt and cinnamon into a bowl. Stir in the sugars. Make a well in the centre.

3 Beat together the butter, egg and milk in a large bowl until light. Add the flour mixture to it and stir until just combined. Stir in the raspberries and lemon rind.

4 Spoon the batter into the muffin tins, filling them almost to the top.

5 To make the topping, mix the pecans, sugar, flour and cinnamon in a bowl. Stir in the melted butter.

6 Spoon a little of the crumble topping over the top of each muffin. Bake for about 25 minutes.

7 Transfer to a wire rack to cool slightly. Serve the muffins warm.

Raspberry Buttermilk Muffins

Low-fat buttermilk gives these muffins a light and spongy texture. Make them in the summer when fresh raspberries are at their seasonal best.

Makes 10–12
300g/11oz/2¾ cups plain
  (all-purpose) flour
15ml/1 tbsp baking powder
115g/4oz/generous ½ cup caster
  (superfine) sugar
1 egg
250ml/8fl oz/1 cup buttermilk
60ml/4 tbsp sunflower oil
150g/5oz/1 cup raspberries

1 Preheat the oven to 200°C/400°F/Gas 6. Arrange 10–12 paper cases in a muffin tin (pan).

2 Sift the flour and baking powder into a mixing bowl. Stir in the sugar, then make a well in the centre.

3 Mix the egg, buttermilk and sunflower oil together in a bowl, pour into the flour mixture and mix quickly until just combined.

4 Add the raspberries and lightly fold them into the mixture with a metal spoon until just combined. Spoon the mixture into the prepared paper cases, filling them about two-thirds full.

5 Bake for 20–25 minutes, until golden brown and firm in the centre. Transfer to a wire rack and serve warm or cold.

Cook's Tips
• *As with other soft fruits – which can also be used in these delicious muffins – don't buy more raspberries than you require as they deteriorate quickly, although they do freeze well. If they're sold in packs, make sure that there are no squashed ones underneath. Avoid soaking them in water when washing them; just wipe with damp kitchen paper.*
• *Raspberry muffins make a fabulous breakfast treat with butter and honey and are great at teatime when served warm with raspberry jam and thickly whipped cream.*

Raspberry Buttermilk Muffins Energy 132kcal/555kJ; Protein 4g; Carbohydrate 19g, of which sugars 5.7g; Fat 5g, of which saturates 2.7g; Cholesterol 42mg; Calcium 48mg; Fibre 1.5g; Sodium 45mg.
Raspberry Crumble Muffins Energy 225kcal/940kJ; Protein 2.7g; Carbohydrate 25.2g, of which sugars 14.1g; Fat 13.3g, of which saturates 7.3g; Cholesterol 45mg; Calcium 48mg; Fibre 0.9g; Sodium 93mg.

Apple and Cinnamon Muffins

These fruity, spicy muffins are quick and easy to make and are perfect for serving for breakfast or tea. The appetizing aroma as they bake is out of this world.

Makes 6
1 egg, beaten
40g/1½oz/3 tbsp caster (superfine) sugar
120ml/4fl oz/½ cup milk
50g/2oz/¼ cup butter, melted

150g/5oz/1¼ cups plain (all-purpose) flour
7.5ml/1½ tsp baking powder
pinch of salt
2.5ml/½ tsp ground cinnamon
2 small eating apples, peeled, cored and finely chopped

For the topping
12 brown sugar cubes, coarsely crushed
5ml/1 tsp ground cinnamon

1 Preheat the oven to 200°C/400°F/Gas 6. Arrange 6 paper cases in a muffin tin (pan).

2 Mix the egg, sugar, milk and melted butter in a large bowl. Sift in the flour, baking powder, salt and cinnamon. Add the chopped apple and mix roughly.

3 Spoon the mixture into the prepared muffin cases. To make the topping, mix the crushed sugar cubes with the cinnamon. Sprinkle over the uncooked muffins.

4 Bake for 30–35 minutes, until well risen and golden brown on top. Transfer the muffins to a wire rack to cool. Serve them warm or at room temperature.

> **Variation**
> You can also make these muffins with pears or even quinces, both of which go well with cinnamon.

> **Cook's Tip**
> Do not overmix the muffin mixture – it should still be slightly lumpy when spooned into the cases.

Date and Apple Muffins

These spiced muffins are delicious and very filling. If possible, use fresh Medjool dates from Egypt, as they have sweet, dense flesh and a truly opulent flavour.

Makes 12
150g/5oz/1¼ cups self-raising (self-rising) wholemeal (whole-wheat) flour
150g/5oz/1¼ cups self-raising (self-rising) flour

5ml/1 tsp ground cinnamon
5ml/1 tsp baking powder
25g/1oz/2 tbsp butter
75g/3oz/⅓ cup light muscovado (brown) sugar
250ml/8fl oz/1 cup apple juice
30ml/2 tbsp pear and apple jam
1 egg, lightly beaten
1 eating apple
75g/3oz/½ cup chopped dates
15ml/1 tbsp chopped pecan nuts

1 Preheat the oven to 200°C/400°F/Gas 6. Arrange 12 paper cases in a muffin tin (pan).

2 Sift together both flours, the cinnamon and baking powder into a large bowl. Add the butter and rub it in with your fingertips until the mixture resembles fine breadcrumbs. Add the sugar and stir well to mix.

3 In a mixing bowl, stir a little of the apple juice with the pear and apple jam until smooth. Mix in the remaining apple juice, then add to the rubbed-in mixture with the beaten egg.

4 Quarter and core the apple, and peel it if you like, then chop the flesh finely. Add to the batter and stir in the dates. Divide the mixture among the muffin cases.

5 Sprinkle the chopped pecans on top. Bake for 20–25 minutes, until golden brown and firm in the middle. Transfer to a wire rack and serve while still warm.

> **Cook's Tip**
> If self-raising (self-rising) wholemeal (whole-wheat) flour is not available, use more self-raising (self-rising) white flour instead.

Date and Apple Muffins Energy 158kcal/670kJ; Protein 3.2g; Carbohydrate 30.7g, of which sugars 11.7g; Fat 3.4g, of which saturates 0.3g; Cholesterol 16mg; Calcium 45mg; Fibre 1g; Sodium 25mg.
Apple and Cinnamon Muffins Energy 236kcal/995kJ; Protein 4.3g; Carbohydrate 38.2g, of which sugars 19.1g; Fat 8.5g, of which saturates 4.9g; Cholesterol 51mg; Calcium 74mg; Fibre 1.2g; Sodium 73mg.

Apple and Cranberry Muffins

If you choose a really sweet variety of apple, it will provide a lovely contrast with the sharp flavour of the cranberries.

Makes 12

50g/2oz/¼ cup butter
1 egg
90g/3½oz/½ cup caster (superfine) sugar
grated rind of 1 large orange
120ml/4fl oz/½ cup freshly squeezed orange juice
150g/5oz/1¼ cups plain (all-purpose) flour
5ml/1 tsp baking powder
2.5ml/½ tsp bicarbonate of soda (baking soda)
5ml/1 tsp ground cinnamon
2.5ml/½ tsp freshly grated nutmeg
2.5ml/½ tsp ground allspice
1.5ml/¼ tsp ground ginger
pinch of salt
1–2 eating apples
150g/6oz/1½ cups cranberries
50g/2oz/¼ cup walnuts, chopped
icing (confectioners') sugar, for dusting (optional)

1 Preheat the oven to 180°C/350°F/Gas 4. Arrange 12 paper cases in a muffin tin (pan).

2 Melt the butter over a gentle heat. Set aside to cool.

3 In a large bowl, whisk the egg lightly. Add the melted butter and whisk to combine. Add the sugar, orange rind and juice. Whisk to blend, then set aside.

4 In a mixing bowl, sift together the flour, baking powder, bicarbonate of soda, cinnamon, nutmeg, allspice, ginger and salt. Set aside.

5 Make a well in the dry ingredients and pour in the egg mixture. Using a spoon, stir until just blended.

6 Quarter, core and peel the apples. Chop coarsely. Add the apples, cranberries and walnuts, and stir to blend.

7 Fill the cases three-quarters full and bake for 25–30 minutes, until the tops spring back when touched lightly. Transfer to a rack to cool. Dust with icing sugar.

Cranberry and Orange Muffins

These delicious muffins are perfect to eat at any time of day and are a real energy boost for breakfast or as a lunchbox treat. Use fresh or frozen cranberries.

Makes 10–12

350g/12oz/3 cups plain (all-purpose) flour, sifted
15ml/1 tsp baking powder
pinch of salt
115g/4oz/generous ½ cup caster (superfine) sugar
2 eggs
150ml/¼ pint/⅔ cup milk
50ml/2fl oz/¼ cup corn oil
finely grated rind of 1 orange
150g/5oz/1¼ cups cranberries, thawed if frozen

1 Preheat the oven to 190°C/375°F/Gas 5. Arrange 10–12 paper cases in a muffin tin (pan).

2 Sift together the flour, baking powder and salt into a large bowl. Add the sugar and stir well to mix.

3 Lightly beat the eggs with the milk and corn oil in another bowl until thoroughly combined.

4 Make a well in the centre of the dry ingredients and pour in the egg mixture. Stir with a wooden spoon until blended to a smooth batter. Gently fold in the grated orange rind and cranberries with a metal spoon.

5 Divide the mixture among the paper cases and bake for about 25 minutes, until risen and golden. Transfer to a wire rack to cool and serve warm or cold.

Cook's Tip
The flared sides of a proper muffin tin (pan) increase the surface area, encouraging the dough to rise.

Variation
Replace half the cranberries with blueberries or raspberries.

Apple and Cranberry Muffins Energy 149kcal/624kJ; Protein 2.5g; Carbohydrate 20.4g, of which sugars 10.8g; Fat 6.9g, of which saturates 2.6g; Cholesterol 25mg; Calcium 30mg; Fibre 0.9g; Sodium 34mg. **Cranberry and Orange Muffins** Energy 184kcal/780kJ; Protein 4.3g; Carbohydrate 34.4g, of which sugars 12.2g; Fat 4.3g, of which saturates 0.9g; Cholesterol 32mg; Calcium 66mg; Fibre 1.1g; Sodium 19mg.

Dried Cherry Muffins

Cherries are always a great favourite, especially with children, so why not spoil the family. Serve these scrumptious muffins freshly baked and still warm from the oven, smothered with butter and cherry jam. Dried cherries are full of antioxidants and a healthy food to eat.

Makes 16

250ml/8fl oz/1 cup natural (plain) yogurt
225g/8oz/1 cup dried cherries
115g/4oz/½ cup butter, softened
175g/6oz/scant 1 cup caster (superfine) sugar
2 eggs
5ml/1 tsp vanilla extract
200g/7oz/1¾ cups plain (all-purpose) flour
10ml/2 tsp baking powder
5ml/1 tsp bicarbonate of soda (baking soda)
pinch of salt

1 In a mixing bowl, combine the yogurt and dried cherries. Cover with clear film (plastic wrap) and leave to stand for about 30 minutes.

2 Preheat the oven to 180°C/350°F/Gas 4. Arrange 12 paper cases in a muffin tin (pan).

3 Beat together the butter and caster sugar in a bowl until light and fluffy. Add the eggs, one at a time, beating well after each addition until fully incorporated.

4 Add the vanilla extract and yogurt and cherry mixture and stir well until thoroughly mixed.

5 Sift the flour, baking powder, bicarbonate of soda and salt over the batter in batches. Gently fold in using a metal spoon after each addition.

6 Spoon the mixture into the prepared muffin tins, filling them about two-thirds full. Bake for 20 minutes, or until risen and golden and the tops spring back when touched lightly. Transfer to a wire rack to cool completely before serving or storing in an airtight container.

Oat and Raisin Muffins

Often the simplest things are the nicest and that is the case with these flavour-packed muffins.

Makes 12

75g/3oz/scant 1 cup rolled oats
250ml/8fl oz/1 cup buttermilk
115g/4oz/½ cup butter, at room temperature
90g/3½oz/generous ⅓ cup soft dark brown sugar

1 egg, at room temperature
115g/4oz/1 cup plain (all-purpose) flour
5ml/1 tsp baking powder
2.5ml/½ tsp bicarbonate of soda (baking soda)
pinch of salt
25g/1oz/2 tbsp raisins

1 In a bowl, combine the oats and buttermilk, and leave to soak for 1 hour.

2 Preheat the oven to 200°C/400°F/Gas 6. Arrange 12 paper cases in a muffin tin (pan)

3 In a bowl, cream the butter and sugar until light and fluffy. Beat in the egg.

4 Sift the flour, baking powder, bicarbonate of soda and salt into the butter mixture in batches. Alternate with batches of the oat mixture. Stir to combine after each addition. Fold in the raisins. Do not overmix.

5 Fill the prepared cups two-thirds full. Bake for about 20–25 minutes, until a skewer inserted in the centre comes out clean. Transfer to a rack to cool.

> **Cook's Tip**
> *Buttermilk is made from skimmed milk fermented with a special culture under controlled conditions, resulting in an acidic product that helps dough to rise. If it is not available, add 5ml/1 tsp lemon juice or vinegar to milk and leave to stand for a few minutes until curdled.*

Dried Cherry Muffins Energy 196kcal/825kJ; Protein 3.2g; Carbohydrate 32.1g, of which sugars 22.6g; Fat 7g, of which saturates 4g; Cholesterol 39mg; Calcium 67mg; Fibre 0.7g; Sodium 69mg.
Oat and Raisin Muffins Energy 177kcal/742kJ; Protein 3g; Carbohydrate 22.3g, of which sugars 10.4g; Fat 9.1g, of which saturates 5.2g; Cholesterol 37mg; Calcium 51mg; Fibre 0.8g; Sodium 77mg.

Pear and Sultana Bran Muffins

These tasty muffins are best eaten freshly baked and served warm or cold, on their own or spread with a butter, jam or honey.

Makes 12

75g/3oz/³⁄₄ cup plain (all-purpose) wholemeal (whole-wheat) flour, sifted
50g/2oz/¹⁄₂ cup plain (all-purpose) white flour, sifted
50g/2oz/3 cups bran
15ml/1 tbsp baking powder
pinch of salt
50g/2oz/4 tbsp butter
50g/2oz/¹⁄₄ cup soft light brown sugar
1 egg
200ml/7fl oz/scant 1 cup skimmed (low fat) milk
50g/2oz/¹⁄₂ cup ready-to-eat dried pears, chopped
50g/2oz/¹⁄₃ cup sultanas (golden raisins)

1 Preheat the oven to 200°C/400°F/Gas 6. Arrange 12 paper cases in a muffin tin (pan).

2 Mix together the flours, bran, baking powder and salt in a bowl. Set aside.

3 Gently heat the butter in a small pan until melted.

4 Mix together the melted butter, sugar, egg and milk.

5 Pour the butter mixture over the dry ingredients. Gently fold the ingredients together, only enough to combine. The mixture should look quite lumpy.

6 Fold in the pears and sultanas.

7 Spoon the mixture into the prepared muffin tins. Bake for 15–20 minutes, until well risen and golden brown. Turn out on to a wire rack to cool.

> **Cook's Tip**
> *For a quick and easy way to chop dried fruit, chop with kitchen scissors.*

Carrot Buns

Carrots are naturally sweet and have a moistness that makes them an ideal ingredient for cakes and muffins. If you haven't used them when baking before, you are likely to be pleasantly surprised.

Makes 12

175g/6oz/³⁄₄ cup butter, at room temperature, diced
75g/3oz/¹⁄₃ cup soft dark brown sugar
1 egg
15ml/1 tbsp water
275g/10oz/2 cups grated carrots
150g/5oz/1¹⁄₄ cups plain (all-purpose) flour
5ml/1 tsp baking powder
2.5ml/¹⁄₂ tsp bicarbonate of soda (baking soda)
5ml/1 tsp ground cinnamon
1.5ml/¹⁄₄ tsp grated nutmeg
pinch of salt

1 Preheat the oven to 180°C/350°F/Gas 4. Arrange 12 paper cases in a muffin tin (pan).

2 In a large bowl, beat the butter and sugar until light and fluffy. Beat in the egg and water.

3 Stir the grated carrots into the butter mixture until evenly combined. Sift over the flour, baking powder, bicarbonate of soda, cinnamon, nutmeg and salt. Stir to blend evenly.

4 Spoon the batter into the prepared muffin tins, filling them almost to the top.

5 Bake for about 35 minutes, until the tops spring back when touched lightly with your fingers. Leave to stand for 10 minutes before transferring to a wire rack to cool completely.

> **Cook's Tip**
> *Unless the carrots are very old and coarse – in which case, they are probably not suitable for this recipe – you do not need to peel them before grating. Simply trim and wash first. Use the fine side of the grater.*

Pear and Sultana Bran Muffins Energy 121kcal/510kJ; Protein 3g; Carbohydrate 18.7g, of which sugars 9.8g; Fat 4.3g, of which saturates 2.4g; Cholesterol 25mg; Calcium 51mg; Fibre 2.2g; Sodium 42mg.
Carrot Buns Energy 190kcal/791kJ; Protein 2g; Carbohydrate 18.1g, of which sugars 8.5g; Fat 12.7g, of which saturates 7.8g; Cholesterol 47mg; Calcium 32mg; Fibre 0.9g; Sodium 101mg.

Prune Muffins

Muffins with prunes are nutritious as well as delicious and perfect as a weekend breakfast treat. These are made with oil rather than butter, so are very quick to mix.

Makes 12
1 egg
250ml/8fl oz/1 cup milk
50ml/2fl oz/¼ cup vegetable oil

50g/2oz/¼ cup sugar
30ml/2 tbsp soft dark
   brown sugar
225g/8oz/2 cups plain
   (all-purpose) flour
10ml/2 tsp baking powder
pinch of salt
1.5ml/¼ tsp grated nutmeg
150g/5oz/¾ cup cooked prunes,
   or ready-to-eat prunes, chopped

1 Preheat the oven to 200°C/400°F/Gas 6. Arrange 12 paper cases in a muffin tin (pan).

2 Break the egg into a mixing bowl and beat with a fork. Beat in the milk and oil.

3 Stir the sugars into the egg mixture. Set aside. Sift the flour, baking powder, salt and nutmeg into a mixing bowl. Make a well in the centre, pour in the egg mixture and stir. The batter should be slightly lumpy.

4 Gently fold the prunes into the batter until just evenly distributed. Spoon into the prepared muffin tins, filling them two-thirds full.

5 Bake for about 20 minutes, until golden brown. Leave to stand for 10 minutes before transferring to a wire rack. Serve warm or cold.

> **Cook's Tip**
> When cooking prunes, if there is time, soak them overnight in 400ml/14fl oz/1⅔ cups water, then bring to the boil with 5ml/1 tsp lemon juice and 30ml/2 tbsp caster (superfine) sugar, if you like. Simmer for about 10 minutes, until soft.

Yogurt and Honey Muffins

Yogurt and honey are known to boost energy levels, so these muffins go well in lunchboxes.

Makes 12
50g/2oz/4 tbsp butter
75ml/5 tbsp clear honey
250ml/8fl oz/1 cup natural
   (plain) yogurt

1 egg
grated rind of 1 lemon
50ml/2fl oz/¼ cup lemon juice
115g/4oz/1 cup plain
   (all-purpose) flour
115g/4oz/1 cup wholemeal
   (whole-wheat) flour
7.5ml/1½ tsp bicarbonate of
   soda (baking soda)
pinch of grated nutmeg

1 Preheat the oven to 190°C/375°F/Gas 5. Arrange 12 paper cases in a muffin tin (pan).

2 Put the butter and honey into a small pan and heat gently, stirring frequently, until melted and smooth. Remove the pan from the heat and leave to cool slightly.

3 In a large bowl, whisk together the yogurt, egg, lemon rind and juice. Add the butter and honey mixture and whisk well until thoroughly combined.

4 In another bowl, sift together the flours, bicarbonate of soda and nutmeg. Fold the dry ingredients into the yogurt mixture just enough to blend them.

5 Fill the prepared muffin tins two-thirds full. Bake for 20–25 minutes, then leave to cool in the tins for about 5 minutes before transferring to a wire rack.

> **Variations**
> • For Yogurt, Honey and Walnut Muffins, add 50g/2oz/½ cup chopped walnuts, folded in with the flour and substitute ground cinnamon for the nutmeg.
> • For Honey and Hazelnut Muffins, substitute hazelnut yogurt for the natural (plain) yogurt and fold in 50g/2oz/½ cup chopped toasted hazelnuts with the flour.

Prune Muffins Energy 190kcal/801kJ; Protein 3.7g; Carbohydrate 28.1g, of which sugars 10.7g; Fat 7.8g, of which saturates 1.2g; Cholesterol 17mg; Calcium 66mg; Fibre 1.3g; Sodium 17mg.
Yogurt and Honey Muffins Energy 155kcal/652kJ; Protein 4.7g; Carbohydrate 25.4g, of which sugars 6.9g; Fat 4.6g, of which saturates 2.5g; Cholesterol 25mg; Calcium 66mg; Fibre 1.7g; Sodium 50mg.

Raisin Bran Buns

These traditional muffins remain hugely popular. This is hardly surprising as they are delicious served warm and spread with butter and honey.

Makes 15

50g/2oz/¼ cup butter
75g/3oz/¾ cup plain (all-purpose) flour
50g/2oz/½ cup wholemeal (whole-wheat) flour
7.5ml/1½ tsp bicarbonate of soda (baking soda)
pinch of salt
5ml/1 tsp ground cinnamon
25g/1oz/⅓ cup bran
75g/3oz/generous ½ cup raisins
50g/2oz/¼ cup soft dark brown sugar
50g/2oz/¼ cup sugar
1 egg
250ml/8fl oz/1 cup buttermilk
juice of ½ lemon

1 Preheat the oven to 200°C/400°F/Gas 6. Arrange 15 paper cases in a muffin tin (pan).

2 Place the butter in a pan and melt over a low heat. Set aside to cool slightly.

3 In a mixing bowl, sift together both flours, bicarbonate of soda, salt and ground cinnamon. Add the bran, raisins and sugars and stir until blended.

4 In another bowl, mix together the egg, buttermilk, lemon juice and melted butter. Add the buttermilk mixture to the dry ingredients and stir lightly and quickly until just moistened; do not mix until smooth.

5 Spoon the batter into the prepared muffin tins, filling them almost to the top. Bake for about 15 minutes, or until golden. Serve warm or at room temperature.

> **Cook's Tip**
> *Bran is the outer husk of cereal grains removed during milling. Wheat bran is the most widely available and popular variety, but other cereal brans are available from health food stores.*

Spiced Sultana Muffins

Sunday breakfasts will never be the same again, once you have tried these delicious muffins! They are easy to prepare and take only a short time to bake.

Makes 6

75g/3oz/6 tbsp butter
1 small (US medium) egg
120ml/4fl oz/½ cup unsweetened coconut milk
150g/5oz/1¼ cups wholemeal (whole-wheat) flour
7.5ml/1½ tsp baking powder
5ml/1 tsp ground cinnamon
generous pinch of salt
115g/4oz/⅔ cup sultanas (golden raisins)

1 Preheat the oven to 190°C/375°F/Gas 5. Arrange 6 paper cases in a muffin tin (pan).

2 Beat the butter, egg and coconut milk in a bowl until well combined.

3 Sift the wholemeal flour, baking powder, ground cinnamon and salt over the beaten mixture. Fold in carefully, then beat well. Fold in the sultanas. Divide the mixture among the paper cases.

4 Bake for 20 minutes, or until the muffins have risen well and are firm to the touch. Cool slightly on a wire rack before serving warm.

> **Variation**
> *The heath-conscious or those following a slimming plan can substitute the same quantity of low-fat spread for the butter. The muffins will still be utterly delicious although not quite so rich in flavour.*

> **Cook's Tip**
> *These muffins taste equally good cold. They also freeze well, packed in freezer bags. To serve, leave them to thaw overnight, or defrost in a microwave, then warm them briefly in the oven.*

Raisin Bran Buns Energy 89kcal/373kJ; Protein 2g; Carbohydrate 13.4g, of which sugars 8.9g; Fat 3.4g, of which saturates 1.9g; Cholesterol 20mg; Calcium 34mg; Fibre 1.1g; Sodium 36mg.
Spiced Sultana Muffins Energy 240kcal/1006kJ; Protein 4.9g; Carbohydrate 30.3g, of which sugars 14.9g; Fat 11.9g, of which saturates 6.9g; Cholesterol 58mg; Calcium 35mg; Fibre 2.6g; Sodium 114mg.

Sweet Potato Muffins with Raisins

Muffins have been a part of the American breakfast for many years. This variety mixes the great colour and flavour of sweet potatoes with the more usual ingredients.

Makes 12
1 large sweet potato
350g/12oz/3 cups plain
   (all-purpose) flour
15ml/1 tbsp baking powder
1 egg, beaten
225g/8oz/1 cup butter, melted
250ml/8fl oz/1 cup milk
50g/2oz/scant ½ cup raisins
50g/2oz/¼ cup caster
   (superfine) sugar
pinch of salt
icing (confectioners') sugar,
   for dusting

1 Cook the sweet potato in plenty of boiling water for 45 minutes, or until very tender. Drain the potato and when cool enough to handle peel off the skin. Place in a large bowl and mash well.

2 Preheat the oven to 220°C/425°F/Gas 7. Sift the flour and baking powder over the potatoes with a pinch of salt and beat in the egg.

3 Stir the butter and milk together and pour into the bowl. Add the raisins and sugar and mix the ingredients until everything has just come together.

4 Spoon the mixture into 12 paper muffin cases set in a muffin tin (pan).

5 Bake for 25 minutes until golden. Dust with icing sugar and serve warm.

> **Variation**
> *These muffins are delicious made with all sorts of dried fruits and would work particularly well with tropical varieties, such as pineapple, mango or papaya, as well as the more usual blueberries or cranberries.*

Maple Pecan Muffins

The smooth, rich and distinctive flavour of maple syrup complements the nuts superbly. Make sure you buy the pure syrup, as blended varieties are disappointing.

Makes 20
150g/5oz/1¼ cups pecan nuts
300g/11oz/2¾ cups plain
   (all-purpose) flour
5ml/1 tsp baking powder
5ml/1 tsp bicarbonate of soda
   (baking soda)
pinch of salt
1.5ml/¼ tsp ground cinnamon
115g/4oz/½ cup sugar
50g/2oz/½ cup soft light
   brown sugar
45ml/3 tbsp maple syrup
150g/5oz/⅔ cup butter, softened
3 eggs
300ml/½ pint/1¼ cups
   buttermilk
60 pecan nut halves, to decorate

1 Preheat the oven to 180°C/350°F/Gas 4. Arrange 20 paper cases in a muffin tin (pan)

2 Spread the pecan nuts on a baking sheet and toast in the oven for 5 minutes. Leave to cool, then chop coarsely and set aside.

3 In a bowl, sift together the flour, baking powder, bicarbonate of soda, salt and cinnamon. Set aside.

4 Combine the sugar, light brown sugar, maple syrup and butter in a bowl. Beat until light and fluffy. Add the eggs, one at a time, beating well after each addition.

5 Pour half of the buttermilk and half of the dry ingredients into the butter mixture, then stir until blended. Repeat with the remaining buttermilk and dry ingredients. Fold the chopped pecan nuts into the batter. Spoon the mixture into the paper cases, filling them two-thirds full. Top with the pecan nut halves.

6 Bake for 20–25 minutes, until puffed up and golden brown. Leave to stand in the tins for about 5 minutes before transferring the muffins to a wire rack to cool completely before serving.

Sweet Potato Muffins with Raisins Energy 293kcal/1227kJ; Protein 4.1g; Carbohydrate 34.2g, of which sugars 9.3g; Fat 16.5g, of which saturates 10.1g; Cholesterol 57mg; Calcium 70mg; Fibre 1.4g; Sodium 135mg. Maple Pecan Muffins Energy 319kcal/1329kJ; Protein 5g; Carbohydrate 24.6g, of which sugars 12.8g; Fat 23g, of which saturates 5.5g; Cholesterol 45mg; Calcium 64mg; Fibre 1.5g; Sodium 70mg.

Gooey Butterscotch Muffins

Make up the two mixtures for these muffins the night before you need them and stir them together first thing next day for an irresistible mid-morning treat. Instead of butterscotch, you could try adding chocolate chips, marshmallows or blueberries.

Makes 9–12

150g/5oz butterscotch sweets
  (candies)
225g/8oz/2 cups plain
  (all purpose) flour
90g/3½oz/½ cup golden caster
  (superfine) sugar
10ml/2 tsp baking powder
pinch of salt
1 large (US extra large)
  egg, beaten
150ml/¼ pint/⅔ cup milk
50ml/2fl oz/¼ cup sunflower oil
  or melted butter
75g/3oz/¾ cup chopped
  hazelnuts

1 Preheat the oven to 200°C/400°F/Gas 6. Arrange 9–12 paper cases in a muffin tin (pan).

2 With floured fingers, break the butterscotch sweets into small chunks. Toss them in a little flour, if necessary, to prevent them from sticking together.

3 Into a mixing bowl sift together the flour, sugar, baking powder and salt.

4 Whisk together the egg, milk and oil or melted butter, then stir the mixture into the dry ingredients with the sweets and nuts. Only lightly stir together as the mixture should be lumpy.

5 Spoon the batter evenly into the paper cases, filling about half full. Bake for 20 minutes, until well risen and golden brown. Cool in the tin for 5 minutes, then remove and transfer the muffins to a cooling rack.

6 Try spreading these with a Spanish treat called *dulce de leche* (available in larger supermarkets); it is rather like sweetened condensed milk that has been boiled in the can until caramelized. Drizzle over and eat on the day of baking.

Coffee and Macadamia Muffins

These muffins are delicious eaten cold, but are best served still warm from the oven.

Makes 12

25ml/1½ tbsp ground coffee
250ml/8fl oz/1 cup milk
50g/2oz/4 tbsp butter
275g/10oz/2½ cups plain
  (all-purpose) flour
10ml/2 tsp baking powder
150g/5oz/⅔ cup light
  muscovado (brown) sugar
75g/3oz/½ cup macadamia nuts
1 egg, lightly beaten

1 Preheat the oven to 200°C/400°F/Gas 6. Arrange 12 paper cases in a muffin tin (pan).

2 Put the coffee in a heatproof jug (pitcher) or bowl. Heat the milk to near boiling and pour it over. Leave to infuse (steep) for 4 minutes, then strain through a sieve (strainer).

3 Add the butter to the coffee-flavoured milk mixture and stir until melted. Leave until cold.

4 Sift the flour and baking powder into a large mixing bowl. Stir in the sugar and macadamia nuts. Add the egg to the coffee-flavoured milk mixture, pour into the dry ingredients and stir until just combined – do not overmix.

5 Divide the coffee mixture among the paper cases and bake for about 15 minutes, until well risen and firm. Transfer to a wire rack and serve warm or cold.

Variation
Macadamia nuts have a unique buttery flavour but if they are not available, cashews make a good substitute.

Cook's Tip
To cool the coffee-flavoured milk quickly, place the jug (pitcher) in a large bowl of iced or cold water.

Gooey Butterscotch Muffins Energy 224kcal/941kJ; Protein 3.9g; Carbohydrate 31.7g, of which sugars 14.6g; Fat 10g, of which saturates 2.1g; Cholesterol 19mg; Calcium 66mg; Fibre 1g; Sodium 55mg.
Coffee and Macademia Muffins Energy 221kcal/929kJ; Protein 4g; Carbohydrate 32.2g, of which sugars 14.7g; Fat 9.4g, of which saturates 3.3g; Cholesterol 26mg; Calcium 70mg; Fibre 1g; Sodium 59mg.

Chunky Chocolate and Banana Muffins

Luxurious but not overly sweet, these muffins are simple and quick to make. Serve warm, while the chocolate is still gooey.

Makes 12
90ml/6 tbsp semi-skimmed (low-fat) milk
2 eggs
150g/5oz/²/₃ cup unsalted butter, melted
225g/8oz/2 cups plain (all-purpose) flour
pinch of salt
5ml/1 tsp baking powder
150g/5oz/³/₄ cup golden caster (superfine) sugar
150g/5oz plain (semisweet) chocolate, cut into large chunks
2 small bananas, mashed

1 Preheat the oven to 200°C/400°F/Gas 6. Arrange 12 paper cases in a muffin tin (pan).

2 Place the milk, eggs and melted butter in a bowl and whisk until combined.

3 Sift together the flour, salt and baking powder into a separate bowl. Add the sugar and chocolate to the flour mixture and stir to combine. Gradually stir in the milk mixture, but do not beat it. Fold in the mashed bananas.

4 Spoon the mixture into the paper cases. Bake for about 20 minutes until golden. Cool on a wire rack.

Cook's Tips
• *Use ripe bananas for this recipe and do not peel them before you are ready to use them or they will discolour. Slice thickly into a bowl before mashing with a fork; do not try to mash them while they are still whole as they are likely to slide about and fly across the kitchen.*
• *You can use plain (semisweet) chocolate chips instead of chunks if you prefer.*

Chocolate Chip Muffins

Nothing could be easier – or nicer – than these classic muffins. The muffin mixture is plain, with a surprise layer of chocolate chips in the middle.

Makes 10
115g/4oz/½ cup butter
75g/3oz/¹/₃ cup sugar
30ml/2 tbsp soft dark brown sugar
2 eggs
175g/6oz/1½ cups plain (all-purpose) flour
5ml/1 tsp baking powder
120ml/4fl oz/½ cup milk
175g/6oz/1 cup plain (semisweet) chocolate chips

1 Preheat the oven to 190°C/375°F/Gas 5. Arrange 10 paper cases in a muffin tin (pan).

2 In a large bowl, beat the butter until pale. Add both sugars and beat until light and fluffy. Beat in the eggs, one at a time, beating well after each addition.

3 Sift the flour and baking powder together, twice. Fold into the butter mixture, alternating with the milk.

4 Divide half of the mixture among the paper cases. Sprinkle the chocolate chips on top, dividing them equally among the muffins, then cover with the remaining mixture.

5 Bake for about 25 minutes, until lightly coloured. Leave to stand for 5 minutes before transferring to a wire rack to cool.

Variation
To make Chocolate Chip and Apple Muffins, sift 2.5ml/½ tsp ground cinnamon, a pinch of grated nutmeg and 1.5ml/¼ tsp mixed spice (apple pie spice) with the dry ingredients in step 2. Halve the quantity of chocolate. Peel, core and grate two eating apples and stir into the batter with the chopped chocolate in step 3. Bake as given in the recipe, but check that the muffins are cooked by inserting a skewer into the centre of one of them. If it comes out clean, then they are ready.

Chunky Chocolate and Banana Muffins Energy 240kcal/1003kJ; Protein 3.7g; Carbohydrate 26.3g, of which sugars 11.6g; Fat 14.1g, of which saturates 8.4g; Cholesterol 59mg; Calcium 47mg; Fibre 1g; Sodium 92mg. **Chocolate Chip Muffins** Energy 296kcal/1238kJ; Protein 4.3g; Carbohydrate 36.4g, of which sugars 22.9g; Fat 15.8g, of which saturates 3.4g; Cholesterol 40mg; Calcium 56mg; Fibre 1g; Sodium 113mg.

Chocolate Walnut Muffins

Walnuts and chocolate are a delicious combination and provide both smoothness and crunch while vanilla and almond extract provide extra flavour.

Makes 12
175g/6oz/3/4 cup unsalted
  butter, diced
150g/5oz plain (semisweet)
  chocolate, chopped
225g/8oz/1 cup sugar
50g/2oz/1/4 cup soft dark
  brown sugar
4 eggs
5ml/1 tsp vanilla extract
1.5ml/1/4 tsp almond extract
75g/3oz/3/4 cup plain
  (all-purpose) flour
115g/4oz/1 cup walnuts,
  coarsely chopped

1 Preheat the oven to 180°C/350°F/Gas 4. Arrange 12 paper cases in a muffin tin (pan).

2 Melt the butter with the chocolate in a heatproof bowl set over a pan of gently simmering water. Transfer to a large mixing bowl.

3 Stir both the sugars into the chocolate mixture. Mix in the eggs, one at a time, beating well after each addition, then add the vanilla and almond extracts.

4 Sift the flour over the chocolate mixture and fold in with a flexible spatula until evenly combined. Stir the walnuts into the mixture.

5 Fill the paper cases almost to the top and bake for 30–35 minutes. Leave to stand for 5 minutes before transferring to a wire rack to cool.

> **Variation**
> For Chocolate Mint and Nut Muffins, omit the vanilla and almond extracts and add 2.5ml/1/2 tsp peppermint extract instead and substitute the same quantity of blanched almonds or hazelnuts for the walnuts.

Chocolate Blueberry Muffins

Blueberries are one of the many fruits that combine deliciously with the richness of chocolate, while still retaining their own distinctive flavour. These muffins are best served warm.

Makes 12
115g/4oz/1/2 cup butter
75g/3oz plain (semisweet)
  chocolate, chopped
200g/7oz/scant 1 cup sugar
1 egg, lightly beaten
250ml/8fl oz/1 cup buttermilk
10ml/2 tsp vanilla extract
275g/10oz/2 1/2 cups plain
  (all-purpose) flour
5ml/1 tsp bicarbonate of soda
  (baking soda)
175g/6oz/generous 1 cup fresh or
  thawed frozen blueberries
25g/1oz plain (semisweet)
  chocolate, melted, to decorate

1 Preheat the oven to 190°C/375°F/Gas 5. Arrange 12 paper cases in a muffin tin (pan).

2 Melt the butter and chocolate in a pan over a medium heat, stirring frequently until smooth. Remove from the heat and leave to cool slightly.

3 Stir the sugar, egg, buttermilk and vanilla extract into the melted chocolate mixture. Gently fold in the flour and bicarbonate of soda until just blended. (The mixture should be slightly lumpy.) Gently fold in the blueberries.

4 Spoon the batter into the paper cases. Bake for 25–30 minutes, until a skewer inserted in the centre comes out with just a few crumbs attached. Transfer the muffins to a wire rack.

5 To decorate, drizzle with the melted chocolate and serve warm or at room temperature.

> **Cook's Tip**
> Do not keep the batter waiting once you have folded in the blueberries. Bake the muffins immediately or they won't rise very well during cooking.

Chocolate Walnut Muffins Energy 374kcal/1563kJ; Protein 4.9g; Carbohydrate 37.1g, of which sugars 32.2g; Fat 24g, of which saturates 10.8g; Cholesterol 95mg; Calcium 46mg; Fibre 0.8g; Sodium 115mg.
Chocolate Blueberry Muffins Energy 279kcal/1172kJ; Protein 4.1g; Carbohydrate 43.5g, of which sugars 25.4g; Fat 11g, of which saturates 6.6g; Cholesterol 38mg; Calcium 73mg; Fibre 1.2g; Sodium 75mg.

Chocolate Mint-filled Muffins

For extra mint flavour, chop 8 mint cream-filled after-dinner mints and fold into the cake batter.

Makes 12
150g/5oz/²⁄₃ cup unsalted
  butter, softened
300g/11oz/1¹⁄₂ cups caster
  (superfine) sugar
3 eggs
5ml/1 tsp peppermint extract
225g/8oz/2 cups plain
  (all-purpose) flour
pinch of salt
5ml/1 tsp bicarbonate of soda
  (baking soda)

50g/2oz/¹⁄₂ cup unsweetened
  cocoa powder
250ml/8fl oz/1 cup milk

For the mint cream filling
300ml/10fl oz/1¹⁄₄ cups double
  (heavy) or whipping cream
5ml/1 tsp peppermint extract

For the chocolate mint glaze
175g/6oz plain (semisweet)
  chocolate
115g/4oz/¹⁄₂ cup unsalted butter
5ml/1 tsp peppermint extract

1 Preheat the oven to 180°C/350°F/Gas 4. Arrange 12 paper cases in a muffin tin (pan).

2 In a bowl, beat together the butter and sugar until light and creamy. Add the eggs one at a time, beating well after each addition. Stir in the peppermint extract. Sift together the flour, salt, bicarbonate of soda and unsweetened cocoa powder over the batter and mix well.

3 Fill the paper cases with the batter. Bake for 12–15 minutes, until a skewer inserted into the centre comes out clean. Remove to a wire rack and leave to cool.

4 To make the filling, in a small bowl whip the cream with the peppermint extract until stiff peaks form. Spoon into a piping (pastry) bag fitted with a plain nozzle. Pipe 15ml/1 tbsp into the centre of each muffin.

5 To make the glaze, in a pan over a low heat melt the chocolate and butter. Remove from the heat, stir in the peppermint. Leave to cool. Spread on top of each muffin.

Chocolate Muffins

These magical little treats are sure to enchant adults and children alike.

Makes 24
175g/6oz/³⁄₄ cup butter, softened
150ml/¹⁄₄ pint/²⁄₃ cup milk
5ml/1 tsp vanilla extract
115g/4oz plain (semisweet)
  chocolate, broken into pieces
15ml/1 tbsp water
275g/10oz/2¹⁄₂ cups plain
  (all-purpose) flour
5ml/1 tsp baking powder

2.5ml/¹⁄₂ tsp bicarbonate of soda
  (baking soda)
pinch of salt
300g/11oz/1¹⁄₂ cups caster
  (superfine) sugar
3 eggs

For the icing
40g/1¹⁄₂ oz/3 tbsp butter
115g/4oz/1 cup icing
  (confectioners') sugar
2.5ml/¹⁄₂ tsp vanilla extract
15–30ml/1–2 tbsp milk

1 Preheat the oven to 180°C/350°F/Gas 4. Arrange 24 paper cases in a small muffin tin (pan).

2 In a bowl, beat the butter until light and fluffy. Add the milk and vanilla extract.

3 Melt the chocolate with the water in a heatproof bowl set over a pan of simmering water. Remove from the heat. Add the chocolate mixture to the butter mixture.

4 Sift the flour, baking powder, bicarbonate of soda, salt and sugar over the batter in batches and stir well to combine. Add the eggs, one at a time, and beat well after each addition. Divide the mixture evenly among the paper cases.

5 Bake for 20–25 minutes or until a skewer inserted into the centre of a cake comes out clean. Cool in the tins for 10 minutes, then turn out to cool completely on a wire rack.

6 To make the icing, in a bowl beat the butter and icing sugar together with the vanilla extract. Beat in just enough milk to make a creamy mixture.

7 Spread the top of each cake with the icing.

Chocolate Mint-filled Muffins Energy 511kcal/2129kJ; Protein 5.4g; Carbohydrate 45.2g, of which sugars 30.4g; Fat 35.6g, of which saturates 21.7g; Cholesterol 130mg; Calcium 85mg; Fibre 1.2g; Sodium 204mg. Chocolate Muffins Energy 210kcal/884kJ; Protein 2.5g; Carbohydrate 30.4g, of which sugars 21.6g; Fat 9.7g, of which saturates 5.8g; Cholesterol 44mg; Calcium 39mg; Fibre 0.5g; Sodium 67mg.

Double Chocolate Chip Muffins

These marvellous muffins are flavoured with cocoa and packed with chunky chips of plain and white chocolate so they are sure to be a success. Serve them on their own or with cherry or raspberry jam.

Makes 16
400g/14oz/3½ cups plain (all-purpose) flour
15ml/1 tbsp baking powder
30ml/2 tbsp unsweetened cocoa powder, plus extra for dusting
115g/4oz/½ cup muscovado (molasses) sugar
2 eggs
150ml/¼ pint/⅔ cup sour cream
150ml/¼ pint/⅔ cup milk
60ml/4 tbsp sunflower oil
175g/6oz white chocolate
175g/6oz plain (semisweet) chocolate

1 Preheat the oven to 190°C/375°F/Gas 5. Arrange 16 paper cases in a muffin tin (pan).

2 Sift the flour, baking powder and cocoa into a bowl and stir in the sugar. Make a well in the centre.

3 In a separate bowl, beat the eggs with the sour cream, milk and sunflower oil. Add the egg mixture to the well in the dry ingredients. Gradually incorporate the flour mixture to make a thick batter. The batter should be slightly lumpy.

4 Finely chop the white and plain chocolate and stir into the batter. Spoon the mixture into the muffin cases, filling them almost to the top.

5 Bake for 25–30 minutes, until well risen and firm to the touch. Transfer to a wire rack to cool, then dust lightly with cocoa powder before serving.

> **Cook's Tip**
> If sour cream is not available, sour 150ml/¼ pint/⅔ cup single (light) cream by stirring in 5ml/1 tsp lemon juice and letting the mixture stand until thickened.

Nutty Muffins with Walnut Liqueur

These muffins are slightly spicy and topped with a delicious crunchy sugar and nut mixture. If you're making them for children simply omit the walnut liqueur and add more milk.

Makes 12
225g/8oz/2 cups plain (all-purpose) flour
20ml/4 tsp baking powder
2.5ml/½ tsp mixed spice (apple pie spice)
pinch of salt
115g/4oz/½ cup soft light brown sugar
75g/3oz/¾ cup chopped walnuts
50g/2oz/¼ cup butter
2 eggs
175ml/6fl oz/¾ cup milk
30ml/2 tbsp walnut liqueur

For the topping
30ml/2 tbsp soft dark brown sugar
25g/1oz/¼ cup chopped walnuts

1 Preheat the oven to 200°C/400°F/Gas 6. Arrange 12 paper cases in a muffin tin (pan).

2 Sift the flour, baking powder, mixed spice and salt into a bowl. Stir in the sugar and walnuts.

3 In a small pan melt the butter over a low heat. Beat in the eggs, milk and liqueur.

4 Pour the butter mixture into the dry mixture and stir for just long enough to combine the ingredients. The batter should be lumpy. Fill the paper cases two-thirds full, then top with a sprinkling of sugar and walnuts.

5 Bake for 15 minutes, until the muffins are golden brown. Leave in the tins for a few minutes, then transfer to a wire rack to cool.

> **Cook's Tip**
> Probably the best-known walnut liqueur is brou de noix from France, which is made from green walnut husks and flavoured with cinnamon and nutmeg. Other versions are also produced.

Double Chocolate Chip Muffins Energy 281kcal/1183kJ; Protein 4.7g; Carbohydrate 41.3g, of which sugars 21.9g; Fat 11.9g, of which saturates 5.7g; Cholesterol 7mg; Calcium 94mg; Fibre 1.3g; Sodium 40mg. **Nutty Muffins with Walnut Liqueur** Energy 225kcal/946kJ; Protein 4.6g; Carbohydrate 29g, of which sugars 14.7g; Fat 10.6g, of which saturates 3.1g; Cholesterol 41mg; Calcium 64mg; Fibre 0.9g; Sodium 45mg.

Jam Tarts

"The Queen of Hearts, she made some tarts, all on a summer's day; the Knave of Hearts, he stole those tarts, and took them quite away!" So goes the nursery rhyme. Jam tarts have long been a treat at birthday parties and are often a child's first attempt at baking.

Makes 12

175g/6oz/1½ cups plain
 (all purpose) flour, plus extra
 for dusting
pinch of salt
30ml/2 tbsp caster
 (superfine) sugar
85g/3oz/6 tbsp butter, diced
1 egg, lightly beaten
jam

1 Sift together the flour and salt into a large bowl and stir in the caster sugar. Add the butter and rub it in with your fingertips until the mixture resembles fine breadcrumbs. Stir in the beaten egg and gather the mixture together into a smooth ball of dough.

2 Wrap the dough in clear film (plastic wrap) and chill in the refrigerator for about 30 minutes.

3 Meanwhile, preheat the oven to 220°C/425°F/Gas 7 and lightly grease a 12-cup bun tin (muffin pan).

4 Roll out the dough on a lightly floured surface to about 3mm/⅛in thick. Using a 7.5cm/3in fluted cookie cutter, stamp out rounds. Re-roll the scraps and stamp out more rounds to make a total of 12. Gently press the dough rounds into the prepared tray. Put a teaspoon of jam into each.

5 Bake for 15–20 minutes, until the pastry is firm and light golden brown and the jam has spread to fill the tarts. Using a metal spatula with a flexible blade, carefully transfer the tarts to a wire rack and leave to cool completely.

Cook's Tip
Take care not to overfill the tarts with jam or it will boil over, spoiling the pastry and making a sticky mess.

Maids of Honour

These little delicacies were allegedly being enjoyed by Anne Boleyn's maids of honour when the English king, Henry VIII, first met her in Richmond Palace in Surrey, and he is said to have named them. Originally they would have been made with strained curds, made by adding rennet to milk.

Makes 12

250g/9oz ready-made puff
 pastry, thawed if frozen
250g/9oz/generous 1 cup curd
 (farmer's) cheese
60ml/4 tbsp ground almonds
45ml/3 tbsp caster
 (superfine) sugar
finely grated rind of
 1 small lemon
2 eggs
15g/½ oz/1 tbsp butter, melted
icing (confectioners') sugar, to dust

1 Preheat the oven to 200°C/400°F/Gas 6. Lightly grease a 12-cup bun tray (muffin pan).

2 Roll out the dough very thinly on a lightly floured surface and, using a 7.5cm/3in cookie cutter, stamp out 12 rounds. Press the dough rounds into the prepared tray and prick well with a fork. Chill while you make the filling.

3 Put the curd cheese into a bowl and add the almonds, sugar and lemon rind. Lightly beat the eggs with the butter and add to the cheese mixture. Mix well.

4 Spoon the mixture into the pastry cases (tart shells). Bake for about 20 minutes, until the pastry is well risen and the filling is puffed up, golden brown and just firm to the touch.

5 Transfer to a wire rack (the filling will sink down as it cools). Serve warm or at room temperature, dusted with a little sifted icing sugar.

Variation
Sprinkle the filling with a little freshly grated nutmeg at the end of step 4.

Jam Tarts Energy 114kcal/479kJ; Protein 1.1g; Carbohydrate 18.8g, of which sugars 12.5g; Fat 4.3g, of which saturates 2.6g; Cholesterol 18mg; Calcium 16mg; Fibre 0.3g; Sodium 39mg.
Maids of Honour Energy 236kcal/993kJ; Protein 2.5g; Carbohydrate 36.7g, of which sugars 22.4g; Fat 9.8g, of which saturates 5.2g; Cholesterol 37mg; Calcium 43mg; Fibre 1g; Sodium 70mg.

Ricotta and Marsala Tarts

These sweet, melt-in-the-mouth tarts have a crisp puff pastry base. The light cheese filling is flavoured in the Italian way with Marsala.

Makes 12
375g/13oz ready-made puff pastry, thawed if frozen
250g/9oz/generous 1 cup ricotta cheese
1 egg, plus 2 egg yolks
45–60ml/3–4 tbsp caster (superfine) sugar
30ml/2 tbsp Marsala
grated rind of 1 lemon
50g/2oz/scant ½ cup sultanas (golden raisins)

1 Preheat the oven to 190°C/375°F/Gas 5. Lightly grease a muffin tin (pan).

2 Roll out the pastry. Stamp out 12 9cm/3½in rounds of pastry and line the prepared tin. Leave to rest in the refrigerator for 20 minutes.

3 Put the ricotta cheese in a bowl and add the egg, extra yolks, sugar, Marsala and lemon rind. Whisk until smooth, then stir in the sultanas.

4 Spoon the mixture into the lined tins. Bake for about 20 minutes, or until the filling has risen and the pastry is golden and crisp.

5 Cool the tarts slightly before easing each one out with a metal spatula. Serve warm.

Variations
• You could use ready-made shortcrust pastry instead of puff, but the tarts will not be quite so light or crisp.
• Instead of Marsala, you could use Madeira or sweet sherry, but if you prefer a non-alcoholic version, substitute 5ml/1 tsp vanilla extract.
• You can substitute curd (farmer's) cheese, strained cottage cheese or mascarpone for the ricotta but neither the texture nor the flavour will be quite the same.

Chocolate Whirls

These cookies are so easy to make. They're made with ready-made puff pastry rolled up with a chocolate filling. They're not too sweet and are similar to Danish pastries, so you could even make them as a special treat for breakfast.

Makes about 20
75g/3oz/scant ½ cup golden caster (superfine) sugar
40g/1½oz/⅓ cup unsweetened cocoa powder
2 eggs
500g/1lb 2oz ready-made puff pastry, thawed if frozen
25g/1oz/2 tbsp butter, softened
75g/3oz/generous ½ cup sultanas (golden raisins)
90g/3½oz milk chocolate, broken into small pieces

1 Preheat the oven to 220°C/425°F/Gas 7. Lightly grease two baking sheets.

2 Put the sugar, cocoa powder and eggs in a bowl and mix to a paste. Set aside.

3 Roll out the pastry on a lightly floured surface to make a 30cm/12in square. Trim off any rough edges using a sharp knife.

4 Dot the pastry all over with the butter, then spread the chocolate paste evenly over the pastry surface. Sprinkle the sultanas over the top.

5 Roll the pastry into a sausage, then cut the roll into 1cm/½in slices.

6 Place the slices on the baking sheets, spacing them apart. Bake the cookies for 10 minutes, until risen and pale golden. Transfer to a wire rack and leave to cool.

7 Melt the chocolate in a heatproof bowl set over a pan of gently simmering water.

8 Spoon or pipe lines of melted chocolate over the cookies, taking care not to completely hide the swirls of chocolate filling.

Chocolate Whirls Energy 165kcal/689kJ; Protein 2.9g; Carbohydrate 18.6g, of which sugars 9.4g; Fat 9.5g, of which saturates 1.9g; Cholesterol 23mg; Calcium 34mg; Fibre 0.4g; Sodium 117mg.
Ricotta and Marsala Tarts Energy 222kcal/928kJ; Protein 29g; Carbohydrate 27.3g, of which sugars 10.1g; Fat 11.4g, of which saturates 3.4g; Cholesterol 16mg; Calcium 64mg; Fibre 1.7g; Sodium 119mg.

Filo Crackers

These can be prepared a day in advance, brushed with melted butter and kept covered with clear film in the refrigerator or freezer before baking.

Makes 24
2 x 275g/10oz packets frozen filo pastry, thawed
115g/4oz/½ cup butter, melted
thin foil ribbon, to decorate
sifted icing (confectioners') sugar, to decorate

For the filling
450g/1lb eating apples, peeled, cored and finely chopped

5ml/1tsp ground cinnamon
25g/1oz/2 tbsp soft light brown sugar
50g/2oz/½ cup pecan nuts, chopped
50g/2oz/1 cup fresh white breadcrumbs
25g/1oz/3 tbsp sultanas (golden raisins)
25g/1oz/2 tbsp currants

For the lemon sauce
115g/4oz/ generous ½ cup caster (superfine) sugar
finely grated rind of 1 lemon
juice of 2 lemons

1 Unwrap the filo pastry and cover it with clear film (plastic wrap) and a damp cloth to prevent it from drying out. Mix all the filling ingredients together in a bowl.

2 Take one sheet of pastry at a time and cut it into 15 x 30cm/ 6 x 12in strips. Brush with butter. Place a spoonful of the filling at one end and fold in the sides, so the pastry measures 13cm/5in across. Brush the edges with butter and roll up. Pinch the "frill" at each end and tie with ribbon. Brush with butter.

3 Place the crackers on baking trays, cover and chill for 10 minutes. Preheat the oven to 190°C/375°F/Gas 5. Brush each cracker with melted butter. Bake the crackers for 30–35 minutes, or until they are golden brown. Let them cool slightly on the baking trays and then transfer them to a wire rack to cool completely.

4 To make the lemon sauce, put all the ingredients in a small pan and heat gently to dissolve the sugar. Serve the sauce warm. Finally, dust the crackers with sifted icing sugar.

Mince Tarts

Taste the difference in these luxurious pies filled with homemade mincemeat.

Makes 36
425g/15oz/3¾ cups plain (all-purpose) flour
150g/5oz/1¼ cups icing (confectioners') sugar
350g/12oz/1½ cups butter, chilled and diced
grated rind and juice of 1 orange
milk, for glazing

For the filling
175g/6oz/1½ cups finely chopped blanched almonds
150g/5oz/⅔ cup ready-to-eat dried apricots, chopped
175g/6oz/generous 1 cup raisins

150g/5oz/⅔ cup currants
150g/5oz/scant 1 cup glacé (candied) cherries, chopped
150g/5oz/scant 1 cup cut mixed (candied) peel, chopped
115g/4oz/⅔ cup chopped suet
grated rind and juice of 2 lemons
grated rind and juice of 1 orange
200g/7oz/scant 1 cup soft dark brown sugar
4 cooking apples, peeled, cored and chopped
10ml/2 tsp ground allspice
250ml/8fl oz/1 cup brandy
225g/8oz/1 cup cream cheese
30ml/2 tbsp caster (superfine) sugar
icing (confectioners') sugar, for dusting

1 Mix the first 13 filling ingredients together. Cover and leave in a cool place for 2 days.

2 For the pastry, sift the flour and icing sugar into a bowl. Rub in the butter. Stir in the orange rind and enough juice to bind. Chill for 20 minutes.

3 Preheat the oven to 220°C/425°F/Gas 7. Lightly grease two or three bun trays (muffin pans).

4 Roll out the dough, stamp out 36 8cm/3in rounds and put into the trays. Half fill with mincemeat. Beat the cream cheese and sugar and add a teaspoonful to each pie. Roll out the trimmings and stamp out 36 5cm/2in rounds. Brush the edges with milk and cover the pies. Cut a slit in each.

5 Brush lightly with milk. Bake for 15–20 minutes, then leave to cool. Dust with icing sugar.

Filo Crackers Energy 149kcal/629kJ; Protein 2.2g; Carbohydrate 23.9g, of which sugars 9.6g; Fat 5.7g, of which saturates 2.7g; Cholesterol 10mg; Calcium 34mg; Fibre 1g; Sodium 46mg.
Mince Tarts Energy Energy 301kcal/1258kJ; Protein 2.9g; Carbohydrate 33g, of which sugars 23.5g; Fat 16.8g, of which saturates 8.8g; Cholesterol 29mg; Calcium 58mg; Fibre 1.6g; Sodium 96mg.

Simple Mince Pies

These small pies have become synonymous with Christmas. To eat one per day for the 12 days of Christmas was thought to bring happiness for the coming year.

Makes 12

225g/8oz/2 cups plain (all-purpose) flour, plus extra for dusting
pinch of salt
45ml/3 tbsp caster (superfine) sugar, plus extra for dusting
115g/4oz/½ cup butter, diced
1 egg, lightly beaten
about 350g/12oz mincemeat

1 Sift the flour and salt and stir in the sugar. Rub in the butter until the mixture resembles breadcrumbs. Stir in the egg and gather into a smooth dough.

2 Chill the dough for 30 minutes. Meanwhile, preheat the oven to 220°C/425°F/Gas 7 and lightly grease a 12-cup bun tray (muffin pan).

3 Roll out the dough on a lightly floured surface to about 3mm/⅛in thick and, using a 7.5cm/3in cutter, cut out 12 rounds. Press into the prepared tray. Gather up the scraps and roll out again, cutting slightly smaller rounds to make 12 lids. Spoon mincemeat into each case (shell), dampen the edges and top with a pastry lid. Make a small slit in each pie.

4 Bake for 15–20 minutes until light golden brown. Transfer to a wire rack to cool and serve dusted with sugar.

Galettes

These simple round flat pastries, whose name comes from the French word for a flat weather-worn pebble, are made from a sweet pastry such as pâte sucrée.

Makes 10

150g/5oz/1¼ cups plain (all-purpose flour)
pinch of salt
75g/3oz/6 tbsp chilled butter, diced
25g/1oz/¼ cup icing (confectioners') sugar, sifted
2 egg yolks

1 Sift the flour and salt together. Make a well in the centre and put in the butter and sugar, then the egg yolks on top.

2 Rub in the mixture until it resembles scrambled eggs, and then a smooth paste. Work quickly. Lightly knead the dough for about 1 minute.

3 Shape the dough into a ball, then flatten slightly to make it easier to start rolling out. Wrap in clear film (plastic wrap) and chill for 1 hour. Preheat the oven to 200°C/400°F/Gas 6.

4 Roll out the dough to 5mm/¼in thick. Stamp out 6cm/2½in rounds. Place on a baking sheet and prick with a fork. Gather up the scraps and roll out more cookies. Bake for 10 minutes, until golden brown.

Almond Mincemeat Tarts

These little tartlets are a welcome change from traditional mince pies. Serve them warm with brandy butter. They freeze well and can be reheated for serving.

Makes 36

275g/10oz/2½ cups plain (all-purpose) flour, plus extra for dusting
75g/3oz/generous ¾ cup icing (confectioners') sugar
5ml/1tsp ground cinnamon
175g/6oz/¾ cup butter
50g/2oz/½ cup ground almonds
1 egg yolk

45ml/3 tbsp milk
450g/1lb mincemeat
15ml/1 tbsp brandy or rum

For the filling
115g/4oz/½ cup butter
115g/4oz/generous ½ cup caster (superfine) sugar
175g/6oz/1½ cups self-raising (self-rising) flour
2 large (US extra large) eggs
finely grated rind of 1 large lemon

For the icing
115g/4oz/1 cup icing (confectioners') sugar
15ml/1 tbsp lemon juice

1 Sift the flour, icing sugar and cinnamon into a bowl or a food processor and rub in the butter until it resembles fine breadcrumbs. Add the ground almonds and bind with the egg yolk and milk to a soft dough. Knead the dough until smooth, wrap in clear film (plastic wrap) and chill for 30 minutes.

2 Preheat the oven to 190°C/375°F/Gas 5.

3 On a lightly floured surface, roll out the pastry and stamp out 36 rounds with a cookie cutter. Mix the mincemeat with the brandy or rum and put a teaspoonful in the bottom of each pastry case (tart shell). Chill.

4 For the filling, whisk all the ingredients together until smooth. Spoon on top of the mincemeat, dividing it evenly, and level the tops. Bake for 20–30 minutes, or until golden brown and springy to the touch. Remove and leave to cool on a wire rack.

5 For the icing, sift the icing sugar and mix with the lemon juice to a smooth, thick, coating consistency. Spoon into a piping (pastry) bag and drizzle a zig-zag pattern over each tart.

Simple Mince Pies Energy 182kcal/758kJ; Protein 5.2g; Carbohydrate 12.6g, of which sugars 5.1g; Fat 12.9g, of which saturates 3g; Cholesterol 43mg; Calcium 31mg; Fibre 0.4g; Sodium 85mg.
Almond Mincemeat Tarts Energy 177kcal/746kJ; Protein 1.8g; Carbohydrate 26.4g, of which sugars 16.9g; Fat 7.8g, of which saturates 4.4g; Cholesterol 34mg; Calcium 32mg; Fibre 0.6g; Sodium 57mg.
Galettes Energy 83kcal/352kJ; Protein 3.4g; Carbohydrate 14.3g, of which sugars 2..9g; Fat 1.75g, of which saturates 0.4g; Cholesterol 43mg; Calcium 27.9mg; Fibre 4..9g; Sodium 6mg.

Mini Mille Feuilles

This pâtisserie classic is a delectable combination of crisp puff pastry with luscious pastry cream. As a large one is difficult to cut, making individual servings is a great solution.

Serves 4
450g/1lb ready-made puff pastry, thawed if frozen
6 egg yolks

65g/2½oz/⅓ cup caster (superfine) sugar
45ml/3 tbsp plain (all-purpose) flour
350ml/12fl oz/1½ cups milk
30ml/2 tbsp Kirsch or cherry liqueur
450g/1lb/2⅔ cups raspberries
icing (confectioners') sugar, for dusting

1 Lightly grease two large baking sheets and sprinkle them with a little very cold water.

2 On a lightly floured surface, roll out the pastry to a thickness of 3mm/⅛in. Using a 10cm/4in cookie cutter, stamp out 12 rounds. Place on the baking sheets and prick each with a fork. Chill for 30 minutes. Preheat the oven to 200°C/400°F/Gas 6.

3 Bake the pastry rounds for 15–20 minutes, until golden, then transfer to wire racks to cool.

4 Whisk the egg yolks and sugar for 2 minutes until light and creamy, then whisk in the flour until just blended. Bring the milk to the boil over a medium heat and pour it over the egg mixture, whisking to blend. Return to the pan, bring to the boil and boil for 2 minutes, whisking constantly.

5 Remove from the heat and whisk in the Kirsch or liqueur. Pour into a bowl and press a piece of clear film (plastic wrap) on to the surface to prevent a skin from forming. Set aside.

6 To assemble, carefully split the pastry rounds in half. Spread each round with a little pastry cream. Arrange a layer of raspberries over the cream and top with a second pastry round. Spread with a little more cream and a few more raspberries. Top with a third pastry round and dust with icing sugar.

Almond Cream Puffs

These sweet little pies consist of crisp, flaky layers of pastry surrounding a delicious, creamy filling. They are best served warm, so reheat any that become cold before eating.

Makes 10
275g/10oz ready-made puff pastry, thawed if frozen
2 egg yolks

15ml/1 tbsp plain (all-purpose) flour
30ml/2 tbsp ground almonds
30ml/2 tbsp caster (superfine) sugar
a few drops of vanilla or almond extract
150ml/¼ pint/⅔ cup double (heavy) cream, whipped
milk, to glaze
icing (confectioners') sugar, for dusting

1 Preheat the oven to 200°C/400°F/Gas 6. Lightly grease a patty or cupcake tin (pan).

2 Roll out the pastry thinly on a lightly floured surface, and stamp out ten 7.5cm/3in plain rounds and ten 6.5cm/2½in fluted rounds. Keep the smaller fluted rounds for the lids and use the larger ones to line the tin. Chill in the refrigerator for about 10 minutes.

3 Whisk the egg yolks with the flour, almonds, sugar and vanilla extract. Fold in the cream and spoon into the pastry cases (pie shells).

4 Brush the rims with milk, add the lids and seal the edges. Glaze with milk.

5 Bake for 20–25 minutes, until puffed up and golden. Using a metal spatula carefully transfer the puffs to a wire rack to cool slightly. Dust with icing sugar.

Variations
Other tasty options are to use desiccated (dry unsweetened shredded) coconut or ground hazelnuts instead of ground almonds in the filling.

Mini Mille Feuilles Energy 702kcal/2943kJ; Protein 16.5g; Carbohydrate 79.1g, of which sugars 30.4g; Fat 37.8g, of which saturates 3.4g; Cholesterol 308mg; Calcium 258mg; Fibre 3.2g; Sodium 406mg.
Almond Cream Puffs Energy 225kcal/933kJ; Protein 3.2g; Carbohydrate 14.9g, of which sugars 3.9g; Fat 17.6g, of which saturates 5.5g; Cholesterol 61mg; Calcium 39mg; Fibre 0.3g; Sodium 91mg.

Surprise Fruit Baskets

Almost too pretty to eat, these crisp filo baskets are filled with fresh fruit set on a rich creamy base with a surprise flavour.

Serves 6

4 large or 8 small sheets of
   frozen filo pastry, thawed
65g/2½oz/5 tbsp butter, melted
250ml/8fl oz/1 cup double
   (heavy) or whipping cream
45ml/3 tbsp strawberry jam
15ml/1 tbsp Cointreau or other
   orange-flavoured liqueur

For the topping

15g/4oz seedless black
   grapes, halved
115g/4oz seedless white
   grapes, halved
150g/5oz fresh pineapple,
   cubed, or drained canned
   pineapple chunks
115g/4 oz/⅔ cup raspberries
30ml/2 tbsp icing
   (confectioners') sugar
6 sprigs of fresh mint,
   to decorate

1 Preheat the oven to 350°F/180°C/Gas 4. Lightly grease six cups of a bun tray (muffin pan).

2 Stack the filo sheets and cut with a sharp knife or scissors into 24 squares each 11cm/4¼in.

3 Place 4 squares of pastry in each of the six greased cups. Press the pastry firmly into the cups, rotating slightly to make star-shaped baskets.

4 Lightly brush the pastry baskets with melted butter. Bake for about 5–7 minutes, until the pastry is crisp and golden brown. Using a metal spatula, carefully transfer the baskets to a wire rack to cool.

5 In a bowl, lightly whip the cream until soft peaks form. Gently fold the strawberry jam and Cointreau into the cream with a flexible spatula.

6 Just before serving, spoon a little of the cream mixture into each pastry basket. Top with the grapes, pineapple and raspberries. Sprinkle with icing sugar and decorate each basket with a small sprig of mint.

Plum and Marzipan Pastries

These Danish pastries can be made with any stoned fruit. Try apricots, cherries, damsons or greengages, adding a glaze made from clear honey or a complementary jam.

Makes 6

375g/13oz ready-made puff
   pastry, thawed if frozen
90ml/6 tbsp plum jam

115g/4oz/¾ cup white
   marzipan, coarsely grated
3 red plums, halved and
   stoned (pitted)
1 egg, beaten
50g/2oz/½ cup flaked
   (sliced) almonds

For the glaze

30ml/2 tbsp plum jam
15ml/1 tbsp water

1 Preheat the oven to 220°C/425°F/Gas 7.

2 Roll out the pastry, cut it into six equal squares and place on one or two dampened baking sheets.

3 Spoon 15ml/1 tbsp jam into the centre of each pastry square. Divide the marzipan among them. Place half a plum, hollow side down, on top of each marzipan mound.

4 Brush the edges of the pastry with beaten egg. Bring up the corners and press them together lightly, then open out the pastry corners at the top.

5 Brush the pastries all over with a little beaten egg to glaze. Divide the flaked almonds between the six pastries and press all over the tops and sides.

6 Bake the pastries for 20–25 minutes, until crisp and golden brown. Keep a close eye on them towards the end of the cooking time as the almonds can scorch quite quickly, spoiling the appearance and flavour of the pastries.

7 To make the glaze, heat the jam and water in a small pan, stirring until smooth. Press the mixture through a sieve (strainer) into a small bowl, then brush it over the tops of the pastries while they are still warm. Leave to cool on a wire rack.

Surprise Fruit Baskets Energy 619kcal/2569kJ; Protein 3.9g; Carbohydrate 37.9g, of which sugars 15.6g; Fat 50.9g, of which saturates 20.9g; Cholesterol 80mg; Calcium 76mg; Fibre 1.6g; Sodium 80mg.
Plum and Marzipan Pastries Energy 416kcal/1746kJ; Protein 6.6g; Carbohydrate 51.8g, of which sugars 29.2g; Fat 22.4g, of which saturates 0.6g; Cholesterol 0mg; Calcium 73mg; Fibre 1.2g; Sodium 205mg.

Marzipan Buns

These delicious buns are perfumed with aromatic light spices, and filled with thick cream and marzipan.

Makes 12
275ml/9fl oz/generous 1 cup double (heavy) cream
40g/1½oz fresh yeast
100g/4oz/½ cup unsalted (sweet) butter, melted
5ml/1 tsp ground cardamom
30ml/2 tbsp sugar

450g/1lb/4 cups plain (all-purpose) flour, plus extra for dusting
pinch of salt
1 egg, beaten
icing (confectioners') sugar, to decorate

For the filling
100g/4oz good quality marzipan
275ml/16fl oz/2 cups double (heavy) cream

1 Pour the cream into a pan and heat until warm to the touch.

2 In a large bowl, blend the yeast with a little of the warmed cream and then add the butter, cardamom and sugar. Add the flour and salt and mix together to form a dough.

3 Turn the dough on to a lightly floured surface and knead for 10 minutes, until firm and elastic. Shape into a ball, put in a clean bowl and cover with a clean dish towel. Leave to rise in a warm place for about 1½ hours, until the dough has doubled in size.

4 Turn the dough on to a lightly floured surface and knead for 2–3 minutes. Divide into 12 equal pieces. Shape each into a round bun and place on a greased baking sheet. Cover and leave to rise in a warm place until doubled in size.

5 Preheat the oven to 180°C/350°F/Gas 4. Brush the tops of the buns with beaten egg, then bake for about 10 minutes until golden brown. Transfer to a wire rack and leave to cool.

6 To serve, cut the tops off the buns and reserve. Remove half of the crumbs from the buns and put in a bowl. Grate the marzipan on top and mix. Replace the mixture in the buns. Whisk the cream until stiff, top the buns with the cream and then replace the tops. Sprinkle the icing sugar on top.

Apricot Triangles

These quite substantial pastries have a luscious filling of dried apricots poached with cinnamon, but a variety of other fillings are also popular. If serving them as snacks, you can make the pastry cases smaller and more delicate.

Makes about 24
115g/4oz/½ cup unsalted butter, softened
250g/9oz/generous 1cup sugar
30ml/2 tbsp milk
1 egg, beaten

5ml/1 tsp vanilla extract
pinch of salt
200–250g/7–9oz/1¼–2¼ cups plain (all-purpose) flour, plus extra for dusting
icing (confectioners') sugar, for dusting (optional)

For the filling
250g/9oz/generous 1 cup dried apricots
1 cinnamon stick
45ml/3 tbsp sugar

1 Beat the butter and sugar until pale and fluffy. In another bowl mix together the milk, egg, vanilla extract and salt.

2 Add one-third of the flour, stir, then add the rest in batches, alternating with the milk mixture. Cover and chill for 1 hour.

3 To make the filling, put the ingredients in a pan and add enough water to cover. Heat gently, then simmer for 15 minutes, until the apricots are tender and most of the liquid has evaporated. Remove the cinnamon stick, then purée the apricots in a food processor or blender with a little of the cooking liquid until they form a consistency like thick jam.

4 Preheat the oven to 180°C/350°F/Gas 4. On a lightly floured surface, roll out the dough to 5mm/¼in thick, then cut into 7.5cm/3in rounds using a cookie cutter.

5 Place 15–30ml/1–2 tbsp of filling in the centre of each round, then pinch the pastry together to form three corners.

6 Place on a baking sheet and bake for 15 minutes, or until pale golden. Serve warm or cold, dusted with icing sugar.

Marzipan Buns Energy 465kcal/1938kJ; Protein 5.3g; Carbohydrate 38.2g, of which sugars 9.6g; Fat 33.4g, of which saturates 19.9g; Cholesterol 96mg; Calcium 85mg; Fibre 1.3g; Sodium 69mg.
Apricot Triangles Energy 125kcal/528kJ; Protein 1.6g; Carbohydrate 21.3g, of which sugars 14.9g; Fat 4.4g, of which saturates 2.6g; Cholesterol 18mg; Calcium 28mg; Fibre 0.9g; Sodium 35mg.

Mallorcan Ensaimadas

These spiral-shaped sweet breads are a popular Spanish breakfast treat. The butter adds a delicious richness.

Makes 16

225g/8oz/2 cups strong white
   bread flour, plus extra
   for dusting
pinch of salt
50g/2oz/¼ cup caster
   (superfine) sugar
15g/½ oz fresh yeast
75ml/5 tbsp lukewarm milk
1 egg
30ml/2 tbsp sunflower oil
50g/2oz/¼ cup butter, melted
icing (confectioners') sugar,
   for dusting

1 Lightly grease two baking sheets. Sift the flour and salt into a large bowl. Stir in the sugar. Make a well in the centre.

2 Cream the yeast with the milk, pour into the centre of the flour, then sprinkle a little of the flour mixture over the top of the liquid. Leave in a warm place for 15 minutes, or until frothy.

3 In a small bowl, beat the egg and sunflower oil together. Add to the flour mixture and mix to a smooth dough. Turn out on to a lightly floured surface and knead for 8–10 minutes, until smooth and elastic. Place in a lightly oiled bowl, cover with lightly oiled clear film (plastic wrap) and leave to rise in a warm place for 1 hour, or until doubled in bulk.

4 Turn out the dough on to a lightly floured surface. Knock back (punch down) and divide into 16 equal pieces. Shape each piece into a rope about 38cm/15in long. Pour the melted butter on to a plate and dip the ropes into the butter to coat.

5 On the baking sheets, curl each rope into a loose spiral, spacing well apart. Tuck the ends under to seal. Cover with lightly oiled clear film and leave to rise in a warm place for about 45 minutes, or until doubled in size.

6 Preheat the oven to 190°C/375°F/Gas 5. Brush the rolls with water and dust with icing sugar. Bake for 10 minutes, or until light golden brown. Cool on a wire rack. Dust again with icing sugar and serve warm.

Saffron Buns

Sweet, filling and infused with saffron, these delicious buns are great for eating at any time of day

Makes 20

300ml/½ pint/1¼ cups milk
130g/4½oz/9 tbsp unsalted
   butter
a pinch of saffron threads
50g/2oz fresh yeast
700g/1½lb/6 cups plain
(all-purpose) flour, plus extra
   for dusting
5ml/1 tsp salt
150g/5oz/¾ cup caster
   (superfine) sugar
40 raisins
beaten egg, to glaze

1 Put the milk and butter in a pan and heat until the butter has melted. Remove from the heat, add the saffron threads and leave to cool until warm to the touch.

2 In a large bowl, blend the fresh yeast with a little of the warm saffron milk. Add the remaining saffron milk, then add the flour, salt and sugar. Mix together to form a dough that comes away from the sides of the bowl.

3 Turn the dough on to a lightly floured surface and knead for about 10 minutes, until the dough feels firm and elastic. Shape into a ball, put in a clean bowl and cover with a clean dish towel. Leave to rise in a warm place for about 1 hour, until the dough has doubled in size.

4 Turn the dough on to a lightly floured surface and knead again for 2–3 minutes. Divide the dough into 20 equal pieces. Roll each into an S shape and place on greased baking sheets.

5 Place a raisin at the end of each bun. Cover with a clean dish towel and leave to rise in a warm place for about 40 minutes, until doubled in size.

6 Preheat the oven to 200°C/400°F/Gas 6. Brush the tops of the buns with beaten egg to glaze and bake for 15 minutes, until golden brown.

Mallorcan Ensaimadas Energy 327kcal/1371kJ; Protein 8.7g; Carbohydrate 38.6g, of which sugars 4.3g; Fat 16.1g, of which saturates 9.3g; Cholesterol 117mg; Calcium 172mg; Fibre 1.4g; Sodium 162mg.
Saffron Buns Energy 423kcal/1788kJ; Protein 9.2g; Carbohydrate 81.7g, of which sugars 15.1g; Fat 8.8g, of which saturates 5g; Cholesterol 20mg; Calcium 161mg; Fibre 2.8g; Sodium 69mg.

Chocolate Eclairs

These crisp pastry fingers are filled with fresh cream, sweetened with vanilla.

Makes 12
65g/2½oz/9 tbsp plain (all-purpose) flour
pinch of salt
50g/2oz/¼ cup butter, diced
150ml/¼ pint/⅔ cup water
2 eggs, lightly beaten

For the filling
300ml/½ pint/1¼ cups double (heavy) cream
10ml/2 tsp icing (confectioners') sugar, sifted
1.5ml/¼ tsp vanilla extract

For the glaze
115g/4oz plain (semisweet) chocolate
25g/1oz/2 tbsp butter

1 Preheat the oven to 200°C/400°F/Gas 6. Grease and line a baking sheet. For the pastry, sift the flour and salt on to a sheet of baking parchment.

2 Melt the butter with the water in a pan, then bring to a rolling boil. Remove from the heat, add all the flour and beat until combined. Return to a low heat, beating until the mixture leaves the side of the pan and forms a ball. Leave to cool for 2–3 minutes. Gradually beat in the eggs to make a smooth, shiny paste.

3 Spoon the pastry into a piping (pastry) bag fitted with a 2.5cm/1in plain nozzle. Pipe 10cm/4in lengths on to the baking sheet. Use a wet knife to cut off the pastry at the nozzle. Bake for 25–30 minutes, until risen and golden.

4 Make a slit along the side of each éclair to release the steam, lower the oven temperature to 180°C/350°F/Gas 4 and bake for 5 minutes more. Cool on a wire rack.

5 For the filling, whip the cream with the sugar and vanilla. Spoon into a piping bag and use to fill the éclairs.

6 Melt the chocolate with 30ml/2 tbsp water in a heatproof bowl over a pan of simmering water. Remove from the heat and gradually stir in the butter. Dip the top of each éclair in the chocolate. Leave to cool until set.

Chocolate Profiteroles

These mouthwatering desserts are served with ice cream and drizzled with chocolate sauce.

Serves 4–6
75g/3oz/¾ cup plain (all-purpose) flour
pinch of salt
pinch of ground nutmeg
175ml/6fl oz/¾ cup water

75g/6 tbsp unsalted butter, diced
3 eggs

For the filling and glaze
275g/10oz plain (semisweet) chocolate
120ml/4fl oz/½ cup water
750ml/1¼ pints/3 cups vanilla ice cream

1 Preheat the oven to 200°C/400°F/Gas 6. Lightly grease a large baking sheet.

2 To make the profiteroles, sift the flour, salt and nutmeg into a bowl.

3 In a medium pan, bring the water and butter to a boil. Remove from the heat and add the dry ingredients all at once. Beat with a wooden spoon for about 1 minute, until well blended, then set the pan over a low heat and cook for about 2 minutes, beating constantly. Remove from the heat.

4 Beat one egg in a small bowl and set aside. Add the remaining eggs, one at a time, to the flour mixture, beating well after each addition. Add the beaten egg by teaspoonfuls until the dough is smooth and shiny; it should pull away and fall slowly when dropped from a spoon.

5 Using a tablespoon, drop the dough on to the baking sheet in 12 mounds. Bake for 25–30 minutes until the pastry is well risen and browned. Turn off the oven and leave the puffs to cool with the door open.

6 To make the sauce, melt the chocolate and water in a heatproof bowl over a pan of gently simmering water, stirring occasionally. Split the pastry in half, add a scoop of ice cream and pour over the chocolate sauce.

Chocolate Eclairs Energy 253kcal/1050kJ; Protein 2.5g; Carbohydrate 11.6g, of which sugars 7.4g; Fat 22.2g, of which saturates 13.5g; Cholesterol 80mg; Calcium 29mg; Fibre 0.4g; Sodium 56mg.
Chocolate Profiteroles Energy 647kcal/2707kJ; Protein 11.7g; Carbohydrate 68.2g, of which sugars 52.4g; Fat 36.9g, of which saturates 22.7g; Cholesterol 155mg; Calcium 182mg; Fibre 1.7g; Sodium 189mg.

Double Chocolate Cream Puffs

These cream puffs are made with double helpings of chocolate and cream.

Makes 12
150g/5oz/1¼ cups plain (all-purpose) flour
25g/1oz/2 tbsp unsweetened cocoa powder
250ml/8fl oz/1 cup water
2.5ml/½ tsp salt
15ml/1 tbsp sugar
115g/4oz/½ cup unsalted butter, diced
4–5 eggs

For the cream
150g/5oz plain (semisweet) chocolate, melted

475ml/16fl oz/2 cups milk
6 egg yolks
100g/3½oz/scant ½ cup sugar
50g/2oz/½ cup plain (all-purpose) flour
120ml/4fl oz/½ cup whipping cream

For the glaze
300ml/10fl oz/1¼ cups whipping cream
55g/2oz/4 tbsp unsalted butter, diced
225g/8oz plain (semisweet) chocolate, chopped
15ml/1 tbsp golden (light corn) syrup

1 Preheat the oven to 200°C/400°F/Gas 6. Lightly grease a large baking sheet. To make the cream puffs, sift the flour and cocoa powder into a bowl.

2 In a medium pan, bring the water, salt, sugar and butter to a boil. Continue to make and bake the cream puffs following the recipe for Chocolate Profiteroles.

3 To make the cream, melt the chocolate and set it aside. Bring the milk to a boil. In a bowl, beat the egg yolks with the sugar until pale and thick. Stir in the flour. Slowly pour over half of the hot milk, stirring constantly. Return the yolk mixture to the milk pan and cook until boiling. Stir in the melted chocolate. Cool to room temperature. Whip the cream. Fold into the cooled custard mixture. Fill each puff with pastry cream using a piping (pastry) bag.

4 Melt the glaze ingredients in a medium pan over a low heat, stir until smooth. Cool slightly and pour over the cream puffs.

Coffee Cream Profiteroles

Crisp-textured coffee choux pastry puffs are filled with cream and drizzled with a white chocolate sauce.

Serves 6
65g/2½oz/9 tbsp plain (all-purpose) flour
pinch of salt
50g/2oz/¼ cup butter, diced
150ml/¼ pint/⅔ cup freshly brewed coffee
2 eggs, lightly beaten

For the filling and sauce
50g/2oz/¼ cup sugar
100ml/3½fl oz/scant ½ cup water
150g/5oz good-quality white chocolate, broken up
25g/1oz/2 tbsp butter
300ml/½ pint/1¼ cups double (heavy) cream
30ml/2 tbsp coffee liqueur, such as Tia Maria or Kahlúa

1 Preheat the oven to 220°C/425°F/Gas 7. To make the pastry, sift the flour and salt on to a sheet of baking parchment and set aside. Put the butter into a pan with the coffee. Bring to a rolling boil, then remove from the heat and add all the flour. Beat vigorously with a wooden spoon until the mixture forms a ball and comes away from the side. Let stand for 2 minutes.

2 Gradually add the beaten eggs to the flour mixture, beating thoroughly after each addition. Spoon into a piping (pastry) bag fitted with a 1cm/½in plain nozzle.

3 Pipe 24 buns on to a damp baking sheet and bake for about 20 minutes. Transfer to a wire rack. Pierce each one to let out the steam. Leave to cool.

4 To make the sauce, put the sugar and water in a pan and heat until the sugar has dissolved. Bring to the boil, then simmer for 3 minutes. Remove from the heat and add the chocolate and butter, stirring until smooth. Stir in 45ml/3 tbsp of the cream and the coffee liqueur.

5 To assemble, whip the remaining cream in a small bowl until soft peaks form. Spoon into a piping bag and use to fill the buns through the slits in the sides. Pour a little sauce over.

Double Chocolate Cream Puffs Energy 576kcal/2401kJ; Protein 9.2g; Carbohydrate 46.9g, of which sugars 33.7g; Fat 40.4g, of which saturates 23.5g; Cholesterol 235mg; Calcium 133mg; Fibre 1.6g; Sodium 166mg. Coffee Cream Profiteroles Energy 579kcal/2401kJ; Protein 6g; Carbohydrate 32.6g, of which sugars 24.4g; Fat 46.8g, of which saturates 28.4g; Cholesterol 159mg; Calcium 123mg; Fibre 0.3g; Sodium 138mg.

Nutty Cream Cheese Spirals

These light and sweet cream cheese and nut-filled spirals taste heavenly.

1 egg white beaten with
    15ml/1 tbsp water, for glazing
sugar, for sprinkling

Makes 32
225g/8oz/1 cup butter
225g/8oz/1 cup cream cheese
10ml/2 tsp sugar
225g/8oz/ 2 cups plain
    (all-purpose) flour, plus extra
    for dusting

For the filling
115g/4oz/1 cup walnuts or
    pecans, finely chopped
75g/3oz/1/2 cup light brown sugar
5ml/1 tsp ground cinnamon

1 In a bowl, beat the butter, cream cheese and sugar until pale and creamy.

2 Sift over the flour and mix to a form a dough. Gather into a ball and divide into two. Flatten each piece, wrap in clear film (plastic wrap) and chill in the refrigerator for at least 30 minutes.

3 To make the filling, mix together the chopped walnuts, or pecans, brown sugar and cinnamon.

4 Preheat the oven to 190°C/375°F/Gas 5. Lightly grease two baking sheets.

5 On a lightly floured surface, roll out each half of dough thinly into a circle about 28cm/11in in diameter. Trim the edges with a knife using a dinner plate as a guide.

6 Brush the surface with egg white glaze and sprinkle the dough evenly with half the filling.

7 Cut the dough into quarters and each quarter into four sections to form 16 triangles. Starting from the base of the triangles (the rounded end) roll up to form spirals.

8 Place on the prepared baking sheets and brush with the remaining glaze. Sprinkle with sugar. Bake for 15–20 minutes until golden. Transfer to a wire rack to cool completely.

Spiced Nut Palmiers

Created at the beginning of the last century, these dainty French cookies are designed to be served with afternoon tea. They are said to look like the foliage of palm trees.

Makes 40
75g/3oz/3/4 cup chopped
    almonds, walnuts or hazelnuts
30ml/2 tbsp caster (superfine)
    sugar, plus extra for sprinkling
2.5ml/1/2 tsp ground cinnamon
225g/8oz ready-made rough-puff
    or puff pastry dough, thawed
    if frozen
1 egg, lightly beaten

1 Lightly butter two large baking sheets, preferably non-stick. In a food processor fitted with a metal blade, process the nuts, sugar and cinnamon until finely ground.

2 Sprinkle the work surface with caster sugar and roll out the dough to a rectangle 50 × 20cm/20 × 8in and about 3mm/1/8in thick. Lightly brush the dough all over with beaten egg and sprinkle evenly with about half of the nut mixture.

3 Fold in the long edges of the dough to meet in the centre and flatten with the rolling pin. Brush with egg and sprinkle with most of the remaining nut mixture. Fold in the folded edges to meet in the centre, brush with egg and sprinkle with the remaining nut mixture. Fold one side of the dough over the other.

4 Cut the dough crossways into 8mm/3/8in slices and place 2.5cm/1in apart on the baking sheets.

5 Spread the dough edges apart to form dough wedges. Chill the palmiers for at least 15 minutes. Preheat the oven to 220°C/425°F/Gas 7.

6 Bake the palmiers for about 8–10 minutes, until the pastry is crisp and golden. Carefully turn them over halfway through the cooking time using a metal spatula. Keep a watchful eye on them as the sugar can easily scorch. Carefully transfer to a wire rack to cool completely.

Nutty Cream Cheese Spirals Energy 150kcal/621kJ; Protein 1.7g; Carbohydrate 9.7g, of which sugars 4.3g; Fat 11.8g, of which saturates 6g; Cholesterol 28mg; Calcium 24mg; Fibre 0.3g; Sodium 67mg.
Spiced Nut Palmiers Energy 37kcal/155kJ; Protein 0.9g; Carbohydrate 3g, of which sugars 0.9g; Fat 2.6g, of which saturates 0.1g; Cholesterol 5mg; Calcium 9mg; Fibre 0.1g; Sodium 20mg.

Tunisian Almond Cigars

These light-as-air pastries are filled with a subtly flavoured almond mixture that is sure to delight your guests but will also keep them guessing.

Makes 8–12
250g/9oz almond paste
1 egg, lightly beaten
15ml/1 tbsp rose water or orange flower water
5ml/1 tsp ground cinnamon
1.5ml/¼ tsp almond extract
8–12 sheets filo pastry, thawed if frozen
melted butter, for brushing
icing (confectioners') sugar and ground cinnamon, for dusting

1 Knead the almond paste until soft, then put in a bowl and mix in the egg, flower water, cinnamon and almond extract. Chill for 1–2 hours.

2 Preheat the oven to 190°C/375°F/Gas 5. Lightly grease a baking sheet.

3 Place a sheet of filo pastry on a piece of baking parchment, keeping the remaining pastry covered with a damp cloth, and brush with the melted butter.

4 Shape 30–45ml/2–3 tbsp of the filling into a cylinder and place at one end of the pastry. Fold the pastry over to enclose the ends of the filling, then roll up to form a cigar. Place on the baking sheet and make 7–11 more cigars in the same way.

5 Bake for about 15 minutes, or until golden brown. Leave to cool completely, then serve, dusted with icing sugar and ground cinnamon.

> **Variation**
> *Instead of dusting with sugar, drench the pastries in syrup. In a pan, dissolve 250g/9oz/generous 1 cup sugar in 250ml/ 8fl oz/1 cup water and boil until thickened. Stir in a squeeze of lemon juice and a few drops of rose water and pour over the pastries. Leave the syrup to soak in before serving.*

Butterfly Cookies

Melt-in-the-mouth puff pastry interleaved with sugar, nuts and cinnamon produces a slightly outrageous-looking cookie that teams well with ice creams and fruit salads.

Makes about 12
500g/1¼lb ready-made puff pastry, thawed if frozen
1 egg, beaten
115g/4oz/½ cup sugar
25g/1oz/¼ cup chopped mixed nuts
5ml/1 tsp ground cinnamon

1 Preheat the oven to 200°C/400°F/Gas 6.

2 Roll out the puff pastry dough on a lightly floured surface to a rectangle 50 × 17cm/20 × 6½in. Using a sharp knife, cut the rectangle widthways into four pieces. Lightly brush each piece with the beaten egg.

3 Mix together 75g/3oz/6 tbsp of the sugar, the nuts and cinnamon in a bowl. Sprinkle this mixture evenly over three of the pieces of dough. Place the pieces one on top of the other, ending with the uncoated piece, placing this one egg side down on the top of the stack. Press lightly together with the rolling pin.

4 Cut the stack of dough sheets widthways into 5mm/¼in slices. Carefully place one strip on a non-stick baking sheet and place the next strip over it at an angle. Place a third strip on top at another angle so that it looks like a butterfly. Don't worry if the strips separate slightly when you are transferring them to the baking sheet. However, try to handle the dough as little as possible.

5 Using your fingers, press the centre very flat. Sprinkle with a little of the reserved sugar. Continue in this way to make more cookies until all the dough is used up.

6 Bake the cookies for about 10–15 minutes, or until golden brown all over. Leave to cool completely on the baking sheet before serving with a dessert such as ice cream or fruit salad.

Tunisian Almond Cigars Energy 109kcal/458kJ; Protein 2.2g; Carbohydrate 18.9g, of which sugars 14.2g; Fat 3.2g, of which saturates 0.4g; Cholesterol 16mg; Calcium 25mg; Fibre 0.6g; Sodium 10mg.
Butterfly Cookies Energy 212kcal/889kJ; Protein 3.4g; Carbohydrate 25.6g, of which sugars 10.6g; Fat 11.8g, of which saturates 0.2g; Cholesterol 16mg; Calcium 37mg; Fibre 0.2g; Sodium 136mg.

Rugelach

These crisp, flaky cookies, rolled around a sweet filling, resemble a croissant. They are thought to have come from Poland, where they are a traditional sweet treat. Chocolate chip rugelach are very popular in the United States.

Makes 48–60
115g/4oz/½ cup unsalted
  butter
115g/4oz/½ cup full-fat soft
  white (farmer's) cheese
15ml/1 tbsp sugar

1 egg
pinch of salt
about 250g/9oz/2¼ cups plain
  (all-purpose) flour, plus extra
  for dusting
about 250g/9oz/generous 1 cup
  butter, melted
250g/9oz/scant 2 cups sultanas
  (golden raisins)
130g/4½oz/generous 1 cup
  chopped walnuts
about 225g/8oz/generous 1 cup
  caster (superfine) sugar
10–15ml/1–2 tsp ground
  cinnamon

1 To make the pastry, put the butter and cheese in a bowl and beat until creamy. Beat in the sugar, egg and salt.

2 Fold the flour into the mixture, a little at a time, until the dough can be worked with the hands. Continue adding the flour, kneading with the hands, until it is a consistency that can be rolled out. (Add only as much flour as needed.)

3 Shape the dough into a ball, then cover with clear film (plastic wrap) and chill in the refrigerator for at least 2 hours or overnight. Preheat the oven to 180°C/350°F/Gas 4.

4 Divide the dough into six equal pieces. On a lightly floured surface, roll out each piece into a round about 3mm/⅛in thick, then brush with a little of the melted butter and sprinkle over the sultanas, chopped walnuts, a little sugar and the cinnamon.

5 Cut the rounds into eight to ten wedges and carefully roll the large side of each wedge towards the tip. (Some of the filling will fall out.) Arrange on baking sheets, brush with a little butter and sprinkle with the sugar. Bake for 15–30 minutes, until lightly browned. Leave to cool before serving.

Fig and Date Ravioli

These irresistible cushions of sweet pastry are filled with a delicious mixture of figs, dates and walnuts and dusted with icing sugar. They are ideal for serving with coffee.

Makes about 20
375g/13oz ready-made sweet
  shortcrust pastry dough,
  thawed if frozen

milk, for brushing
icing (confectioners') sugar, sifted,
  for dusting

For the filling
115g/4oz/⅔ cup ready-to-eat
  dried figs
50g/2oz/scant ½ cup stoned
  (pitted) dates
15g/½oz/1 tbsp chopped walnuts
10ml/2 tsp lemon juice
15ml/1 tbsp clear honey

1 Preheat the oven to 180°C/350°F/Gas 4. To make the filling, put all the ingredients into a food processor and blend to a paste.

2 Roll out just under half of the shortcrust pastry dough on a lightly floured surface to a square. Place spoonfuls of the fig paste on the dough in neat rows at equally spaced intervals.

3 Roll out the remaining dough to a slightly larger square. Dampen all around each spoonful of filling, using a pastry brush dipped in cold water. Place the second sheet of dough on top and press together around each mound of filling.

4 Using a zig-zag pastry wheel, cut squares between the mounds of filling. Place the cookies on non-stick baking sheets and lightly brush the top of each with a little milk. Bake for 15–20 minutes, until golden.

5 Using a metal spatula, transfer the cookies to a wire rack to cool. When cool, dust with icing sugar.

Cook's Tip
If you don't have a pastry wheel, use a sharp knife to cut out the ravioli, although it will not produce a fluted edge.

Rugelach Energy 143kcal/596kJ; Protein 1.9g; Carbohydrate 13.2g, of which sugars 5.3g; Fat 9.5g, of which saturates 4.7g; Cholesterol 18mg; Calcium 32mg; Fibre 0.6g; Sodium 48mg.
Fig and Date Ravioli Energy 111kcal/464kJ; Protein 1.5g; Carbohydrate 13.9g, of which sugars 5.3g; Fat 5.9g, of which saturates 1.7g; Cholesterol 3mg; Calcium 31mg; Fibre 0.9g; Sodium 79mg.

Baked Sweet Ravioli

These rich pastries are flavoured with lemon and filled with ricotta cheese, fruit and chocolate, for a sweet and rich treat.

Serves 4
225g/8oz/2 cups plain
(all-purpose) flour
65g/2½oz/⅓ cup caster
(superfine) sugar
90/3½oz/scant ½ cup
butter, diced
2 eggs
5ml/1 tsp finely grated lemon
rind, plus extra for sprinkling

For the filling
175g/6oz/¾ cup ricotta cheese
50g/2oz/¼ cup caster
(superfine) sugar
4ml/¾ tsp vanilla extract
1 egg yolk, beaten
15ml/1 tbsp mixed candied fruits
25g/1oz dark (bittersweet)
chocolate, finely chopped
icing (confectioners') sugar,
for sprinkling
grated dark (bittersweet)
chocolate, for sprinkling

1 For the dough, process the flour, sugar and butter in a food processor. Add one egg and the lemon rind and process to form a dough. Wrap in clear film (plastic wrap) and chill.

2 Press the cheese through a sieve (strainer) into a bowl. Stir in the sugar, vanilla, egg yolk, fruits and chocolate.

3 Halve the dough and roll out each half between sheets of clear film to a 15 x 56cm/6 x 22in rectangle.

4 Preheat the oven to 180°C/350°F/Gas 4. Lightly grease a baking sheet.

5 Place mounds of filling, 2.5cm/1in apart, in two rows on one dough strip. Beat the remaining egg and brush between the mounds. Top with the second dough strip and press to seal. Stamp out ravioli around each mound with a 6cm/2½in cookie cutter. Gently pinch to seal the edges.

6 Place on the baking sheet and bake for 15 minutes, until golden. Sprinkle with lemon rind, icing sugar and chocolate.

Gazelles' Horns

Originating from Morocco, these horn-shaped pastries are filled with fragrant sweet almond paste – an unusual and lovely treat.

Makes about 16
200g/7oz/1¾ cups plain
(all-purpose) flour, plus extra
for dusting
pinch of salt
25g/1oz/2 tbsp butter, melted
about 30ml/2 tbsp orange
flower water

1 egg yolk, beaten
60–90ml/4–6 tbsp chilled water

For the filling
200g/7oz/scant 2 cups
ground almonds
115g/4oz/1 cup icing
(confectioners') sugar, plus
extra for dusting
30ml/2 tbsp orange flower water
25g/1oz/2 tbsp butter, melted
2 egg yolks, beaten
2.5ml/½ tsp ground cinnamon

1 Mix the almonds, icing sugar, orange flower water, butter, egg yolks and cinnamon in a bowl to make a smooth paste.

2 To make the dough, sift the flour and salt into a large bowl, then stir in the melted butter, orange flower water and about three-quarters of the egg yolk. Stir in enough chilled water to make a fairly soft dough.

3 Quickly and lightly, knead the dough until it is smooth and elastic, then place it on a lightly floured surface and roll it out thinly. Cut the dough into long strips 7.5cm/3in wide. Preheat the oven to 180°C/350°F/Gas 4. Grease a baking sheet.

4 Roll small pieces of the almond paste into thin sausages about 7.5cm/3in long with tapering ends. Place these in a line along one side of the strips of dough, about 3cm/1¼in apart. Dampen the dough edges with water, then fold the other half of the strip over the filling and press the edges together firmly.

5 Cut around each dough sausage to make a crescent shape. Make sure that the edges are firmly pinched together. Prick the crescents with a fork and place on the baking sheet. Brush with the remaining egg yolk and bake for 12–16 minutes until lightly coloured. Leave to cool, then dust with icing sugar.

Baked Sweet Ravioli Energy 628kcal/2636kJ; Protein 13.1g; Carbohydrate 81.4g, of which sugars 38.5g; Fat 30.1g, of which saturates 17.7g; Cholesterol 162mg; Calcium 119mg; Fibre 2.1g; Sodium 186mg.
Gazelles' Horns Energy 182kcal/762kJ; Protein 4.4g; Carbohydrate 18.1g, of which sugars 8.2g; Fat 10.7g, of which saturates 2.5g; Cholesterol 44mg; Calcium 56mg; Fibre 1.3g; Sodium 23mg.

Fruit-filled Empanadas

Imagine biting through crisp buttery pastry to discover a rich fruity filling flavoured with oranges and cinnamon.

Makes 12

275g/10oz/2½ cups plain
(all-purpose) flour, plus extra
for dusting
25g/1oz/2 tbsp sugar
90g/3½ oz/scant ½ cup butter,
chilled and diced
1 egg yolk
iced water

milk, to glaze
caster (superfine) sugar,
for sprinkling
whole almonds and orange
wedges, to serve

For the filling

25g/1oz/2 tbsp butter
3 ripe plantains, peeled
and mashed
2.5ml/½ tsp ground cloves
5ml/1 tsp ground cinnamon
225g/8oz/1⅓ cups raisins
grated rind and juice of 2 oranges

1 Combine the flour and sugar in a mixing bowl. Add the butter and rub in with your fingertips until the mixture resembles fine breadcrumbs.

2 Beat the egg yolk and add to the flour mixture. Add iced water to make a smooth dough. Shape it into a ball.

3 For the filling, melt the butter in a pan. Add the plantains, cloves and cinnamon and cook over a medium heat for 2–3 minutes. Stir in the raisins, with the orange rind and juice. Lower the heat so that the mixture barely simmers. Cook for about 15 minutes, until the raisins are plump and the juice has evaporated. Set aside to cool.

4 Preheat the oven to 200°C/400°F/Gas 6. Roll out the dough on a lightly floured surface. Stamp out 10cm/4in rounds using a cookie cutter. Place on a baking sheet and spoon on a little of the filling. Dampen the rim of the dough rounds with water, fold the dough over the filling and crimp the edges to seal.

5 Brush with milk. Bake in batches if necessary, for about 15 minutes, or until they are golden. Leave to cool a little, sprinkle with caster sugar and serve warm, with whole almonds and orange wedges.

Microwave Date-filled Pastries

Made traditionally these pastries are labour-intensive, but making a small quantity in the microwave is not such a lengthy procedure.

Makes about 25

75g/3oz/6 tbsp butter, softened
175g/6oz/1½ cups plain
(all-purpose) flour
5ml/1 tsp rose water
5ml/1 tsp orange flower water

45ml/3 tbsp water
20ml/4 tsp sifted icing
(confectioners') sugar, for
sprinkling

For the filling

115g/4oz/⅔ cup stoned (pitted)
dried dates
50ml/2fl oz/¼ cup boiling water
2.5ml/½ tsp orange flower water

1 To make the filling, chop the dates finely and place in a bowl. Add the boiling water and orange flower water, then beat the mixture vigorously with a wooden spoon. Set aside and leave to cool.

2 For the pastries, rub the butter into the flour with your fingertips. Mix in the rose and orange flower waters and the water to make a firm dough.

3 Shape the dough into about 25 small balls.

4 Press your finger into a ball of dough to make a small container, pressing the sides round and round to make the sides thinner. Put 1.5ml/¼ tsp of the date mixture into the dough. Seal by pressing the pastry together.

5 Repeat with the remaining dough and filling.

6 Arrange the date pastries, seam side down, on lightly greased baking parchment and prick each one with a fork. Microwave on HIGH (100 per cent) power for 3–5 minutes, rearranging twice during cooking. Leave to stand for 5 minutes before transferring to a rack to cool.

7 Put the cooled pastries on a plate and sprinkle over the icing sugar. Shake lightly to make sure they are covered.

Fruit-filled Empanadas Energy 276kcal/1161kJ; Protein 4g; Carbohydrate 45.4g, of which sugars 15.7g; Fat 9.9g, of which saturates 5.9g; Cholesterol 40mg; Calcium 59mg; Fibre 1.7g; Sodium 80mg.
Microwave Date-filled Pastries Energy 59kcal/246kJ; Protein 0.8g; Carbohydrate 8.6g, of which sugars 3.3g; Fat 2.6g, of which saturates 1.6g; Cholesterol 6mg; Calcium 12mg; Fibre 0.4g; Sodium 19mg.

Greek Fruit and Nut Pastries

Aromatic Greek pastries are packed with candied citrus peel and walnuts, soaked in a coffee syrup.

Makes 16
450g/1lb/4 cups plain
  (all-purpose) flour, plus extra
  for dusting
2.5ml/½ tsp ground cinnamon
2.5ml/½ tsp baking powder
pinch of salt
150g/5oz/10 tbsp unsalted
  butter
30ml/2 tbsp caster (superfine)
  sugar
1 egg
120ml/4fl oz/½ cup milk, chilled

For the filling
60ml/4 tbsp clear honey
60ml/4 tbsp strong freshly
  brewed coffee
75g/3oz/½ cup mixed candied
  citrus peel, finely chopped
175g/6oz/1½ cups
  walnuts, chopped
1.5ml/¼ tsp freshly-grated
  nutmeg
milk, to glaze
caster (superfine) sugar,
  for sprinkling

1 Preheat the oven to 180°C/350°F/Gas 4. To make the dough, sift the flour, ground cinnamon, baking powder and salt into a bowl. Rub in the butter until the mixture resembles fine breadcrumbs. Stir in the sugar. Make a well in the middle.

2 Beat the egg and milk together and add to the well in the dry ingredients. Mix to a soft dough. Divide the dough into two and wrap in clear film (plastic wrap). Chill for 30 minutes.

3 To make the filling, mix the honey and coffee. Add the peel, walnuts and nutmeg. Stir well and leave to soak for 20 minutes.

4 Roll out a portion of dough on a lightly floured surface to about 3mm/⅛in thick. Stamp out 10cm/4in rounds.

5 Place a heaped teaspoonful of filling on one side of each round. Brush the edges with milk, then fold over and press the edges together to seal. Repeat until all the filling is used.

6 Put the pastries on non-stick baking sheets, brush with milk and sprinkle with caster sugar. Prick each with a fork and bake for 35 minutes. Cool on a wire rack.

Fruit and Nut Turnovers

A tasty mixture of dried fruit and nuts is enclosed in crisp little pastry crescents.

Makes 16
225g/8oz/2 cups plain
  (all-purpose) flour
1.5ml/¼ tsp baking powder
pinch of salt
10ml/2 tsp caster (superfine)
  sugar
50g/2oz/4 tbsp unsalted
  butter, chilled
25g/1oz/2 tbsp white cooking fat
120–175ml/4–6fl oz/½–¾ cup
  iced water

For the filling
350g/12oz/2 cups mixed
  dried fruit, such as apricots
  and prunes
75g/3oz/generous ½ cup raisins
115g/4oz/½ cup soft light
  brown sugar
65g/2½oz/generous ½ cup pine
  nuts or chopped almonds
2.5ml/½ tsp ground cinnamon
oil, for frying
45ml/3 tbsp caster (superfine)
  sugar mixed with 5ml/1 tsp
  ground cinnamon, for sprinkling

1 For the dough, sift the flour, baking powder, salt and sugar into a bowl and rub in the fats until the mixture resembles fine breadcrumbs. Mix in enough iced water to form a dough. Shape into a ball, cover and chill for 30 minutes.

2 Place the dried fruit in a pan and add cold water to cover. Bring to the boil, then simmer for 30 minutes, until the fruit is soft enough to purée. Drain and place in a food processor or blender. Process until smooth, then return the purée to the pan.

3 Add the brown sugar and cook for 5 minutes, stirring constantly, until thick. Remove from the heat and stir in the nuts and cinnamon. Leave to cool.

4 Roll out the dough to 3mm/⅛in thick. Stamp out rounds with a 10cm/4in cookie cutter. Put a spoonful of fruit in the centre of each round. Brush the edges of the rounds with water, fold in half and crimp the edges with a fork.

5 Heat a 1cm/½in depth of oil in a frying pan. Fry the pastries, in batches, for 1½ minutes on each side, until golden. Drain, sprinkle with cinnamon sugar and serve.

Greek Fruit and Nut Pastries Energy 278kcal/1162kJ; Protein 5g; Carbohydrate 30.2g, of which sugars 8.7g; Fat 16.1g, of which saturates 5.7g; Cholesterol 32mg; Calcium 69mg; Fibre 1.5g; Sodium 80mg. **Fruit and Nut Turnovers** Energy 199kcal/840kJ; Protein 3.2g; Carbohydrate 33.6g, of which sugars 22.7g; Fat 6.7g, of which saturates 2.5g; Cholesterol 8mg; Calcium 54mg; Fibre 2.2g; Sodium 27mg.

Pan Dulce

These "sweet breads" of various shapes are made throughout Mexico and are eaten as a snack or with jam or marmalade for breakfast.

Makes 12
120ml/4fl oz/½ cup lukewarm milk
10ml/2 tsp active dried yeast
450g/1lb/4 cups strong white bread flour, plus extra for dusting
75g/3oz/scant ½ cup caster (superfine) sugar
25g/1oz/2 tbsp butter, softened
4 large (US extra large) eggs, beaten

For the topping
75g/3oz/6 tbsp butter, softened
115g/4oz/½ cup sugar
1 egg yolk
5ml/1 tsp ground cinnamon
115g/4oz/1 cup plain (all-purpose) flour

1 Pour the milk into a small bowl, stir in the dried yeast and leave in a warm place until frothy.

2 Put the flour and sugar in a mixing bowl, add the yeast mixture, butter and eggs and mix to a soft, sticky dough.

3 Place the dough on a lightly floured surface and dredge it with flour until it is completely covered. Cover it with lightly oiled clear film (plastic wrap) and leave to rest for 20 minutes.

4 Meanwhile, make the topping. Beat the butter and sugar in a bowl, then mix in the egg yolk, cinnamon and flour.

5 Grease two baking sheets. Divide the dough into 12 equal pieces and shape each of them into a round. Space well apart on the baking sheets. Sprinkle the topping over the breads, dividing it more or less equally among them, then press it lightly into the surface.

6 Leave the rolls in a warm place to stand for about 30 minutes, until they are about one and a half times their previous size. Preheat the oven to 200°C/400°F/Gas 6 and bake the breads for about 15 minutes. Leave to cool slightly.

Baklava

Turkish coffee is black, thick, very sweet and often spiced. Here it is used in this famous pastry confection served throughout the Middle East.

Makes 16
50g/2oz/½ cup blanched almonds, chopped
50g/2oz/½ cup pistachio nuts, chopped
75g/3oz/scant ½ cup caster (superfine) sugar
115g/4oz filo pastry, thawed if frozen
75g/3oz/6 tbsp unsalted butter, melted and cooled

For the syrup
115g/4oz/generous ½ cup caster (superfine) sugar
7.5cm/3in piece cinnamon stick
1 whole clove
2 cardamom pods, crushed
75ml/5 tbsp strong freshly brewed coffee

1 Preheat the oven to 180°C/350°F/Gas 4. Lightly grease an 18 × 28cm/7 × 11in tin (pan) with melted butter.

2 Mix the nuts and sugar together. Cut the pastry to fit the tin. Place a sheet of pastry in the tin and brush with butter. Repeat with three more sheets and spread with half the nut mixture.

3 Layer up three more sheets of pastry as before, then spread the remaining nut mixture over them. Top with the remaining pastry and butter. Press down the edges to seal. Mark the top into diamonds. Bake for 20–25 minutes, until golden.

4 Put the syrup ingredients in a pan and heat gently until the sugar dissolves. Cover and leave to stand for 20 minutes.

5 Remove from the oven. Re-heat the syrup and strain over the pastry. Leave to cool in the tin. Cut into diamonds, remove from the tin and serve.

Cook's Tip
Keep the filo pastry covered with a damp cloth to stop it drying out and becoming brittle, which makes it difficult to use.

Baklava Energy 161kcal/675kJ; Protein 2.3g; Carbohydrate 21.3g, of which sugars 16.3g; Fat 8g, of which saturates 2.6g; Cholesterol 8mg; Calcium 27mg; Fibre 0.7g; Sodium 70mg.
Pan Dulce Energy 358kcal/1510kJ; Protein 6.5g; Carbohydrate 65.2g, of which sugars 17.6g; Fat 9.6g, of which saturates 5.6g; Cholesterol 39mg; Calcium 110mg; Fibre 1.9g; Sodium 68mg.

Churros

Churros are long, golden doughnuts which are deep-fried and rolled in sugar while still hot.

Serves 2
200g/7oz/1¾ cups plain (all-purpose) flour
150ml/¼ pint/⅔ cup milk
150ml/¼ pint/⅔ cup water
2 eggs, beaten
vegetable oil, for deep-frying
caster (superfine) sugar, for dusting

1 Sift the flour on to a sheet of baking parchment.

2 Bring the milk and water to a boil in a pan. Pour in the flour and beat vigorously with a wooden spoon, stirring until the dough forms a ball.

3 Remove the pan from the heat and let the dough cool a little. Gradually beat in the eggs, adding just enough to give a piping consistency. Spoon the mixture into a piping (pastry) bag fitted with a large fluted nozzle.

4 Preheat the oven to 150°C/300°F/Gas 2.

5 To cook the churros, heat the oil in a deep-fat-fryer or heavy frying pan to 190°C/375°F or until a piece of dough sizzles as soon as it hits the oil. Squeeze the piping bag over the deep-fryer or pan, snipping off 10cm/4in lengths with kitchen scissors. Fry the churros, in batches of four to six, for 3–4 minutes, until golden brown.

6 Remove with a slotted spoon and drain on kitchen paper. Dust with caster sugar and keep warm in the oven while you cook the remaining batches.

Cook's Tip
Kids will love these served Spanish-style scooped into a cone of rolled paper – perhaps with a mug of hot chocolate.

Brioches au Chocolat

These lovely buttery and chocolate-filled breads are the ultimate luxury breakfast treat.

Makes 12
250g/9oz/2¼ cups strong white bread flour, plus extra for dusting
pinch of salt
30ml/2 tbsp caster (superfine) sugar
1 sachet easy-blend dried yeast
3 eggs, beaten, plus extra beaten egg, for glazing
45ml/3 tbsp hand-hot milk
115g/4oz/½ cup unsalted butter, diced
175g/6oz plain (semisweet) chocolate, broken into squares

1 Sift the flour and salt into a large bowl and stir in the sugar and yeast. Make a well in the centre and add the eggs and milk. Beat the egg and milk mixture well, gradually incorporating the surrounding dry ingredients to make a fairly soft dough.

2 Turn the dough on to a lightly floured surface and knead well for about 5 minutes, until smooth and elastic.

3 Add the butter to the dough, a few pieces at a time, kneading until each addition is absorbed before adding the next. When all the butter has been incorporated and small bubbles appear in the dough, wrap it in clear film (plastic wrap) and chill for at least 1 hour.

4 Lightly grease 12 individual brioche tins (pans) set on a baking sheet. Divide the dough into 12 and shape each into a smooth round. Place a chocolate square in the centre of each round. Bring up the sides of the dough and press the edges firmly together to seal, use a little beaten egg if necessary.

5 Place the brioches, join side down, in the prepared tins. Cover and leave them in a warm place for about 30 minutes, or until doubled in size. Preheat the oven to 200°C/400°F/Gas 6.

6 Brush the brioches with beaten egg. Bake for 12–15 minutes, until well risen and golden brown. Leave to cool slightly on wire racks.

Churros Energy 378kcal/1561kJ; Protein 9.1g; Carbohydrate 40.7g, of which sugars 2.6g; Fat 20.6g, of which saturates 3.2g; Cholesterol 10mg; Calcium 130mg; Fibre 1.6g; Sodium 53mg.
Brioches Au Chocolat Energy 236kcal/988kJ; Protein 4.3g; Carbohydrate 27g, of which sugars 11g; Fat 13.1g, of which saturates 7.6g; Cholesterol 69mg; Calcium 48mg; Fibre 1g; Sodium 79mg.

Buñuelos

These lovely little puffs look like miniature doughnuts and taste so good it is hard not to over-indulge. Make them for brunch, or simply serve them with coffee

Makes 12

225g/8oz/2 cups plain
    (all-purpose) flour, plus extra
    for dusting
pinch of salt

5ml/1 tsp baking powder
2.5ml/½ tsp ground aniseed
115g/4oz/½ cup caster
    (superfine) sugar
1 large (US extra large) egg
120ml/4fl oz/½ cup milk
50g/2oz/¼ cup butter, melted
oil, for deep frying
10ml/2 tsp ground cinnamon
cinnamon sticks, to decorate

1 Sift the flour, salt, baking powder and ground aniseed into a mixing bowl. Add 30ml/2 tbsp of the caster sugar.

2 Place the egg and milk in a small jug (pitcher) and whisk together well. Pour the egg mixture gradually into the flour, stirring constantly, then add the butter. Mix with a wooden spoon and then with your hands to make a soft dough. Turn out the dough on to a lightly floured surface and knead for about 10 minutes, until smooth.

3 Divide the dough into 12 pieces and roll into balls. Slightly flatten each ball with your hand and then make a hole in the centre with the floured handle of a wooden spoon.

4 Heat the oil to 190°C/375°F, or until a cube of dried bread, added to the oil, floats and then turns golden in 30–60 seconds. Fry the buñuelos in small batches until they are puffy and golden brown, turning them once or twice during cooking. As soon as they are golden, lift them out of the oil using a slotted spoon and place on a double layer of kitchen paper to drain.

5 Mix the remaining caster sugar with the ground cinnamon in a small bowl. Add the buñuelos, one at a time, while they are still warm, toss them in the mixture until they are lightly coated and either serve at once or leave to cool. Decorate with cinnamon sticks.

Chocolate Cinnamon Doughnuts

Packed with flavour, these doughnuts really are an extra special treat.

Makes 16

500g/1¼lb/5 cups strong white
    bread flour, plus extra
    for dusting
30ml/2 tbsp unsweetened
    cocoa powder
pinch of salt
1 sachet easy-blend dried yeast
300ml/½ pint/1¼ cups
    lukewarm milk

40g/1½oz/3 tbsp butter, melted
1 egg, beaten
115g/4oz plain (semisweet)
    chocolate, broken into
    16 pieces
sunflower oil, for deep-frying

For the coating
45ml/3 tbsp caster
    (superfine) sugar
15ml/1 tbsp unsweetened
    cocoa powder
5ml/1 tsp ground cinnamon

1 Sift the flour, cocoa and salt into a large bowl. Stir in the yeast. Make a well in the centre and add the milk, melted butter and egg. Stir, gradually incorporating the surrounding dry ingredients, to make a soft and pliable dough.

2 Knead the dough on a lightly floured surface for about 5 minutes, until smooth and elastic. Return to the clean bowl, cover and leave to rise in a warm place for 1 hour.

3 Knead the dough lightly again, then divide into 16 pieces. Shape each into a round, press a piece of plain chocolate into the centre, then fold the dough over to enclose the filling, pressing firmly to make sure the edges are sealed. Re-shape the doughnuts when sealed, if necessary.

4 Heat the oil for frying to 180°C/350°F or until a cube of day-old bread browns in 30–45 seconds. Deep fry the doughnuts in batches. As each doughnut rises and turns golden brown, turn it over carefully to cook the other side. Drain the cooked doughnuts well on kitchen paper.

5 Mix the sugar, cocoa and cinnamon in a shallow bowl. Toss the doughnuts in the mixture to coat them evenly. Pile on a plate and serve warm.

Buñuelos Energy 296kcal/1235kJ; Protein 9.9g; Carbohydrate 22.5g, of which sugars 0.6g; Fat 18.9g, of which saturates 10.5g; Cholesterol 184mg; Calcium 156mg; Fibre 0.9g; Sodium 223mg.
Chocolate Cinnamon Doughnuts Energy 235kcal/989kJ; Protein 5.1g; Carbohydrate 33.2g, of which sugars 9g; Fat 10.1g, of which saturates 2.7g; Cholesterol 14mg; Calcium 76mg; Fibre 1.5g; Sodium 48mg.

Lover's Knots

These attractive cookies are eaten at carnival time in Italy but as they are so charming they're sure to be welcome at any time of year.

Makes 24
150g/5oz/1¼ cups plain
    (all-purpose) flour, plus extra
    for dusting
2.5ml/½ tsp baking powder
pinch of salt
30ml/2 tbsp caster (superfine)
    sugar, plus extra for dusting
1 egg, beaten
about 25ml/1½ tbsp rum
vegetable oil, for deep-frying

1 Sift the flour, baking powder and salt into a bowl, then stir in the sugar. Add the egg. Stir with a fork until it is evenly mixed with the flour, then add the rum gradually and continue mixing until the dough draws together.

2 Knead the dough on a lightly floured surface until it is smooth. Divide the dough into quarters.

3 Roll each piece out to a 15 x 7.5cm/6 x 3in rectangle and trim to make them straight. Cut each rectangle lengthways into six strips, 1cm/½in wide, and tie into a simple knot without stretching the dough.

4 Heat the oil in a frying pan to a temperature of 190°C/375°F or until a cube of day-old bread browns in about 30 seconds. Deep-fry the knots, in batches, for 1–2 minutes, until crisp and golden. Transfer to kitchen paper with a slotted spoon. Serve warm, dusted with sugar.

Variations
• If you don't like the flavour of rum, substitute another sweet spirit or liqueur, such as Amaretto or Kirsch.
• For a chocolate treat, replace 30ml/2 tbsp of the flour with the same quantity of unsweetened cocoa powder and use crème de cacao instead of rum.

Ladies' Navels

This is a classic fried pastry, an invention from the Topkapı Palace kitchens. Garnish it with whole or chopped pistachios and serve with cream.

175g/6oz/1½ cups plain
    (all-purpose) flour
60g/2oz/⅓ cup semolina
2 eggs
sunflower oil, for deep-frying

For the syrup
450g/1lb/scant 2¼ cups sugar
juice of 1 lemon

Serves 4–6
50g/2oz/¼ cup butter
pinch of salt

1 To make the syrup, put the sugar and 300ml/½ pint/1¼ cups water into a heavy pan and bring to the boil, stirring constantly. When the sugar has dissolved, stir in the lemon juice and lower the heat, then simmer for about 10 minutes, until the syrup has thickened a little. Leave to cool.

2 Put the butter, salt and 250ml/8fl oz/1 cup water in another heavy pan and bring to the boil. Remove from the heat and add the flour and semolina, beating all the time, until the mixture becomes smooth. Leave to cool.

3 Beat the eggs into the cooled mixture so that it gleams. Add 15ml/1 tbsp of the cooled syrup and beat well.

4 Pour enough oil for deep-frying into a deep-sided pan. Heat until just warm, then remove from the heat. Wet your hands and take an apricot-size piece of dough. Roll it into a ball, flatten it, then make an indentation in the middle.

5 Drop the dough into the pan of warmed oil. Repeat with the rest of the mixture to make about 12 navels.

6 Place the pan back over the heat. As the oil heats up, the pastries will swell, retaining the dip in the middle. Swirl the oil until the navels turn golden all over.

7 Remove with a slotted spoon. Toss them in the cooled syrup. Leave to soak for a few minutes, and spoon some syrup over.

Lover's Knots Energy 56kcal/236kJ; Protein 0.9g; Carbohydrate 6.2g, of which sugars 1.4g; Fat 3.1g, of which saturates 0.4g; Cholesterol 8mg; Calcium 11mg; Fibre 0.2g; Sodium 3mg.
Ladies' Navels Energy 517kcal/2190kJ; Protein 6.3g; Carbohydrate 108.8g, of which sugars 78.9g; Fat 9.3g, of which saturates 4.9g; Cholesterol 81mg; Calcium 93mg; Fibre 1.1g; Sodium 80mg.

French Quarter Beignets

These airy puffs are even lighter than fritters, so they're sure to disappear in no time at all.

Makes about 20

225g/8oz/2 cups plain (all-purpose) flour, plus extra for dusting
pinch of salt
15ml/1 tbsp baking powder
5ml/1 tsp ground cinnamon
2 eggs
50g/2oz/¼ cup sugar
175ml/6fl oz/¾ cup milk
2.5ml/½ tsp vanilla extract
oil for deep-frying
icing (confectioners') sugar, for sprinkling

1 To make the dough, sift the flour, salt, baking powder and ground cinnamon into a medium mixing bowl.

2 In a separate bowl, beat together the eggs, sugar, milk and vanilla. Pour the egg mixture into the dry ingredients and mix together quickly to form a ball.

3 Turn the dough out on to a lightly floured surface and knead until it is smooth and elastic.

4 Heat the oil in a deep-fryer or large, heavy pan to 190°C/375°F.

5 Roll out the dough to 5mm/¼in thick. Slice diagonally into diamonds about 7.5cm/3in long.

6 Fry in the hot oil, turning once, until golden brown on both sides. Remove with tongs or a slotted spoon and drain well on kitchen paper. Sprinkle the beignets with icing sugar before serving warm.

> **Cook's Tip**
> For a special treat, heat a few tablespoons of strawberry or raspberry jam or golden (light corn) or maple syrup until runny. Pour into a sauceboat and serve with the warm beignets for a delicious dessert.

Chelsea Buns

Soft, sweet and scrumptious, no wonder these lightly spiced buns are so popular.

Makes 12

225g/8oz/2 cups strong white bread flour, plus extra for dusting
pinch of salt
40g/1½oz/3 tbsp unsalted butter
7.5ml/1½ tsp easy-blend (rapid-rise) dried yeast
120ml/4fl oz/½ cup milk
1 egg, beaten
75g/3oz/½ cup mixed dried fruit
25g/1oz/2½ tbsp chopped mixed (candied) peel
50g/2oz/¼ cup soft light brown sugar
clear honey, to glaze

1 Sift the flour and salt into a bowl, then rub in 25g/1oz/2 tbsp of the butter until the mixture resembles breadcrumbs.

2 Stir in the yeast and make a well in the centre. Slowly pour the milk and egg into the well, stirring the ingredients together, then beat until the dough leaves the sides of the bowl clean.

3 Turn out the dough on to a lightly floured surface and knead until smooth and elastic. Place in an oiled bowl, cover with oiled clear film (plastic wrap) and leave at room temperature for about 2 hours, until doubled in volume. Place on a lightly floured surface, then roll out to a rectangle about 30 × 23cm/12 × 9in.

4 Mix the dried fruit, peel and sugar. Melt the remaining butter and brush over the dough. Sprinkle over the fruit mixture, leaving a 2.5cm/1in border. Starting at a long side, roll up the dough. Seal the edges, then cut into 12 slices.

5 Lightly grease a 18cm/7in round tin (pan). Put the slices, cut side up, in the prepared tin. Cover with a clean dish towel and leave to rise in a warm place for about 30 minutes, until doubled in size.

6 Preheat the oven to 190°C/375°F/Gas 5. Bake for 30 minutes, until a rich golden brown. Brush the tops with honey and leave to cool slightly in the tin before turning out.

French Quarter Beignets Energy 99kcal/415kJ; Protein 2g; Carbohydrate 11.8g, of which sugars 3.2g; Fat 5.2g, of which saturates 0.8g; Cholesterol 20mg; Calcium 30mg; Fibre 0.4g; Sodium 11mg.
Chelsea Buns Energy 287kcal/1208kJ; Protein 6.1g; Carbohydrate 43.5g, of which sugars 16.6g; Fat 11.1g, of which saturates 2.3g; Cholesterol 26mg; Calcium 85mg; Fibre 1.3g; Sodium 243mg.

Sticky Buns

Sweet, gooey and sheer delight, these lightly spiced buns are irresistible.

Makes 18
170ml/5½fl oz/scant ¾ cup milk
15ml/1 tbsp active dried yeast
30ml/2 tbsp caster (superfine)
  sugar
425–450g/15oz–1lb/3½–4 cups
  strong white bread flour, plus
  extra for dusting
pinch of salt
115g/4oz/½ cup butter, diced

2 eggs, lightly beaten
grated rind of 1 lemon

For the topping and filling
275g/10oz/1¼ cups soft dark
  brown sugar
65g/2½oz/5 tbsp butter
120ml/4fl oz/½ cup water
75g/3oz/½ cup walnuts, chopped
45ml/3 tbsp caster
  (superfine) sugar
10ml/2 tsp ground cinnamon
165g/5½oz/generous 1 cup
  raisins

1 Heat the milk to lukewarm. Add the yeast and sugar, and leave until frothy, about 15 minutes.

2 Put the flour and salt in a bowl. Rub in the butter until the mixture forms breadcrumbs. Make a well in the centre and add the yeast mixture, eggs and lemon rind. Mix to a rough dough.

3 Transfer to a floured surface and knead until smooth and elastic. Cover with a plastic bag and leave to rise in a warm place until doubled in volume, about 2 hours.

4 To make the topping, boil the sugar, butter and water in a pan for 10 minutes, until thick. Put 15ml/1 tbsp of the syrup in each muffin cup. Sprinkle lightly with nuts. Mix the remaining nuts with the sugar, cinnamon and raisins in a bowl.

5 Knock back (punch down) the dough. Roll out to a 45 × 30cm/18 × 12in rectangle. Sprinkle the filling over it and roll up from a long side. Cut into 2.5cm/1in rounds and put into the muffin cups, cut side up. Leave to rise in a warm place for 30 minutes. Preheat the oven to 180°C/350°F/Gas 4.

6 Bake for 25 minutes. Invert on a baking sheet, leave for 3–5 minutes, then remove the tins. Transfer the buns to a wire rack.

Banana and Apricot Chelsea Buns

Old favourites are given a low-fat twist with a delectable fruit filling.

Serves 9
225g/8oz/2 cups strong white
  bread flour, plus extra
  for dusting
10ml/2 tsp ground allspice
pinch of salt
2.5ml/½ tsp easy-blend
  (rapid-rise) dried yeast

25g/1oz/2 tbsp butter
75g/3oz /scant ½ cup caster
  (superfine) sugar
90ml/6 tbsp skimmed
  (low-fat) milk
1 egg

For the filling
1 large ripe banana
175g/6oz/¾ cup chopped
  ready-to-eat dried apricots
30ml/2 tbsp light brown sugar

1 Sift the flour, allspice and salt into a bowl and stir in the yeast. Rub in the butter, then stir in 50g/2oz/¼ cup of the sugar. Make a well in the centre. Lightly beat the milk and egg, pour into the well and gradually mix in the flour.

2 Turn the dough on to a floured surface. Knead for 5 minutes, until smooth and elastic. Return to the clean bowl, cover and leave in a warm place to rise for 2 hours.

3 Turn out and knead the dough on a floured surface for 2 minutes. Roll out to a 30 × 23cm/12 × 9in rectangle.

4 Mash the banana in a bowl, stir in the apricots and sugar and spread the filling over the dough. Roll up lengthways like a Swiss (jelly) roll, with the join underneath. Cut the roll into nine slices. Grease an 18cm/7in square cake tin (pan). Put the slices in the tin, cut side down, cover and leave to rise in a warm place for 30 minutes.

5 Preheat the oven to 200°C/400°F/Gas 6. Bake the buns for 20–25 minutes, until golden.

6 Meanwhile, mix the remaining caster sugar with 30ml/2 tbsp water in a pan. Bring to the boil, stirring constantly, then boil for 2 minutes. Brush the glaze over the buns, then transfer to a wire rack to cool.

Sticky Buns Energy 438kcal/1844kJ; Protein 6.1g; Carbohydrate 66.3g, of which sugars 37.6g; Fat 18.4g, of which saturates 8.6g; Cholesterol 64mg; Calcium 100mg; Fibre 1.7g; Sodium 119mg.
Banana and Apricot Chelsea Buns Energy 193kcal/816kJ; Protein 4.3g; Carbohydrate 38.3g, of which sugars 19.1g; Fat 3.5g, of which saturates 0.3g; Cholesterol 22mg; Calcium 70mg; Fibre 2.1g; Sodium 147mg.

Cheese and Pineapple Wholemeal Scones

These cheese and pineapple scones are delicious eaten freshly baked, warm or cold, with a little butter and jam.

Makes 14–16
225g/8oz/2 cups self-raising (self-rising) wholemeal (whole-wheat) flour, sifted, plus extra for dusting
5ml/1 tsp baking powder, sifted

pinch of salt
40g/1½oz/3 tbsp butter
5ml/1 tsp mustard powder
75g/3oz/¾ cup mature (sharp) Cheddar cheese, finely grated
50g/2oz/¼ cup ready-to-eat dried pineapple, finely chopped
150ml/¼ pint/⅔ cup skimmed (low fat) milk

1 Preheat the oven to 220°C/425°F/Gas 7. Line a baking sheet with baking parchment.

2 Sift the flour, baking powder and salt into a bowl.

3 Rub in the fat until the mixture resembles breadcrumbs.

4 Fold in the mustard powder, cheese, pineapple and enough milk to make a fairly soft dough.

5 Turn the dough on to a lightly floured surface and knead lightly. Lightly roll out to 2cm/¾in thickness.

6 Using a 5cm/2in cookie cutter, stamp out rounds and place them on the prepared baking sheet.

7 Brush the tops with milk and bake for about 10 minutes, until well risen and golden brown. Transfer to a wire rack to cool and serve warm or cold.

> **Variation**
> Other mature (sharp) cheese, such as Emmenthal, Mahon, Appenzeller or Gouda, would also taste good in these scones.

Wholemeal Parmesan Scones

These are very good warm with a little butter and are ideal for children's lunches and for picnics. Fill them with ham, cheese, chicken or salad.

Makes 15
450g/1lb/4 cups wholemeal (whole-wheat) flour, plus extra for dusting
pinch of salt
10ml/2 tsp baking powder
115g/4oz Parmesan cheese, finely grated
50g/2oz/¼ cup butter
150–300ml/¼–½ pint/⅔– 1¼ cups buttermilk

1 Preheat the oven to 200°C/400°F/Gas 6.

2 Mix the flour, salt, baking powder and Parmesan cheese in a bowl and rub in the butter with your fingertips until the mixture resembles breadcrumbs. Working quickly and lightly, stir in enough of the buttermilk to make a moist dough using a knife at first and then gathering up the dough with your fingertips.

3 Pat out the dough on a lightly floured board to a thickness of about 4cm/1½in.

4 Using a 7cm/2¾in cutter, stamp out 15 rounds. Place the rounds on a floured baking sheet and bake for about 10 minutes. The exact cooking time will depend on the depth of the scones. They should be well risen and lightly browned. Serve warm, cut in half, spread with butter.

> **Cook's Tips**
> • These scones will keep well in an airtight container for up to 3 days. Before serving, reheat them for 4–5 minutes in a preheated oven at 200°C/400°F/Gas 6.
> • Baked scones can also be frozen for up to 3 months. Thaw thoroughly at room temperature and reheat before serving, as described above.

Cheese and Pineapple Wholemeal Scones Energy 99Kcals/418KJ; Protein 4.22g; Fat 3.62g; Saturated Fat 1.05g; Carbohydrate 13.28g; Fibre 1.74g; Added Sugar 1.33g; Sodium 0.06g.
Wholemeal Parmesan Scones Energy 160kcals/674kJ; Fat, total 5.95g; saturated fat 2.25g; polyunsaturated fat 1.55g; monounsaturated fat 1.7g; Carbohydrate 20.4g; sugar, total 1.65g; starch 18.8g; Fibre 2.7g; Sodium 196.6mg.

Cornmeal Scones

These are delicious served hot, straight from the oven, and spread with butter. They are great for breakfast and also go well with soup for a light lunch.

Makes 12
50g/2oz/½ cup cornmeal, plus extra for sprinkling
175g/6oz/1¼ cups plain (all-purpose) flour, plus extra for dusting
12.5ml/2½ tsp baking powder
pinch of salt
175g/6oz/¾ cup butter, diced
175ml/6fl oz/¾ cup milk

1 Preheat the oven to 230°C/450°F/Gas 8. Sprinkle a large baking sheet lightly with a little cornmeal.

2 Sift together the flour, baking powder and salt into a bowl. Stir in the cornmeal. Add the butter and rub into the dry ingredients with your fingertips until the mixture resembles coarse breadcrumbs.

3 Make a well in the centre and pour in the milk. Stir in quickly with a wooden spoon until the dough begins to pull away from the sides of the bowl.

4 Turn the dough out on to a lightly floured surface and knead lightly 8–10 times only. Roll it out to a thickness of 1cm/½in. Stamp out into rounds with a floured 5cm/2in cookie cutter.

5 Arrange the dough rounds on the prepared baking sheet, spacing them about 2.5cm/1in apart. Sprinkle with a little cornmeal, then bake for about 10–12 minutes, until golden brown.

Cook's Tip
Cornmeal usually has a beautiful golden colour that makes the scones look particularly appetizing. Blue cornmeal, once used exclusively by Native Americans, is blue-black in colour and could also be used with striking results.

Cheese Scones

These delicious scones make a good teatime treat. They are best served fresh and still slightly warm.

Makes 12
225g/8oz/2 cups plain (all-purpose) flour, plus extra for dusting
12.5ml/2½ tsp baking powder
2.5ml/½ tsp dry mustard powder
pinch of salt
50g/2oz/4 tbsp butter, chilled and diced
75g/3oz/¾ cup mature (sharp) Cheddar cheese, grated
150ml/¼ pint/⅔ cup milk
1 egg, beaten

1 Preheat the oven to 230°C/450°F/Gas 8.

2 Sift the flour, baking powder, mustard powder and salt into a mixing bowl. Add the butter and rub into the flour mixture until the mixture resembles breadcrumbs.

3 Stir 50g/2oz/½ cup of the cheese into the butter and flour mixture.

4 Make a well in the centre and gently stir in the milk and egg with a wooden spoon until a soft dough forms. Turn the dough on to a lightly floured surface.

5 Roll out the dough and cut it into triangles or squares with a sharp knife. Put the scones on to one or two baking sheets, brush lightly with milk and sprinkle evenly with the remaining grated cheese. Leave to rest for 15 minutes, then bake for 15 minutes, until well risen and golden.

Cook's Tip
While ready-grated cheese is convenient, it does dry out quickly once the packet has been opened and it is rarely a top-quality variety. For maximum flavour, it is always better to grate cheese freshly just before you are going to use it and there's likely to be less waste, too.

Cornmeal Scones Energy 180kcal/750kJ; Protein 2.3g; Carbohydrate 15.2g, of which sugars 1g; Fat 12.6g, of which saturates 7.8g; Cholesterol 32mg; Calcium 41mg; Fibre 0.5g; Sodium 95mg.
Cheese Scones Energy 133kcal/557kJ; Protein 4.3g; Carbohydrate 15.2g, of which sugars 0.9g; Fat 6.4g, of which saturates 3.8g; Cholesterol 32mg; Calcium 91mg; Fibre 0.6g; Sodium 82mg.

Feta Cheese and Chive Scones

Salty feta cheese makes an excellent substitute for butter in these tangy savoury scones. They not only go well with hot soup, but also make a delicious snack at any time of day.

Makes 9
115g/4oz/1 cup self-raising (self-rising) flour, plus extra for dusting
150g/5oz/1¼ cup self-raising wholemeal (self-rising whole-wheat) flour
pinch of salt
75g/3oz feta cheese
15ml/1 tbsp chopped fresh chives
150ml/¼ pint/⅔ cup skimmed (low fat) milk, plus extra for glazing
1.5ml/¼ tsp cayenne pepper

1 Preheat the oven to 200°C/400°F/Gas 6.

2 Sift together both the flours and the salt into a large bowl, adding any bran left over from the flour in the sieve (strainer).

3 Coarsely crumble the feta cheese into the bowl and rub it into the dry ingredients with your fingertips until the mixture resembles breadcrumbs. Stir in the chives, then add the milk and mix lightly with a wooden spoon or your hands to form a soft, but not sticky dough.

4 Turn out the dough on to a floured surface and knead lightly until smooth. Roll out to 2cm/¾in thick and stamp out nine scones with a floured 6cm/2½in cookie cutter.

5 Transfer to a non-stick baking sheet. Lightly brush the tops with skimmed milk, then sprinkle over the cayenne pepper. Bake for 15 minutes, until golden brown. Serve warm or cold.

> **Cook's Tip**
> Try to obtain genuine sheep's milk feta, as it has the best flavour. Much modern feta is made from cow's milk, but some Greek and, surprisingly, Bulgarian feta is still made in the traditional manner.

Cheddar and Chive Scones

These soft scones are delicious warm, split and spread with butter; serve with soup or to accompany a savoury meal.

Makes 20
200g/7oz/1¾ cups plain (all-purpose) flour
10ml/2 tsp baking powder
2.5ml/½ tsp bicarbonate of soda (baking soda)
pinch of salt
1.5ml/¼ tsp black pepper
65g/2½oz/5 tbsp unsalted (sweet) butter, chopped
50g/2oz/½ cup grated mature (sharp) Cheddar cheese
30ml/2 tbsp chopped fresh chives
175ml/6fl oz/¾ cup buttermilk

1 Preheat the oven to 200°C/400°F/Gas 6. Lightly grease two baking sheets.

2 Sift the flour, baking powder, bicarbonate of soda, salt and pepper into a large bowl. Add the butter and rub it into the dry ingredients with your fingertips until the mixture resembles coarse breadcrumbs. Add the grated cheese and chives and stir well to mix.

3 Make a well in the centre of the mixture. Add the buttermilk and stir vigorously until the batter comes away from the sides of the bowl.

4 Drop 30ml/2 tbsp mounds spaced 5–7.5cm/2–3in apart on the prepared baking sheets. Bake for 12–15 minutes, until golden brown.

> **Variations**
> • For Cheddar and Bacon Scones, substitute 45ml/3 tbsp crumbled cooked bacon for the chives.
> • For Cheese and Ham Scones, substitute grated Parmesan or Pecorino for the Cheddar cheese and 50g/2oz/⅓ cup chopped prosciutto for the chives.

Cheese and Marjoram Scones

Amaze unexpected guests with your culinary skills and these mouthwatering made-in-minutes savoury treats.

Makes 18

115g/4oz/1 cup wholemeal
  (whole-wheat) flour
115g/4oz/1 cup self-raising
  (self-rising) flour, plus extra
  for dusting

pinch of salt
40g/1½oz/3 tbsp butter, diced
1.5ml/¼ tsp dry mustard
10ml/2 tsp dried marjoram
50–75g/2–3oz/½–⅔ cup
  mature (sharp) Cheddar
  cheese, finely grated
about 125ml/4fl oz/½ cup milk
50g/2oz/¼ cup pecans or
  walnuts, chopped

1 Sift the two types of flour into a bowl and add the salt. Rub the butter into the flour with your fingertips until the mixture resembles fine breadcrumbs.

2 Add the mustard, marjoram and grated cheese, then mix in sufficient milk to make a soft, but dry dough. Knead the dough lightly.

3 Roll out the dough on a floured surface to 2cm/¾in thick and cut out about 18 scones using a 5cm/2in square cutter. Push the offcuts together and roll out and cut out more scones.

4 Brush the scones with a little milk and sprinkle the chopped pecans or walnuts over the top. Place the scones on a piece of baking parchment in the microwave, spacing them well apart. Microwave on HIGH (100 per cent) power for 3–3½ minutes, repositioning the scones twice during cooking.

5 Brown under a preheated hot grill (broiler) until golden, if you like. Serve warm, split and buttered.

> **Variation**
> For Herb and Mustard Scones, use 30ml/2 tbsp chopped fresh parsley or chives instead of the dried marjoram and 5ml/1 tsp Dijon mustard instead of the dry mustard.

Cheese and Mustard Scones

Depending on their size, these cheese scones can be served as little canapé bases, teatime treats or even as a quick pie topping or cobbler.

Makes 12

250g/9oz/2¼ cups self-raising
  (self-rising) flour, plus extra
  for dusting
5ml/1 tsp baking powder
pinch of salt
40g/1½oz/3 tbsp butter

175g/6oz/1½ cups grated
  mature (sharp) Cheddar
  cheese, plus extra for sprinkling
10ml/2 tsp wholegrain mustard
about 150ml/¼ pint/⅔ cup
  milk, buttermilk or natural
  (plain) yogurt
1 egg yolk beaten with 5ml/1 tsp
  water, to glaze (optional)
ground black pepper
garlic-flavoured cream cheese,
  chopped fresh chives and sliced
  radishes, to serve (optional)

1 Preheat the oven to 220°C/425°F/Gas 7.

2 Sift the flour, baking powder and salt into a bowl, then rub in the butter until the mixture resembles fine breadcrumbs. Season with pepper and stir in the cheese.

3 Mix the mustard with the milk, buttermilk or yogurt. Add to the dry ingredients and mix quickly until the mixture just comes together. Do not over-mix or the scones will be tough.

4 Knead the dough lightly on a lightly floured surface, then pat it out with your hands to a depth of 2cm/¾in. Cut into squares, or use a 5cm/2in cutter to stamp out rounds, re-rolling the dough as necessary.

5 Place the squares or rounds on a non-stick baking sheet. Brush with the egg glaze, if using, and sprinkle with extra grated cheese.

6 Bake for about 10 minutes, until risen and golden. You can test scones by pressing the sides, which should spring back. Transfer to a wire rack to cool.

7 Serve spread with garlic-flavoured cream cheese. Top with chopped chives and sliced radishes, if using.

Cheese and Marjoram Scones Energy 121kcal/504kJ; Protein 3g; Carbohydrate 9.8g, of which sugars 0.9g; Fat 8g, of which saturates 2.4g; Cholesterol 8mg; Calcium 44mg; Fibre 1.1g; Sodium 39mg.
Cheese and Mustard Scones Energy 169kcal/706kJ; Protein 6.4g; Carbohydrate 16.8g, of which sugars 1g; Fat 8.5g, of which saturates 5.2g; Cholesterol 39mg; Calcium 156mg; Fibre 0.7g; Sodium 146mg.

Cheese and Potato Scones

The unusual addition of creamy mashed potato gives these wholemeal scones a light moist texture and a crisp crust. A sprinkling of cheese and sesame seeds adds the finishing touch.

Makes 9
115g/4oz/1 cup wholemeal (whole-wheat) flour, plus extra for dusting
pinch of salt
20ml/4 tsp baking powder
40g/1½oz/3 tbsp unsalted butter
2 eggs, beaten
50ml/2fl oz/¼ cup semi-skimmed (low-fat) milk or buttermilk
115g/4oz/1⅓ cups cooked, mashed potato
45ml/3 tbsp chopped fresh sage
50g/2oz/½ cup grated mature (sharp) Cheddar cheese
sesame seeds, for sprinkling

1 Preheat the oven to 220°C/425°F/Gas 7. Lightly grease a baking sheet.

2 Sift the flour, salt and baking powder into a bowl. Rub in the butter using your fingers until the mixture resembles fine breadcrumbs, then mix in half the beaten eggs and all the milk or buttermilk. Add the mashed potato, sage and half the Cheddar and mix to a soft dough with your hands.

3 Turn out the dough on to a floured surface and knead lightly until smooth. Roll out the dough to 2cm/¾in thick, then stamp out nine scones using a 6cm/2½in fluted cutter.

4 Place the scones on the prepared baking sheet and brush the tops with the remaining beaten egg. Sprinkle the rest of the cheese and the sesame seeds on top and bake for 15 minutes, until golden. Transfer to a wire rack and leave to cool.

Variations
• Use unbleached self-raising (self-rising) flour instead of wholemeal (whole-wheat) flour and baking powder, if you wish.
• Fresh rosemary, basil or thyme can be used in place of the sage.

Caramelized Onion and Walnut Scones

These scones are very good buttered and served with cheese. Make small ones as a base for cocktail canapés, topped with a little soft goat's cheese.

Makes 10–12
90g/3½oz/7 tbsp butter
15ml/1 tbsp olive oil
1 Spanish (Bermuda) onion, chopped
5ml/1 tsp cumin seeds, lightly crushed
200g/7oz/1¾ cups self-raising (self-rising) flour
5ml/1 tsp baking powder
25g/1oz/¼ cup fine oatmeal
5ml/1 tsp light muscovado (molasses) sugar
90g/3½oz/scant 1 cup chopped walnuts
5ml/1 tsp chopped fresh thyme
120–150ml/4–5fl oz/½–⅔ cup buttermilk
a little milk
salt and ground black pepper

1 Melt 15g/½oz/1 tbsp of the butter with the oil in a small pan and cook the onion gently, covered, for 10–12 minutes. Uncover, then continue to cook gently until it begins to brown.

2 Add half the cumin seeds and increase the heat slightly. Continue to cook, stirring occasionally, until the onion begins to caramelize. Cool. Preheat the oven to 200°C/400°F/Gas 6.

3 Sift the flour and baking powder into a bowl and add the oatmeal, sugar, salt and black pepper. Add the remaining butter and rub in until the mixture resembles fine breadcrumbs.

4 Add the cooled onion and cumin mixture, chopped walnuts and chopped fresh thyme, then bind to make a soft, but not sticky, dough with the buttermilk.

5 Roll out the dough to a thickness of 1cm/½in. Stamp out 10–12 scones using a 5–6cm/2–2½in cookie cutter. Place the scones on a floured baking tray, glaze with the milk and sprinkle with a little salt and the remaining cumin seeds. Bake the scones for 12–15 minutes, until well-risen and golden brown. Allow to cool for a few minutes on a wire rack.

Cheese and Potato Scones Energy 124kcal/517kJ; Protein 4.9g; Carbohydrate 10.5g, of which sugars 0.7g; Fat 7.1g, of which saturates 4g; Cholesterol 57mg; Calcium 60mg; Fibre 1.3g; Sodium 87mg.
Caramelized Onion and Walnut Scones Energy 131kcal/543kJ; Protein 1.8g; Carbohydrate 3g, of which sugars 1.3g; Fat 12.6g, of which saturates 4.6g; Cholesterol 17mg; Calcium 23mg; Fibre 0.5g; Sodium 51mg.

Herb and Sesame Seed Triangles

Stuffed with cooked chicken and salad, these make a good lunchtime snack, and are also an ideal accompaniment to a bowl of steaming soup.

Makes 8
225g/8oz/2 cups wholemeal (whole-wheat) flour
115g/4oz/1 cup plain (all-purpose) flour, plus extra for dusting
pinch of salt
2.5ml/½ tsp bicarbonate of soda (baking soda)
5ml/1 tsp cream of tartar
2.5ml/½ tsp chilli powder
50g/2oz/½ cup butter, chilled and diced
60ml/4 tbsp chopped mixed fresh herbs
250ml/8fl oz/1 cup skimmed (low fat) milk
15ml/1 tbsp sesame seeds

1 Preheat the oven to 220°C/425°F/Gas 7. Lightly dust a baking sheet with flour.

2 Put the wholemeal and plain flours in a mixing bowl. Sift in the salt, bicarbonate of soda, cream of tartar and chilli powder, then rub in the butter.

3 Add the herbs and milk and mix to a soft dough. Turn on to a lightly floured surface. Knead only very briefly or the dough will become tough.

4 Roll the dough out to a 23cm/9in round and place on the prepared baking sheet. Brush lightly with water and sprinkle the top evenly with the sesame seeds.

5 Carefully cut the dough round into eight wedges, separate them slightly and bake for 15–20 minutes. Transfer to a wire rack to cool. Serve warm or cold.

Variation
To make Sun-dried Tomato Triangles, replace the fresh mixed herbs with 30ml/2 tbsp drained chopped sun-dried tomatoes in oil and add 15ml/1 tbsp each mild paprika, chopped fresh parsley and chopped fresh marjoram.

Chive and Potato Drop Scones

These little scones should be fairly thin, soft, and crisp on the outside. Serve them for breakfast.

Makes 20
450g/1lb potatoes
115g/4oz/1 cup plain (all-purpose) flour
30ml/2 tbsp olive oil, plus extra for brushing
30ml/2 tbsp chives, chopped
pinch of salt
ground black pepper

1 Cook the potatoes in a pan of salted boiling water for 20 minutes, until tender, then drain thoroughly. Return the potatoes to the clean pan and mash them well with a potato masher. Alternatively, pass them through a potato ricer.

2 Preheat a griddle or heavy frying pan.

3 Add the flour, olive oil, chives and a little salt and pepper to the mashed potato. Mix to a soft dough.

4 Roll out the dough on a well-floured surface to a thickness of 5mm/¼in and stamp out rounds with a floured 5cm/2in plain cookie cutter. Lightly grease the griddle or frying pan with a little olive oil.

5 Reduce the heat to low, add the scones to the pan, in batches, and cook for about 5 minutes on each side, until golden brown and crisp on the outside. Keep the cooked scones warm while you cook the remaining batches. Serve immediately.

Cook's Tips
• Cook the scones over a constant low heat and do not try to hurry them or the outsides will burn before the insides are properly cooked through.
• The easiest way to keep the cooked scones warm is to tuck them into a folded dish towel.

Herb and Sesame Seed Triangles Energy 204kcal/860kJ; Protein 6.4g; Carbohydrate 30.6g, of which sugars 2.2g; Fat 7.1g, of which saturates 3.6g; Cholesterol 14mg; Calcium 84mg; Fibre 3.2g; Sodium 54mg. **Chive and Potato Drop Scones** Energy 45kcal/191kJ; Protein 0.9g; Carbohydrate 8.1g, of which sugars 0.4g; Fat 1.2g, of which saturates 0.2g; Cholesterol 0mg; Calcium 9mg; Fibre 0.4g; Sodium 3mg.

Ham and Potato Scones

These make an ideal accompaniment to soup. Choose a strongly flavoured ham and chop it fairly finely, so that a little goes quite a long way.

Makes 12
225g/8oz/2 cups self-raising (self-rising) flour, plus extra for dusting
5ml/1 tsp dry mustard
5ml/1 tsp paprika, plus extra for sprinkling
pinch of salt
25g/1oz/2 tbsp butter
15ml/1 tbsp chopped fresh basil
50g/2oz/1/2 cup drained sun-dried tomatoes in oil, chopped
50g/2oz/1/3 cup ham, chopped
90–120ml/3–4fl oz/1/2–2/3 cup skimmed (low-fat) milk, plus extra for brushing

1 Preheat the oven to 200°C/400°F/Gas 6. Lightly dust a large baking sheet with flour.

2 Sift the flour, mustard, paprika and salt into a bowl. Add the butter and rub it in with your fingertips until the mixture resembles breadcrumbs.

3 Stir in the basil, sun-dried tomatoes and ham and mix lightly. Pour in enough milk to mix to a soft dough.

4 Turn the dough out on to a lightly floured surface, knead lightly and roll out to a 20 × 15cm/8 × 6in rectangle. Cut into 5cm/2in squares and arrange on the baking sheet.

5 Brush the tops lightly with milk, sprinkle with a little paprika and bake for 12–15 minutes, until golden. Transfer to a wire rack to cool slightly. Serve warm.

> **Cook's Tip**
> *If you want to use sun-dried tomatoes from a packet, rehydrate them first by soaking in hot water until softened. Drain and pat dry before chopping.*

Rosemary Scones

Serve these aromatic scones with a starter or main meal instead of rolls or bread. They're great with lamb dishes.

Makes 12
225g/8oz/2 cups self-raising (self-rising) flour
pinch of salt
5ml/1 tsp baking powder
10ml/2 tsp chopped fresh rosemary
50g/2oz/1/4 cup butter
150ml/1/4 pint/2/3 cup milk
1 egg, beaten

1 Preheat the oven to 230°C/450°F/Gas 8. Lightly grease a baking sheet.

2 Sift together the flour, salt and baking powder into a bowl and stir in the rosemary. Add the butter and rub it in with your fingertips until the mixture resembles breadcrumbs.

3 Add the milk and mix lightly with a wooden spoon or your hands to form a soft, but not sticky dough.

4 Turn out the dough on to a lightly floured surface and knead very gently. Roll out to about 2cm/3/4in thick. Stamp out 12 scones with a 5cm/2in plain round cookie cutter. Lightly brush the tops with beaten egg and place them on the prepared baking sheet.

5 Bake for 8–10 minutes, until risen and golden brown. Transfer the scones to a wire rack to cool slightly, then serve warm.

> **Variations**
> • *When serving these scones with soup, sprinkle the tops with a little grated cheese before baking.*
> • *For scones to serve with fish dishes, substitute 15ml/1 tbsp chopped fresh dill for the rosemary.*
> • *For serving with chicken or vegetarian dishes, substitute 15ml/1 tbsp chopped fresh basil.*

Ham and Potato Scones Energy 103kcal/433kJ; Protein 3.7g; Carbohydrate 15.7g, of which sugars 1.1g; Fat 3.3g, of which saturates 1.4g; Cholesterol 9mg; Calcium 39mg; Fibre 0.7g; Sodium 114mg.
Rosemary Scones Energy 107kcal/449kJ; Protein 2.7g; Carbohydrate 15.2g, of which sugars 0.9g; Fat 4.3g, of which saturates 2.5g; Cholesterol 25mg; Calcium 44mg; Fibre 0.6g; Sodium 37mg.

Sweet Potato Scones

These are scones with a difference. Sweet potato gives them a pale orange colour, and they are meltingly soft in the centre, just waiting for a knob of butter.

Makes about 24
150g/5oz/1¼ cups plain (all-purpose) flour, plus extra for dusting
20ml/4 tsp baking powder
pinch of salt
15g/½oz/1 tbsp soft light brown sugar
150g/5oz mashed sweet potatoes
150ml/¼ pint/⅔ cup milk
50g/2oz/4 tbsp butter, melted

1 Preheat the oven to 230°C/450°F/Gas 8. Lightly grease a baking sheet.

2 Sift together the flour, baking powder and salt into a bowl. Mix in the sugar.

3 In a separate bowl, mix the mashed sweet potatoes with the milk and melted butter. Beat well to blend.

4 Add the flour to the sweet potato mixture and stir to make a dough. Turn out on to a lightly floured surface and knead until soft and pliable.

5 Roll or pat out the dough to a 1cm/½in thickness. Cut into rounds using a 4cm/1½in cutter. Push the offcuts together and roll and cut out more scones.

6 Arrange the rounds on the baking sheet. Bake for about 15 minutes until risen and lightly golden. Serve warm.

> **Cook's Tip**
> *To cook the sweet potatoes, wash them but do not peel. Cook in unsalted boiling water for about 30 minutes, until tender. Drain and leave to cool slightly, then peel off the skins and mash the flesh with a potato masher.*

Three Herb Potato Scones

These flavoursome scones are perfect served warm and split in two with hand-carved ham and Parmesan shavings as a filling.

Makes 12
225g/8oz/2 cups self-raising (self-rising) flour, plus extra for dusting
5ml/1 tsp baking powder
pinch of salt
50g/2oz/4 tbsp butter, diced
25g/1oz potato flakes
15ml/1 tbsp fresh parsley, chopped
15ml/1 tbsp fresh basil, chopped
15ml/1 tbsp fresh oregano, chopped
150ml/¼ pint/⅔ cup milk

1 Preheat the oven to 180°C/350°F/Gas 4. Lightly grease a baking sheet.

2 Sift the flour into a bowl with the baking powder. Add a pinch of salt. Rub in the butter with your fingertips until the mixture resembles fine breadcrumbs.

3 Place the potato flakes in a separate bowl and pour over 200ml/7fl oz/scant 1 cup boiling water. Beat well and cool slightly.

4 Stir the potatoes into the dry ingredients with the parsley, basil, oregano and milk.

5 Bring the mixture together to form a soft dough. Turn out on to a floured surface and knead the dough very gently for a few minutes, until soft and pliable.

6 Roll the dough out on a floured surface to about 4cm/1½in thick and stamp out rounds using a 7.5cm/3in cookie cutter. Reshape any remaining dough and re-roll for more scones. Place the scones on to the prepared baking sheet and brush the surfaces with a little more milk.

7 Bake for 15–20 minutes, until golden brown. Transfer to a wire rack to cool slightly and serve warm. They can be eaten plain, or with a filling.

Sweet Potato Scones Energy 48kcal/200kJ; Protein 0.9g; Carbohydrate 7.1g, of which sugars 1.4g; Fat 1.9g, of which saturates 1.2g; Cholesterol 5mg; Calcium 18mg; Fibre 0.3g; Sodium 18mg.
Three Herb Potato Scones Energy 46kcal/193kJ; Protein 1g; Carbohydrate 8.1g, of which sugars 0.4g; Fat 1.3g, of which saturates 0.2g; Cholesterol 0mg; Calcium 12mg; Fibre 0.5g; Sodium 3mg.

Bacon and Cornmeal Muffins

Serve these tasty muffins fresh from the oven for an extra special breakfast. They would also be ideal as part of a weekend brunch menu, served with scrambled eggs or an omelette.

Makes 14

8 bacon rashers (strips)
50g/2oz/¼ cup butter
50g/2oz/¼ cup margarine
115g/4oz/1 cup plain
    (all-purpose) flour
15ml/1 tbsp baking powder
5ml/1 tsp caster (superfine) sugar
pinch of salt
175g/6oz/1½ cups cornmeal
250ml/8fl oz/1 cup milk
2 eggs

1 Preheat the oven to 200°C/400°F/Gas 6. Lightly grease 14 cups of two muffin tins (pans), or line with paper cases.

2 Remove and discard the bacon rinds, if necessary. Heat a heavy frying pan, add the bacon and cook over a medium heat, turning occasionally, until crisp. Remove with tongs and drain well on kitchen paper. When cool enough to handle, chop into small pieces and set aside.

3 Melt the butter and margarine in a pan over a low heat, then remove from the heat and set aside.

4 Sift together the flour, baking powder, caster sugar and salt into a large mixing bowl. Stir in the cornmeal, then make a well in the centre.

5 Pour the milk into a small pan and heat gently until just lukewarm, then remove from the heat. Lightly whisk the eggs in a small bowl, then add the lukewarm milk. Stir in the melted butter and margarine.

6 Pour the milk and egg mixture into the centre of the well and stir in the dry ingredients until smooth and well blended.

7 Fold in the bacon. Spoon the batter into the prepared tin, filling the cups halfway. Bake for about 20 minutes, until risen and golden.

Chilli Cheese Muffins

Prepare for a whole new taste sensation with these fabulous spicy muffins – they're hot stuff.

Makes 12

115g/4oz/1 cup self-raising
    (self-rising) flour
1 tbsp baking powder
pinch of salt
225g/8oz/2 cups fine cornmeal
150g/5oz/1¼ cups grated
    mature (sharp) Cheddar cheese
50g/2oz/4 tbsp butter, melted
2 large (US extra large)
    eggs, beaten
1 tsp chilli purée (paste)
1 garlic clove, crushed
300ml/½ pint/1¼ cups milk

1 Preheat the oven to 200°C/400°F/Gas 6. Thoroughly grease 12 deep muffin tins (pans) or line the tins with paper cases.

2 Sift the flour, baking powder and salt together into a bowl, then stir in the cornmeal and 115g/4oz/1 cup of the grated cheese until well mixed.

3 Pour the melted butter into a bowl and stir in the eggs, chilli purée, crushed garlic and milk.

4 Pour on to the dry ingredients and mix quickly and lightly until just combined.

5 Spoon the batter into the prepared muffin tins, sprinkle the remaining grated cheese evenly on top and bake for about 20 minutes, until risen and golden brown. Leave to cool for a few minutes in the tin before transferring the muffins to a wire rack to cool completely.

> **Cook's Tip**
> Chilli purée (paste) is available in both jars and tubes from most supermarkets. If you are unable to find it, you can substitute a generous pinch of hot chilli powder, 2.5ml/½ tsp chilli flakes or even a seeded and chopped fresh red or green chilli. Stir any of them into the mixture with the grated cheese in step 2.

Bacon and Cornmeal Muffins Energy 176kcal/735kJ; Protein 5.2g; Carbohydrate 16.7g, of which sugars 1.3g; Fat 10g, of which saturates 3.2g; Cholesterol 43mg; Calcium 39mg; Fibre 0.5g; Sodium 203mg.
Chilli Cheese Muffins Energy 208kcal/871kJ; Protein 7.8g; Carbohydrate 22.3g, of which sugars 1.5g; Fat 9.6g, of which saturates 5.4g; Cholesterol 54mg; Calcium 162mg; Fibre 0.7g; Sodium 176mg.

Corn Muffins with Ham

These delicious little muffins are simple to make. If you like, serve them unfilled with a pot of herb butter.

Makes 24

50g/2oz/scant ½ cup yellow cornmeal
65g/2½ oz/9 tbsp plain (all-purpose) flour
30ml/2 tbsp sugar
7.5ml/1½ tsp baking powder
pinch of salt
50g/2oz/4 tbsp butter, melted
120ml/4fl oz/½ cup whipping cream
1 egg, beaten
1–2 jalapeño or other medium-hot chillies, seeded and finely chopped (optional)
pinch of cayenne pepper
butter, for spreading
grainy mustard or mustard with honey, for spreading
50g/2oz oak-smoked ham

1 Preheat the oven to 200°C/400°F/Gas 6. Lightly grease a muffin tin (pan) with 24 4cm/1½in cups.

2 In a large bowl, combine the cornmeal, flour, sugar, baking powder and salt. In another bowl, whisk together the melted butter, cream, beaten egg, chopped chillies, if using, and the cayenne pepper.

3 Make a well in the cornmeal mixture, pour in the egg mixture and gently stir in just enough to blend (do not over-beat – the batter does not have to be smooth).

4 Drop 15ml/1 tbsp batter into each muffin cup. Bake for 12–15 minutes, until golden. Leave to cool completely.

5 Split the muffins, spread each bottom half with a little butter and mustard and top with ham.

> **Cook's Tip**
> *Muffins can be made in advance and stored in airtight containers. Bring to room temperature or warm slightly before filling and serving.*

Cheese Muffins

Puffed up and golden with their yummy cheese filling and the merest hint of hot spice, these must top the list of everyone's favourite savoury muffins.

Makes 9

50g/2oz/4 tbsp butter
175g/6oz/1½ cups plain (all-purpose) flour
10ml/2 tsp baking powder
30ml/2 tbsp caster (superfine) sugar
pinch of salt
5ml/1 tsp paprika
2 eggs
120ml/4fl oz/½ cup milk
5ml/1 tsp dried thyme
50g/2oz mature (sharp) Cheddar cheese, diced

1 Preheat the oven to 190°C/375°F/Gas 5. Lightly grease a nine-cup muffin tin (pan) or line with paper cases.

2 Melt the butter in a small pan over a low heat. Remove the pan from the heat and set aside to cool slightly.

3 Sift together the flour, baking powder, caster sugar, salt and paprika into a large mixing bowl.

4 Combine the eggs, milk, melted butter and dried thyme in another bowl and beat lightly with a balloon whisk or a fork until thoroughly blended.

5 Add the milk mixture to the bowl of dry ingredients and stir lightly with a wooden spoon until just moistened and combined. Do not mix until smooth.

6 Place a heaped tablespoonful of the mixture in each of the prepared muffin cups. Divide the pieces of cheese equally among them, then top with another spoonful of the mixture, making sure that the cheese is covered.

7 Bake for about 25 minutes, until puffed and golden. Leave to stand for 5 minutes before transferring to a wire rack to cool slightly. These muffins are best served while they are still warm or at room temperature.

Corn Muffins with Ham Energy 54kcal/227kJ; Protein 1.5g; Carbohydrate 6.8g, of which sugars 1.6g; Fat 2.5g, of which saturates 1.4g; Cholesterol 14mg; Calcium 13mg; Fibre 0.2g; Sodium 43mg.
Cheese Muffins Energy 166kcal/698kJ; Protein 5.1g; Carbohydrate 19.3g, of which sugars 4.4g; Fat 8.1g, of which saturates 4.6g; Cholesterol 60mg; Calcium 93mg; Fibre 0.6g; Sodium 96mg.

Praline Pavlova Cookies

Melt-in-the-mouth meringue with a luxurious velvety chocolate filling is topped with nutty praline – just the thing for a special tea party.

Makes 14
2 large (US extra large) egg whites
large pinch of ground cinnamon
90g/3½oz/½ cup caster (superfine) sugar
50g/2oz/½ cup pecan nuts, finely chopped

For the filling
50g/2oz/¼ cup unsalted butter, at room temperature, diced
100g/3½oz/scant 1 cup icing (confectioners') sugar, sifted
50g/2oz plain (semisweet) chocolate

For the praline
60ml/4 tbsp caster (superfine) sugar
15g/½oz/1 tbsp finely chopped toasted almonds

1 Preheat the oven to 140°C/275°F/Gas 1. Line two baking sheets with baking parchment.

2 In a bowl, whisk the egg whites until stiff. Stir the cinnamon into the sugar. Add a spoonful of sugar to the egg whites and whisk. Continue adding sugar, a spoonful at a time, whisking until the mixture is thick and glossy. Stir in the chopped pecan nuts.

3 Place 14 spoonfuls of meringue on the baking sheets, spaced well apart. Using the back of a wetted teaspoon, make a small hollow in the top of each. Bake for 45–60 minutes, until dry and just beginning to colour. Set aside to cool.

4 To make the filling, beat together the butter and icing sugar until light and creamy. Melt the chocolate in a heatproof bowl set over a pan of simmering water and stir occasionally. Remove and leave to cool slightly. Add the chocolate to the butter mixture and combine. Divide among the meringue hollows.

5 To make the praline, heat the sugar gently in a small non-stick pan until melted. When it begins to turn brown, stir in the nuts. When the mixture is a golden brown, remove from the heat. Pour on to a non-stick baking sheet. Leave to cool and then break into small pieces. Sprinkle over the meringues.

Pastel Meringues

A cut-glass cake stand piled high with meringues in pretty pastel shades makes a decorative centrepiece before being dismantled and sampled at the end of the meal.

Makes 30
3 egg whites
175g/6oz/1½ cups icing (confectioners') sugar
mauve and pink food colouring
silver or sugar balls to decorate

1 Preheat the oven to 120°C/250°F/Gas ½. Line two baking sheets with baking parchment.

2 Whisk the egg whites in a heatproof grease-free bowl until they are really stiff, then gently fold in the icing sugar, a little at a time, with a metal spoon. Set the bowl over a pan of gently simmering water and whisk the mixture for a few seconds until it is firm enough for piping. The mixture should form stiff peaks when a metal spoon is pulled away from it.

3 Remove the bowl from the heat and divide the mixture into two batches. Tint one batch with a little mauve food colouring and the other with pink.

4 Gently spoon one batch of meringue into a piping (pastry) bag fitted with a small star nozzle and pipe little mounds of the mixture on to one of the prepared baking sheets. Spoon the second batch of meringue into a clean piping bag fitted with a small plain nozzle and pipe little heart shapes on to the other baking sheet. Decorate the meringues with silver or sugar balls.

5 Bake for 1 hour, until the meringue lifts off the parchment easily. Leave to cool completely, then pile the meringues on to a cake stand.

> **Cook's Tip**
> Use a metal, ceramic or glass bowl for whisking egg whites. Plastic bowls are easily scratched and then it becomes almost impossible to wash away all traces of grease from the bowl.

Praline Pavlova Cookies Energy 148kcal/621kJ; Protein 1.3g; Carbohydrate 21.2g, of which sugars 21.1g; Fat 7g, of which saturates 2.7g; Cholesterol 8mg; Calcium 16mg; Fibre 0.3g; Sodium 32mg.
Pastel Meringues Energy Energy 24kcal/103kJ; Protein 0.3g; Carbohydrate 6.1g, of which sugars 6.1g; Fat 0g, of which saturates 0g; Cholesterol 0mg; Calcium 3mg; Fibre 0g; Sodium 6mg.

Coconut Meringues

Make these tiny meringues to serve with a fruit salad, or make the bigger ones and sandwich with cream or crème fraîche to serve at tea time.

Makes 16

3 egg whites, at room temperature

175g/6oz/1½ cups caster (superfine) sugar
50g/2oz/½ cup desiccated (dry unsweetened shredded) coconut
whipped cream or crème fraîche, and lemon curd (optional), to serve

1 Preheat the oven to 160°C/325°F/Gas 3. Line two baking sheets with baking parchment.

2 Whisk the egg whites in a large, grease-free bowl, until stiff. Whisk in half the sugar until smooth and glossy.

3 Carefully fold in the rest of the sugar and the coconut with a metal spoon. When well blended, place tablespoonfuls, spaced well apart, on the prepared baking sheets.

4 Bake the meringues for 20 minutes, then change the positions of the baking sheets over and reduce the temperature to 140°C/275°F/Gas 1 for a further 40 minutes, or until crisp and slightly golden.

5 Using a metal spatula, carefully remove the meringues from the baking sheets while they are still warm and transfer to a wire rack to cool completely. When they are cold, sandwich the meringues together in pairs with whipped cream, crème fraîche or a mixture of whipped cream and lemon curd. Serve within 30 minutes of filling.

Cook's Tip
You could use this mixture to make one large meringue gâteau. Spread out the mixture in two 18cm/7in rounds and bake as above, then sandwich with one of the suggested fillings.

Muscovado Meringues

These light brown meringues are extremely low in fat and are delicious served on their own or sandwiched together with a fresh fruit and soft cheese filling, or melted chocolate and soft cheese.

Makes about 20

115g/4oz/½ cup light muscovado (brown) sugar
2 egg whites
5ml/1 tsp finely chopped walnuts

1 Preheat the oven to 160°C/325°F/Gas 3. Line two baking sheets with baking parchment.

2 Press the sugar through a metal sieve (strainer) into a bowl.

3 Whisk the egg whites in a grease-free bowl until very stiff and dry, then whisk in the sugar, about 15ml/1 tbsp at a time, until the meringue is very thick and glossy.

4 Spoon small mounds of the mixture on to the prepared baking sheets.

5 Sprinkle the meringues with the chopped walnuts. Bake for 30 minutes. Leave to cool for 5 minutes on the baking sheets, then using a metal spatula, carefully transfer to a wire rack to cool completely.

Cook's Tip
When separating the eggs, make sure that no traces of yolk fall into the egg whites, as this will prevent them from foaming properly when whisked.

Variation
For a sophisticated filling, mix 115g/4oz/½ cup low-fat soft cheese with 15ml/1 tbsp icing (confectioners') sugar. Chop 2 slices of fresh pineapple and add to the mixture. Use to sandwich the meringues together in pairs.

Coconut Meringues Energy 64kcal/270kJ; Protein 0.8g; Carbohydrate 11.6g, of which sugars 11.6g; Fat 1.9g, of which saturates 1.7g; Cholesterol 0mg; Calcium 7mg; Fibre 0.4g; Sodium 13mg.
Muscovado Meringues Energy 26kcal/109kJ; Protein 0.4g; Carbohydrate 6g, of which sugars 6g; Fat 0.2g, of which saturates 0g; Cholesterol 0mg; Calcium 3mg; Fibre 0g; Sodium 6mg.

Mint Chocolate Meringues

These mini meringues are perfect for a buffet dessert at a birthday party and could be tinted pink or green. Alternatively, you could tint the filling with cocoa powder. Any spares are delicious crunched into your next batch of vanilla ice cream.

Makes about 50
2 egg whites

115g/4oz/generous ½ cup caster (superfine) sugar
50g/2oz/16 chocolate mint sticks, chopped
unsweetened cocoa powder, sifted (optional)

For the filling
150ml/¼ pint/⅔ cup double (heavy) or whipping cream
5–10ml/1–2 tsp crème de menthe, or peppermint extract

1 Preheat the oven to 110°C/225°F/Gas ¼. Line two large baking sheets with baking parchment.

2 Whisk the egg whites in a grease-fee bowl until stiff, then gradually whisk in the sugar, a little at a time, until the meringue is thick and glossy. Gently fold in the chopped mint sticks with a metal spoon or flexible spatula. Place teaspoonfuls of the mixture on to the prepared baking sheets, spaced a little apart.

3 Bake for 1 hour, or until crisp. Remove from the oven and allow to cool, then dust with cocoa powder, if using.

4 Lightly whip the cream, stir in the crème de menthe or peppermint extract, and sandwich the meringues together in pairs just before serving.

Cook's Tips
• Crème de menthe may be either a brilliant green or "white", that is, colourless. The flavour is no different, so it is a matter of personal taste which you use to flavour the filling. (Peppermint extract is always colourless.)
• You can store these meringues in an airtight container for several days, but do not fill them until ready to serve.

Orange, Mint and Coffee Meringues

These tiny, crisp meringues are flavoured with orange, coffee and mint chocolate sticks and liqueurs. Pile into dry, airtight glass jars or decorative containers.

Makes 90
25g/1oz/8 chocolate mint sticks
25g/1oz/8 chocolate orange sticks
25g/1oz/8 chocolate coffee sticks
2.5ml/½ tsp crème de menthe
2.5ml/½ tsp orange curaçao or Cointreau
2.5ml/½ tsp Tia Maria
3 egg whites
175g/6oz/¾ cup caster (superfine) sugar
5ml/1 tsp unsweetened cocoa powder

1 Preheat the oven to 110°C/225°F/Gas ¼. Line 2–3 baking sheets with baking parchment.

2 Chop each flavour of chocolate stick separately and place each into separate bowls, reserving a teaspoonful of each flavour stick. Stir in the liquid flavourings to match the chocolate sticks.

3 Place the egg whites in a grease-free bowl and whisk until stiff. Gradually add the sugar, whisking well after each addition until thick. Add a third of the meringue to each bowl of chopped chocolate sticks and fold in gently using a flexible spatula until evenly blended.

4 Place about 30 teaspoons of each mixture on to the baking sheets, spaced well apart. Sprinkle the top of each meringue with the reserved chopped chocolate sticks, matching the flavours to the meringues.

5 Bake for 1 hour, or until crisp. Leave to cool slightly on the baking sheets, then using a metal spatula, carefully transfer the meringues to a wire rack to cool completely. Dust lightly with unsweetened cocoa powder.

Cook's Tip
These meringues are great served with vanilla ice cream.

Mint Chocolate Meringues Energy 30kcal/123kJ; Protein 0.2g; Carbohydrate 3.1g, of which sugars 3.1g; Fat 1.9g, of which saturates 1.2g; Cholesterol 4mg; Calcium 3mg; Fibre 0g; Sodium 3mg.
Orange, Mint and Coffee Meringues Energy 13kcal/54kJ; Protein 0.2g; Carbohydrate 2.6g, of which sugars 2.6g; Fat 0.3g, of which saturates 0.1g; Cholesterol 0mg; Calcium 1mg; Fibre 0g; Sodium 3mg.

Guirlache

This is an Arab sweetmeat from the Pyrenees, combining toasted nuts and caramel to produce a crisp nut brittle – a forerunner of some familiar chocolate bar fillings.

Makes about 24 pieces

115g/4oz/1 cup almonds, half blanched, half unblanched
115g/4oz/1 cup hazelnuts, half blanched, half unblanched
5ml/1 tsp almond oil or a flavourless oil
200g/7oz/1 cup sugar
15ml/1 tbsp lemon juice

1 Preheat the oven to 150°C/300°F/Gas 2. Spread out the nuts on a baking sheet and toast for about 30 minutes, shaking the sheet occasionally. The nuts should smell pleasant and have turned brown and be very dry.

2 Coarsely chop the toasted nuts or crush them coarsely with a rolling pin. Cover another baking tray with foil and grease it generously with the oil.

3 Put the sugar in a pile in a small pan and pour the lemon juice around it. Cook over a high heat, shaking the pan, until the sugar turns a coffee colour. (As it cooks, the pile of sugar will melt and collapse into caramel.) If the heat is too high the sugar will burn and will taste unpleasant.

4 Immediately add the nuts and stir once to mix, then pour the mixture on to the foil and spread out into a thin, even layer with a metal spatula. Leave the mixture to cool completely and harden.

5 Once set, break up the caramel into pieces and store in an airtight container.

> **Cook's Tip**
> *Guirlache may be served as an after-dinner treat. It is also very good pulverized and used as a topping for mousses and whipped cream. It also makes wonderful ice cream.*

Nutty Nougat

Nougat is an almost magical sweetmeat that emerges from honey-flavoured meringue made with boiled syrup. Since any other nuts or candied fruits can be used instead of almonds, as long as you have eggs, sugar and honey, you have the potential for making an impromptu gift or dinner-party treat.

Makes about 500g/1¼lb

225g/8oz/generous 1 cup sugar
225g/8oz/1 cup clear honey or golden (light corn) syrup
1 large (US extra large) egg white
115g/4oz/1 cup flaked (sliced) almonds or chopped pistachio nuts, roasted

1 Line a 17.5cm/7in square cake tin (pan) with rice paper.

2 Place the sugar, honey or syrup and 60ml/4 tbsp water in a large, heavy pan and heat gently, stirring frequently, until the sugar has completely dissolved.

3 Bring the syrup to the boil and boil gently until it reaches the soft crack stage or the temperature registers 129–135°C/264–275°F on a sugar thermometer. To test for soft crack stage, drop a little syrup into a bowl of iced water. If it separates into hard, but not brittle threads that remain supple when pressed between your fingers, it is ready.

4 Meanwhile, whisk the egg white until very stiff, but not crumbly, then slowly drizzle in the syrup while whisking constantly.

5 Quickly stir in the nuts and pour the mixture into the prepared tin. Leave to cool but, before the nougat becomes too hard, cut it into squares. Store in an airtight container.

> **Cook's Tip**
> *Warm the sugar thermometer in hot water (and dry) before placing it in the syrup. Make sure the bulb is covered by the syrup but is not touching the base of the pan, as this would give an inaccurate reading.*

Nutty Nougat Energy 1177kcal/4907kJ; Protein 29.9g; Carbohydrate 85g, of which sugars 83.4g; Fat 82.2g, of which saturates 38.9g; Cholesterol 163mg; Calcium 799mg; Fibre 4.6g; Sodium 483mg.
Guirlache Energy 94kcal/395kJ; Protein 1.7g; Carbohydrate 9.3g, of which sugars 9.1g; Fat 5.8g, of which saturates 0.5g; Cholesterol 0mg; Calcium 23mg; Fibre 0.7g; Sodium 1mg.

Sweet Nutty Confections

If you love chocolate, condensed milk, nuts and crumb crust then these are the cookies for you. It's fortunate that they are incredibly easy to make because they are even easier to eat and are sure to become firm favourites with all the family as a treat for special occasions. Children enjoy helping to make them.

Makes 16–18
250g/9oz digestive biscuits
  (graham crackers)
115g/4oz/½ cup butter, melted
150g/5oz/scant 1 cup milk
  chocolate chips
200g/7oz mixed whole nuts, such
  as pecan nuts, hazelnuts, Brazil
  nuts, walnuts and almonds
200ml/7fl oz/scant 1 cup
  sweetened condensed milk

1 Preheat the oven to 180°C/350°F/Gas 4.

2 Put the digestive biscuits in a plastic bag and crush them with a rolling pin.

3 Put the crumbs in a bowl and stir in the melted butter. Mix well. Press the mixture evenly into the base of a 10 × 36cm/4 × 14in cake tin (pan).

4 Sprinkle the chocolate chips evenly over the crumb base. Arrange the nuts on top and pour the sweetened condensed milk over the top evenly.

5 Bake for 25 minutes, or until bubbling and golden. Cool in the tin, loosen from the sides, then cool completely and slice into thin bars.

Variation
Use crushed ginger nuts (ginger snaps) for the base of the bars.

Cook's Tip
If you prefer, use a shallow 20cm/8in square cake tin (pan) instead, and cut the cookies into squares.

Apple and Date Balls

Although these sweetmeats take quite a long time to cook, they are very easy to make and you are certain to agree that the time spent was worthwhile when you sample this rich, fruity combination of flavours.

Makes 20
1kg/2¼lb cooking apples
115g/4oz/⅔ cup dried, stoned
  (pitted) dates
250ml/8fl oz/1 cup apple juice
5ml/1 tsp ground cinnamon
50g/2oz/½ cup finely
  chopped walnuts

1 Cut the apples in half and core them but do not peel. Put them into a large, heavy pan and add the dates, apple juice and ground cinnamon. Cook over a very low heat, stirring occasionally, for 4–6 hours, or until the mixture has reduced to a dry paste.

2 Remove the pan from the heat and using a metal spatula, scrape the mixture into a bowl. Leave to cool completely.

3 Meanwhile, spread out the nuts on a baking sheet and toast under a preheated grill (broiler) for a few minutes, until golden. Take care that they do not scorch. Remove from the heat and leave to cool.

4 Take spoonfuls of the cooled fruit mixture and roll them into bitesize balls between the palms of your hands. Roll the balls in the toasted nuts to coat.

5 Wrap each apple and date ball in a twist of cellophane and store in an airtight container.

Variations
• Halve the quantity of cinnamon and add 2.5ml/½ tsp ground ginger to the mixture.
• These fruit balls are just as delicious made with pears instead of apples. Try to find a cooking variety or an all-purpose pear. As with apples, the time taken to cook to a dry paste may vary quite considerably.

Sweet Nutty Confections Energy 42kcals/176kJ; Fat, total 2.3g; saturated fat 0.55g; polyunsaturated fat 0.8g; monounsaturated fat 0.8g; Carbohydrate 4.95g sugar, total 4.85g starch 0.05g; Fibre 0.5g Sodium1.9mg. **Apple and Date Balls** Energy 47kcals/198kJ; Fat, total 1.8g; saturated fat 0.15g; polyunsaturated fat1.25g; monounsaturated fat 0.3g; Carbohydrate 7.6g; sugar, total7.6g; starch 0g Fibre 1g; Sodium 1.9mg.

Chocolate Nut Clusters

These delightful chocolate-coated cookies are packed with chunky nuts and are an ideal way to end a dinner party or make the perfect gift for a special friend.

Makes 30

550ml/18fl oz/2¼ cups double (heavy) cream
25g/1oz/2 tbsp unsalted butter, diced
350ml/12fl oz/1½ cups golden (light corn) syrup
200g/7oz/scant 1 cup sugar
90g/3½oz/scant ½ packed cup soft light brown sugar
pinch of salt
15ml/1 tbsp vanilla extract
425g/15oz/3¾ cups hazelnuts, pecan nuts, walnuts, Brazil nuts or unsalted peanuts
400g/14oz plain (semisweet) chocolate, chopped
25g/1oz/2 tbsp white vegetable fat (shortening)

1 Lightly grease two baking sheets. Put the cream, butter, syrup, both kinds of sugar and the salt in a heavy pan and cook over a medium heat, stirring constantly until the sugars dissolve and the butter melts. Bring to the boil and cook, stirring frequently, for about 1 hour, until the caramel reaches 119°C/238°F (soft ball stage) on a sugar thermometer.

2 Plunge the base of the pan into cold water to stop further cooking. Cool slightly, then stir in the vanilla extract.

3 Stir the nuts into the caramel until well coated. Using an oiled tablespoon, drop spoonfuls of the mixture on to the baking sheets, about 2.5cm/1in apart. If the mixture hardens, return to the heat. Chill for 30 minutes, until firm and cold.

4 Transfer to a wire rack placed over a baking sheet. Melt the chocolate with the white vegetable fat in a pan over a low heat, stirring until smooth. Remove from the heat and leave to cool.

5 Using a fork, dip each cluster into the chocolate mixture and lift out, shaking off the excess chocolate.

6 Place the nut clusters on the wire rack over the baking sheet. Leave to set for about 2 hours, until hardened.

Microwave Cinnamon Balls

Ground almonds make these little treats very moist. When cooked, they should be soft inside, with a very strong cinnamon flavour. They harden, however, with keeping, so it is a good idea to freeze some as they can be thawed very quickly when required.

Makes about 15

175g/6oz/1½ cups ground almonds
75g/3oz/scant ½ cup caster (superfine) sugar
15ml/1 tbsp ground cinnamon
2 egg whites
icing (confectioners') sugar, for dusting

1 Mix together the ground almonds, sugar and cinnamon in a bowl. Whisk the egg whites in another grease-free bowl until they begin to stiffen, then fold enough into the almonds to make a fairly firm mixture.

2 Wet your hands with cold water and roll small spoonfuls of the mixture into smooth balls. Place these well apart on baking parchment.

3 Microwave on high (100 per cent) power for 2½–3½ minutes, rearranging their positions twice, until cooked but still slightly soft inside.

4 Slide a metal spatula under the balls to release them from the paper, and leave to cool.

5 Sift a few tablespoons of icing sugar on to a plate and when the cinnamon balls are cold slide them on to the plate. Shake gently to completely cover the cinnamon balls in sugar.

Cook's Tips
• When completely cold, store the cinnamon balls in layers interleaved with baking parchment in an airtight container for 2–3 days.
• To freeze, interleave the cinnamon balls in the same way and freeze for up to 6 months.

Chocolate Nut Clusters Energy 311kcal/1298kJ; Protein 2.7g; Carbohydrate 28.3g, of which sugars 27.9g; Fat 21.6g, of which saturates 9.2g; Cholesterol 27mg; Calcium 36mg; Fibre 1.1g; Sodium 46mg.
Microwave Cinnamon Balls Energy 93kcal/386kJ; Protein 2.9g; Carbohydrate 6g, of which sugars 5.7g; Fat 6.5g, of which saturates 0.5g; Cholesterol 0mg; Calcium 31mg; Fibre 0.9g; Sodium 10mg.

Stuffed Prunes

Chocolate-covered prunes, soaked in brandy liqueur, hide a melt-in-the-mouth coffee filling.

Makes about 30

225g/8oz/1 cup unstoned (unpitted) prunes
50ml/2fl oz/¼ cup Armagnac
30ml/2 tbsp ground coffee
150ml/¼ pint/⅔ cup double (heavy) cream
350g/12oz plain (semisweet) chocolate, broken into squares
10g/¼oz/½ tbsp white vegetable fat (shortening)
30ml/2 tbsp unsweetened cocoa powder, for dusting

1 Put the unstoned prunes in a bowl and pour the Armagnac over. Stir, then cover with clear film (plastic wrap) and set aside for 2 hours, or until the prunes have absorbed the liquid.

2 Make a slit along each prune to remove the stone (pit), making a hollow for the filling, but leaving the fruit intact.

3 Put the coffee and cream in a pan and heat almost to boiling point. Cover, infuse (steep) for 4 minutes, then heat again until almost boiling. Put 115g/4oz of the chocolate into a bowl and pour over the coffee cream through a sieve (strainer).

4 Stir until the chocolate has melted and the mixture is smooth. Leave to cool.

5 Fill a piping (pastry) bag with a small plain nozzle with the chocolate mixture. Pipe into the cavities of the prunes. Chill in the refrigerator for 20 minutes.

6 Melt the remaining chocolate in a bowl over a pan of hot water. Using a fork, dip the prunes one at a time into the chocolate to give them a generous coating. Place on baking parchment to harden. Dust each with a little cocoa powder.

Cook's Tip
Fresh dates can be used instead of prunes, if preferred.

Chocolate-coated Nut Brittle

Equal amounts of pecan nuts and almonds set in crisp caramel, then coated in dark chocolate, make a truly sensational gift – if you can bear to give them away.

Makes 20–24

115g/4oz/1 cup mixed pecan nuts and whole almonds
115g/4oz/generous ½ cup caster (superfine) sugar
60ml/4 tbsp water
200g/7oz plain (semisweet) chocolate, chopped

1 Lightly grease a baking sheet. Mix the nuts, sugar and water in a heavy pan. Cook over a low heat, stirring until the sugar has dissolved.

2 Bring the ingredients to the boil, then lower the heat to medium and cook, without stirring, until the mixture turns a rich golden brown and registers 148°C/300°F on a sugar thermometer.

3 To test without a thermometer, drop a small amount of the mixture into iced water. It should become brittle enough to snap.

4 Quickly remove the pan from the heat and pour the mixture on to the prepared baking sheet, spreading it evenly. Leave until completely cold and set hard. Break the nut brittle into pieces.

5 Place the chocolate in a heatproof bowl set over a pan of gently simmering water and heat gently until melted. Remove the chocolate from the heat and carefully dip the pieces of nut brittle into it to half-coat them. Leave the nut brittle on a sheet of baking parchment to set. Store the nut brittle in an airtight container.

Cook's Tip
This brittle looks best in coarse chunks, so don't worry if the pieces break unevenly, or if there are a few small gaps in the chocolate coating.

Stuffed Prunes Energy 100kcal/419kJ; Protein 0.9g; Carbohydrate 10.1g, of which sugars 9.9g; Fat 6.3g, of which saturates 3.8g; Cholesterol 8mg; Calcium 10mg; Fibre 0.8g; Sodium 7mg.
Chocolate-coated Nut Brittle Energy 94kcal/395kJ; Protein 0.9g; Carbohydrate 10.6g, of which sugars 10.4g; Fat 5.7g, of which saturates 1.7g; Cholesterol 1mg; Calcium 8mg; Fibre 0.4g; Sodium 1mg.

Chocolate Kisses

These rich little balls look attractive mixed together on a plate and dusted with icing sugar. Serve with ice cream or simply with a cup of coffee.

Makes 24

75g/3oz plain (semisweet)
  chocolate, chopped
75g/3oz white chocolate, chopped
115g/4oz/½ cup butter, at room
  temperature, diced
115g/4oz/generous ½ cup caster
  (superfine) sugar
2 eggs, beaten
225g/8oz/2 cups plain
  (all-purpose) flour
icing (confectioners') sugar,
  to decorate

1 Put the plain and white chocolate into separate small, heatproof bowls and melt the chocolates, in turn, over a pan of hot, but not boiling water, stirring until smooth. Remove the bowls from the heat and set them aside to cool slightly.

2 Beat together the butter and caster sugar until pale and fluffy. Beat in the eggs a little at a time, beating well after each addition.

3 Sift the flour over the butter, sugar and egg mixture and mix in lightly and thoroughly.

4 Halve the mixture and divide it between the two bowls of chocolate. Mix each chocolate in well. Knead the doughs until smooth, wrap in clear film (plastic wrap) and chill in the refrigerator for 1 hour.

5 Preheat the oven to 190°C/375°F/Gas 5. Grease two baking sheets.

6 Take rounded teaspoonfuls of the doughs and shape them roughly into balls. Roll the balls between the palms of your hands to make neater ball shapes. Arrange the balls on the prepared baking sheets and bake for about 12 minutes. Remove from the oven.

7 Dust with sifted icing sugar, then, using a metal spatula, transfer the balls to wire racks. Allow to cool completely.

Praline Chocolate Bites

These delicate, mouth-watering little bites never fail to impress guests, but are quite simple to make. They are perfect for serving with coffee after dinner. Dust with icing sugar for a decorative finish, if you like.

Makes 16

115g/4oz/1 cup caster
  (superfine) sugar
115g/4oz/1 cup whole
  blanched almonds
200g/7oz plain (semisweet)
  chocolate

1 Lightly brush a baking sheet with oil. Put the sugar in a heavy pan with 90ml/6 tbsp water. Stir over a gentle heat until the sugar has dissolved. Bring the syrup to the boil and cook for about 5 minutes, without stirring, until the mixture is golden and caramelized.

2 Remove the pan from the heat and add the almonds, gently swirling the pan to immerse them in the caramel. Pour the mixture on to the prepared baking sheet and spread out evenly with a metal spatula. Set aside and leave to cool for about 15 minutes, until hardened.

3 Meanwhile, break the chocolate into pieces and melt in a heatproof bowl set over a pan of gently simmering water. Remove the bowl from the heat.

4 Cover the surface of the hardened caramel with a sheet of clear film (plastic wrap) and hit it with a rolling pin to break it up. Put the pieces in a food processor and process until finely chopped. Transfer to a bowl and stir in the melted chocolate. Chill in the refrigerator until sufficiently set to roll into balls. Roll small pieces of the mixture into 16 balls between the palms of your hands. Place in mini paper cases to serve.

Cook's Tip
The mixture for these bites can be made ahead and stored in the freezer for up to 2 weeks. To use, thaw the mixture at room temperature until soft enough to roll into balls.

Chocolate Kisses Energy 125kcal/524kJ; Protein 1.9g; Carbohydrate 16.1g, of which sugars 9g; Fat 6.4g, of which saturates 3.7g; Cholesterol 26mg; Calcium 28mg; Fibre 0.4g; Sodium 39mg.
Praline Chocolate Bites Energy 544kcal/2280kJ; Protein 8.7g; Carbohydrate 63.8g, of which sugars 62.6g; Fat 30.1g, of which saturates 9.7g; Cholesterol 3mg; Calcium 101mg; Fibre 3.4g; Sodium 9mg.

Rich Chocolate Truffles

These irresistible after-dinner truffles melt in the mouth. Use a good quality chocolate with a high percentage of cocoa solids to give a real depth of fabulous flavour.

Makes 20–30
175ml/6fl oz/³⁄₄ cup double
  (heavy) cream
1 egg yolk, beaten
275g/10oz plain (semisweet)
  chocolate, chopped

25g/1oz/2 tbsp unsalted
  butter, diced

For the coatings
unsweetened cocoa powder
finely chopped pistachio nuts
  or hazelnuts
400g/14oz plain (semisweet),
  milk or white chocolate, or a
  mixture

1 Bring the cream to the boil, then remove the pan from the heat and beat in the egg yolk. Add the chocolate, then stir until melted and smooth. Stir in the butter, then strain into a bowl and leave to cool. Cover and chill for 6–8 hours.

2 Line a large baking sheet with baking parchment. Using two teaspoons, form the mixture into 20–30 balls and place on the paper. Chill if the mixture becomes too soft.

3 To coat the truffles with cocoa, sift some powder into a small bowl, drop in the truffles, one at a time, and roll to coat well. To coat them with nuts, roll the truffles in finely chopped pistachio nuts or hazelnuts.

4 To coat with chocolate, freeze the truffles for at least 1 hour. In a small bowl, melt the plain, milk or white chocolate in a heatproof bowl set over a pan of gently simmering water, stirring until melted and smooth, then leave to cool slightly.

5 Using a fork, dip the frozen truffles into the cooled chocolate, one at a time, tapping the fork on the edge of the bowl to shake off the excess. Place on a baking sheet lined with baking parchment and chill in the refrigerator for several hours before serving.

Liqueur Chocolate Truffles

Truffles can be simply dusted with cocoa, icing sugar, finely chopped nuts or coated in melted chocolate.

**Makes 20 large or
30 medium truffles**
250ml/8fl oz/1 cup double
  (heavy) cream
285g/10oz fine quality dark
  (bittersweet) or plain
  (semisweet) chocolate, chopped

45g/1¹⁄₂oz 3 tbsp unsalted
  butter, diced
45ml/3 tbsp brandy, whisky or
  other liqueur

To decorate
unsweetened cocoa powder,
  for dusting
finely chopped pistachios
400g/14oz dark (bittersweet)
  chocolate

1 In a pan over medium heat, bring the cream to a boil. Remove from the heat and add the chocolate. Stir gently until melted. Stir in the butter until melted, then stir in the brandy or liqueur. Strain into a bowl and leave to cool to room temperature. Cover and chill for 4 hours or overnight.

2 Line one or two baking sheets with baking parchment. Using a small ice cream scoop, scrape up the chocolate mixture into 30 small or 20 medium balls and place them on the prepared baking sheets.

3 If dusting with cocoa, sift a thick layer of unsweetened cocoa powder on to a dish or pie plate. Roll the truffles in the cocoa, rounding them between the palms of your hands. (Dust your hands with cocoa powder to prevent the truffles from sticking.) Do not worry if the truffles are not perfectly round as the irregular shape looks more authentic.

4 Alternatively, roll the truffles in very finely chopped pistachios, to coat.

5 If coating with chocolate, do not roll in cocoa or nuts, but freeze for 1 hour. In a heatproof bowl set over a pan of gently simmering water melt the chocolate. Using a fork, dip each truffle into the melted chcolate. Place on a baking parchment lined baking sheet to set.

Rich Chocolate Truffles Energy 152kcal/634kJ; Protein 1.3g; Carbohydrate 14.4g, of which sugars 14.2g; Fat 10.3g, of which saturates 6.2g; Cholesterol 18mg; Calcium 11mg; Fibre 0.6g; Sodium 8mg.
Liqueur Chocolate Truffles Energy 172kcal/718kJ; Protein 1.3g; Carbohydrate 14.7g, of which sugars 14.4g; Fat 12.1g, of which saturates 7.4g; Cholesterol 16mg; Calcium 12mg; Fibre 0.6g; Sodium 12mg.

Coffee Chocolate Truffles

Because these classic chocolates contain fresh cream, they should be stored in the refrigerator and eaten within a few days.

Makes 24
350g/12oz plain (semisweet) chocolate
75ml/5 tbsp double (heavy) cream

30ml/2 tbsp coffee liqueur, such as Tia Maria, Kahlua or Toussaint
115g/4oz good quality white chocolate
115g/4oz good quality milk chocolate

1 Melt 225g/8oz of the plain chocolate in a bowl over a pan of barely simmering water. Stir in the cream and liqueur, then chill the mixture for 4 hours, until firm.

2 Divide the mixture into 24 equal pieces and quickly roll each into a ball. Chill for 1 more hour, or until they are firm again.

3 Melt the remaining plain, white and milk chocolate in separate small bowls. Using two forks, carefully dip eight of the truffles, one at a time, into the melted milk chocolate.

4 Repeat with the white and plain chocolate. Place the truffles on a board, covered with baking parchment or foil. Leave to set before removing and chill in the refrigerator for several hours before placing in a serving bowl or individual paper cases.

Variations
Ring the changes by adding one of the following to the truffle mixture. Ginger – Stir in 40g/1½ oz/¼ cup finely chopped crystallized (candied) ginger. Candied fruit – Stir in 50g/2oz/⅓ cup finely chopped candied fruit, such as pineapple and orange. Pistachio – Stir in 25g/1oz/¼ cup chopped skinned pistachio nuts. Hazelnut – Roll each ball of chilled truffle mixture around a whole skinned hazelnut.

Fruit and Nut Chocolates

When beautifully boxed, these chocolates make perfect presents.

Makes 20
50g/2oz ready-to-eat prunes or dried apricots
50g/2oz/⅓ cup sultanas (golden raisins) or raisins

25g/1oz/2 tbsp ready-to eat dried apples, figs or dates
25g/1oz/¼ cup flaked (sliced) almonds
25g/1oz/¼ cup hazelnuts or walnuts
30ml/2 tbsp lemon juice
50g/2oz good-quality dark (bittersweet) chocolate

1 Chop the fruit and nuts in a food processor or blender until fairly small. Add the lemon juice and process to mix.

2 Melt the chocolate in a heatproof bowl set over a pan of simmering water. Roll the fruit mixture into small balls. Using tongs, roll the balls in the melted chocolate, then place them on oiled foil to cool and set.

Malt Whisky Truffles

Blending rich chocolate with cool cream and potent whisky makes a mouthwatering end to any meal.

Makes 25–30
200g/7oz dark (bittersweet) chocolate, broken into pieces

150ml/¼ pint/⅔ cup double (heavy) cream
45ml/3 tbsp malt whisky
115g/4oz/1 cup icing (confectioners') sugar
unsweetened cocoa powder, for coating

1 Melt the chocolate in a heatproof bowl set over a pan of simmering water, stirring constantly. Leave to cool slightly.

2 Using a wire whisk, whip the cream with the whisky in a bowl until thick enough to hold its shape. Stir in the melted chocolate and icing sugar and leave until firm enough to handle.

3 Dust your hands with cocoa powder and shape the mixture into bitesize balls. Coat in cocoa powder.

Coffee Chocolate Truffles Energy 143kcal/599kJ; Protein 1.5g; Carbohydrate 15.2g, of which sugars 15.1g; Fat 8.7g, of which saturates 5.3g; Cholesterol 6mg; Calcium 30mg; Fibre 0.4g; Sodium 11mg.
Fruit and Nut Chocolates Energy 33kcal/139kJ; Protein 0.6g; Carbohydrate 4.7g, of which sugars 4.7g; Fat 1.4g, of which saturates 0.5g; Cholesterol 0mg; Calcium 10mg; Fibre 0.4g; Sodium 2mg.
Malt Whisky Truffles Energy 93kcal/387kJ; Protein 0.5g; Carbohydrate 10g, of which sugars 9.9g; Fat 5.5g, of which saturates 3.3g; Cholesterol 9mg; Calcium 8mg; Fibre 0.2g; Sodium 2mg.

Truffle Christmas Puddings

These truffles disguised as Christmas puddings are great fun to make and receive. Make any flavoured truffle, and decorate them as you like.

Makes 20

20 plain (semisweet)
  chocolate truffles
15ml/1 tbsp unsweetened
  cocoa powder
15ml/1 tbsp icing
  (confectioners') sugar
225g/8oz/1⅓ cups white
  chocolate chips, melted
50g/2oz⅓ cup white marzipan
green and red food colourings
yellow food colouring
  dust (optional)

1 Make the rich chocolate truffles following the recipe on the previous page. Sift the cocoa powder and sugar together and coat the truffles in the mixture.

2 Spread about two-thirds of the melted white chocolate over a piece of baking parchment with a metal spatula. Carefully pick up the corners of the parchment and shake gently to level the surface. Leave until just set.

3 Using a 2.5cm/1in daisy cookie cutter, stamp out 20 shapes. Place a truffle on the centre of each daisy shape, securing it with a little of the reserved melted white chocolate. Leave to set completely.

4 Colour two-thirds of the marzipan green and one-third red using the food colourings. Roll out the green marzipan thinly and stamp out 40 leaves using a tiny holly leaf cutter. Mark the veins with a knife. Mould lots of tiny red beads.

5 If you like, colour the remaining melted white chocolate with yellow food colouring dust and spoon into a baking parchment piping (pastry) bag. Fold down the top, cut off the point and pipe the chocolate over the top of each truffle to resemble custard. Alternatively, leave the melted chocolate uncoloured and pipe it to resemble cream. Arrange two marzipan holly leaves and some red berries on the top.

Gingered Truffles

Wonderfully creamy, these rich chocolate truffles are flecked with ginger, coated in dark chocolate and piped with swirls of melted white chocolate.

Makes about 30

150ml/¼ pint/⅔ cup double
  (heavy) cream
150g/5oz dark (bittersweet)
  chocolate
25g/1oz/2 tbsp butter, diced
30ml/2 tbsp brandy
15ml/1 tbsp glacé (candied)
  ginger or preserved stem
  ginger, finely chopped

To decorate
15ml/1 tbsp unsweetened
  cocoa powder
225g/8oz dark (bittersweet)
  chocolate, broken into pieces
glacé (candied) ginger, chopped
50g/2oz white chocolate

1 Put the cream in a heavy pan and bring it to the boil. Remove the pan from the heat. Break the dark chocolate into pieces and add to the cream with the butter. Leave to stand for 5 minutes, stirring occasionally, until the chocolate and butter have melted.

2 Gradually stir in the brandy and then, using an electric whisk, beat for 5–10 minutes, until the mixture is thick. Stir in the ginger. Cover and chill for 2–3 hours, until firm.

3 Put the cocoa powder on a plate. Lightly dip a teaspoonful of mixture in cocoa and then roll it into a ball with your hands. Continue until all the mixture is used up. Chill the truffles for several hours until hard.

4 Melt the chocolate pieces in a heatproof bowl set over a pan of gently simmering water. Hold a truffle on a fork and coat it completely with chocolate. Transfer to a baking sheet lined with baking parchment.

5 To decorate, coarsely chop the ginger, sprinkle it over the truffles and then leave to cool and harden. Melt the white chocolate in the same way. Spoon the chocolate into a baking parchment piping (pastry) bag, snip off the tip and pipe squiggly lines over the truffles. Chill to harden.

Truffle Christmas Puddings Energy 148kcal/616kJ; Protein 1.3g; Carbohydrate 11.9g, of which sugars 10.3g; Fat 10.5g, of which saturates 6.2g; Cholesterol 22mg; Calcium 19mg; Fibre 0.5g; Sodium 31mg.
Gingered Truffles Energy 118kcal/490kJ; Protein 1g; Carbohydrate 10.3g, of which sugars 10.1g; Fat 8.1g, of which saturates 4.9g; Cholesterol 10mg; Calcium 13mg; Fibre 0.4g; Sodium 14mg.

Truffle-filled Filo Tulips

These cups can be prepared a day ahead and stored in an airtight container.

Makes about 24
3–6 sheets filo pastry, thawed
   if frozen
45g/1½oz/3 tbsp unsalted
   butter, melted
sugar for sprinkling
lemon rind, to decorate

For the truffles
250ml/8fl oz/1 cup double
   (heavy) cream
225g/8oz dark (bittersweet)
   or plain (semisweet)
   chocolate, chopped
55g/2oz/4 tbsp unsalted
   butter, diced
30ml/2 tbsp brandy or
   other liqueur

1 In a pan over a medium heat, bring the cream to the boil. Remove from the heat and add the chocolate, stirring until melted. Beat in the butter and add the brandy. Strain into a bowl. Chill for 1 hour until thick

2 Preheat the oven to 200°C/400°F/Gas 6. Grease a bun tray (muffin pan) with 24 × 4cm/1½in cups.

3 Place the filo sheets on a work surface. Cut each sheet into 6cm/2½in squares. Cover the sheets with a damp dish towel to prevent them from drying out while you are working. Keeping the filo squares covered, place one square on a work surface. Brush lightly with melted butter, turn over and brush the other side in the same way. Sprinkle with sugar. Brush melted butter on another square, place it over the first at an angle and sprinkle with sugar. Butter a third square and place it over the first two squares, so that the corners form an uneven edge. Press the layered square into the tray. Continue to fill the tray with filo squares in this way.

4 Bake the filo cups for 4–6 minutes, until golden. Cool for 10 minutes on a wire rack in the tray. Remove from the tray and leave to cool completely.

5 Stir the chocolate mixture; it should be just thick enough to pipe. Spoon it into a piping (pastry) bag with a star nozzle and pipe a swirl into each cup. Decorate with lemon rind.

Chocolate Christmas Cups

These charming petits fours, served with coffee, provide the perfect finishing touch to an elegant festive meal and – most importantly – they taste just as wonderful as they look.

Makes 35
275g/10oz plain (semisweet)
   chocolate, broken into pieces
175g/6oz cooked, cold
   Christmas pudding
75ml/5 tbsp brandy or whisky
chocolate leaves and crystallized
   (candied) cranberries,
   to decorate

1 Place the chocolate in a heatproof bowl set over a pan of gently simmering water and heat gently until melted.

2 Using a pastry brush, brush the bottom and sides of about 35 paper petit fours cases with the melted chocolate. Leave to set, then repeat, reheating the melted chocolate if necessary, applying a second coat. Leave to cool and set completely, for 4–5 hours or overnight. Reserve the remaining chocolate.

3 Crumble the Christmas pudding into a small bowl, sprinkle with brandy or whisky and leave to stand for 30–40 minutes, until the brandy is absorbed.

4 Spoon a little of the pudding mixture into each chocolate cup, smoothing the top. Reheat the remaining chocolate and spoon over the top of each cup to cover the surface of each cup to the edge. Leave to set.

5 When completely set, carefully peel off the cases and place in clean foil cases. Decorate with chocolate leaves and crystallized cranberries.

Cook's Tip
To crystallize (candy) cranberries, beat an egg white until frothy. Dip each berry first in the egg white, then in caster (superfine) sugar. Leave to dry completely on a sheet of baking parchment before using.

Truffle-filled Filo Tulips Energy 147kcal/612kJ; Protein 1.1g; Carbohydrate 9.4g, of which sugars 6.1g; Fat 11.7g, of which saturates 7.2g; Cholesterol 24mg; Calcium 15mg; Fibre 0.4g; Sodium 28mg.
Chocolate Christmas Cups Energy Energy 59kcal/249kJ; Protein 0.6g; Carbohydrate 7.5g, of which sugars 6.6g; Fat 2.7g, of which saturates 1.3g; Cholesterol 0mg; Calcium 7mg; Fibre 0.3g; Sodium 10mg.

Chocolate Box Cookies

These prettily decorated, bitesize cookies look as though they've come straight out of a box of chocolates.

Makes about 50
175g/6oz/1½ cups self-raising (self-rising) flour, plus extra for dusting
25g/1oz/¼ cup unsweetened cocoa powder
5ml/1 tsp mixed spice (apple pie spice)
50g/2oz/¼ cup unsalted butter, softened, diced
115g/4oz/generous ½ cup caster (superfine) sugar
1 egg
1 egg yolk

For the decoration
150g/5oz milk chocolate
150g/5oz white chocolate
100g/3¾oz plain (semisweet) chocolate
whole almonds or walnuts
unsweetened cocoa powder, for dusting

1 Preheat the oven to 180°C/350°F/ Gas 4. Lightly grease two baking sheets.

2 Put the flour, cocoa powder, spice and butter into a food processor. Process until the ingredients are thoroughly blended. Add the sugar, egg and egg yolk and mix to a smooth dough.

3 Turn out on to a lightly floured surface and knead. Cut the dough in half and roll out each piece into a 33cm/13in long log. Cut each log into 1cm/½in slices. Place on the baking sheets, spaced slightly apart, and chill for 30 minutes. Bake for 10 minutes, until slightly risen. Transfer to a wire rack to cool.

4 To decorate, melt the chocolate in three separate heatproof bowls set over pans of gently simmering water.

5 Divide the cookies into six batches. Completely coat three batches, then half-coat the other three batches in plain, milk and white chocolate. Place on a sheet of baking parchment. Press a nut on to the tops of the plain chocolate-coated cookies. Drizzle white chocolate lines over some cookies. Dust the white chocolate-coated cookies with cocoa powder.

White Chocolate Snowballs

These little spherical cookies are particularly popular during the Christmas season. They're simple to make, yet utterly delicious and bursting with creamy, buttery flavours. If you like, make them in advance of a special meal as they will keep well in the refrigerator for a few days.

Makes 16
200g/7oz white chocolate
25g/1oz/2 tbsp butter, diced
90g/3½oz/generous 1 cup desiccated (dry unsweetened shredded) coconut
90g/3½oz syrup sponge or Madeira cake
icing (confectioners') sugar, for dusting

1 Break the chocolate into pieces and put in a heatproof bowl with the butter. Set the bowl over a pan of gently simmering water and stir frequently until melted. Remove the bowl from the heat and set aside for a few minutes.

2 Meanwhile, put 50g/2oz/⅔ cup of the coconut on a plate and set aside. Crumble the cake and add to the melted chocolate with the remaining coconut. Mix well to form a chunky paste.

3 Take spoonfuls of the mixture and roll into balls, about 2.5cm/1in in diameter, and immediately roll them in the reserved coconut. Place the balls on baking parchment and leave to set.

4 Before serving, dust the snowballs generously with plenty of sifted icing sugar.

Cook's Tips
• *You'll need to shape the mixture into balls as soon as you've mixed in the coconut and cake; the mixture sets very quickly and you won't be able to shape it once it hardens.*
• *If you have any brandy or rum butter left over from Christmas lunch, substitute it for the plain butter to give these cookies an extra special flavour.*

Chocolate Box Cookies Energy 74kcal/312kJ; Protein 1.2g; Carbohydrate 9.9g, of which sugars 7.2g; Fat 3.6g, of which saturates 2.1g; Cholesterol 11mg; Calcium 23mg; Fibre 0.2g; Sodium 19mg.
White Chocolate Snowballs Energy 133kcal/554kJ; Protein 1.6g; Carbohydrate 10.9g, of which sugars 9.7g; Fat 9.5g, of which saturates 6.6g; Cholesterol 3mg; Calcium 38mg; Fibre 0.8g; Sodium 46mg.

Rose Petal Truffles

An indulgent treat that demands the finest quality chocolate with at least 60 per cent cocoa solids.

Makes 80
500g/1¼lb plain (semisweet) chocolate
300ml/½ pint/1¼ cups double (heavy) cream
15ml/1 tbsp triple-distilled rose water
2 drops rose essential oil
250g/9oz plain (semisweet) chocolate, for coating
crystallized (candied) rose petals

1 Melt the chocolate and cream together in a heatproof bowl set over a pan of gently simmering water. Add the rose water and essential oil.

2 Pour into a baking tin lined with baking parchment. Leave to cool and when the mixture is nearly firm, shape teaspoonfuls of it into balls. Chill the truffles.

3 To finish, melt the chocolate in a heatproof bowl set over a pan of gently simmering water. Skewer a truffle and dip it into the melted chocolate, coating it completely. Place a crystallized rose petal on each before the chocolate sets.

Swedish Rose Chocolate Balls

This is a very rich and delicious chocolate sweet.

Makes 20–30
150g/5oz good quality milk chocolate
30ml/2 tbsp ground almonds
30ml/2 tbsp caster (superfine) sugar
2 egg yolks
10ml/2 tsp strong coffee or coffee extract
15ml/1 tbsp dark rum
15ml/1 tbsp triple-distilled rose water
40g/1½ oz/¼ cup chocolate vermicelli

1 Grind the chocolate in a processor and add to the other ingredients except the rose water and vermicelli. Make into tiny balls by rolling small spoonfuls between your fingers. Chill well. Dip into the rose water and roll in the chocolate vermicelli.

Chocolate and Cherry Colettes

Luxurious and sophisticated, these unique handmade petits fours add that indefinable distinctive touch to any special occasion meal.

Makes 18–20
115g/4oz plain (semisweet) or dark (bittersweet) chocolate, chopped into small pieces
75g/3oz white or milk chocolate, chopped into small pieces
25g/1oz/2 tbsp unsalted butter, melted
15ml/1 tbsp Kirsch
60ml/4 tbsp double (heavy) cream
18–20 maraschino cherries or liqueur-soaked cherries
milk chocolate curls, to decorate

1 Melt the plain or dark chocolate in a heatproof bowl set over a pan of gently simmering water, stirring occasionally. Remove the bowl from the heat.

2 Spoon the melted chocolate into 18–20 foil petits four cases, dividing it equally among them. Using a small brush, spread the chocolate evenly up the sides of the cases, then leave to cool until the chocolate has set completely.

3 Put the white or milk chocolate and the butter in another heatproof bowl and melt over a pan of gently simmering water, stirring occasionally. Remove from the heat and leave to cool slightly. Stir in the Kirsch, then stir in the cream. Leave to cool until the mixture is just thick enough to hold its shape.

4 When the chocolate cups are set, carefully peel off and discard the foil cases. Place one cherry in each chocolate cup. Spoon the chocolate and cream mixture into a piping (pastry) bag fitted with a small star nozzle. Pipe the mixture over the cherries to fill each of the cases, then pipe a generous swirl on top to decorate. Top each colette with two or three milk chocolate curls. Leave to set before serving.

Variation
Substitute brandy or Drambuie for the Kirsch, if you like.

Rose Petal Truffles Energy 47kcal/197kJ; Protein 0.9g; Carbohydrate 5g, of which sugars 3.9g; Fat 2.5g, of which saturates 1.1g; Cholesterol 15mg; Calcium 16mg; Fibre 0.1g; Sodium 5mg.
Swedish Rose Chocolate Balls Energy 66kcal/276kJ; Protein 0.5g; Carbohydrate 6.01g, of which sugars 5.93g; Fat 4.63g, of which saturates 0.01g; Cholesterol 5.7mg; Calcium 4.9mg; Fibre 0.23g; Sodium 1.38mg.
Chocolate and Cherry Colettes Energy 79kcal/327kJ; Protein 0.7g; Carbohydrate 6.8g, of which sugars 6.8g; Fat 5.4g, of which saturates 3.3g; Cholesterol 7mg; Calcium 14mg; Fibre 0.2g; Sodium 13mg.

Double Chocolate Dipped Fruit

Make the most of your favourite soft seasonal fruit by double dipping them in chocolate – a perfect and light dessert or treat.

Makes 24 coated pieces
fruits – about 24 pieces
  (strawberries, cherries, orange
  segments, large seedless
grapes, physalis, kumquats,
  stoned (pitted) prunes, stoned
  (pitted) dates, dried apricots,
  dried peaches or dried pears)
115g/4oz white chocolate,
  chopped into small pieces
115g/4oz dark (bittersweet) or
  plain (semisweet) chocolate,
  chopped into small pieces

1 Clean and prepare fruits; wipe strawberries with a soft cloth or brush gently with a pastry brush. Wash firm-skinned fruits such as cherries and grapes and dry well. Peel and leave whole or cut up any other fruits being used.

2 Put the white chocolate into a heatproof bowl and melt over a pan of gently simmering water. Remove from the heat and cool, stirring frequently, until tepid (about 29°C/84°F).

3 Line a baking sheet with baking parchment. Holding each fruit by the stem or end and at an angle, dip one by one into the melted chocolate so that they are about two-thirds coated. Allow the excess to drop off back into the bowl, then place on the prepared baking sheet. Chill in the refrigerator for about 20 minutes, until the chocolate has set.

4 Put the pieces of dark or plain chocolate into a heatproof bowl and melt over a pan over gently simmering water, stirring frequently until smooth. Remove the bowl from the heat and leave the chocolate to cool to just below body temperature (about 30°C/86°F).

5 Take each white chocolate-coated fruit in turn from the baking sheet and, holding by the stem or end and at the opposite angle, dip the bottom third of each piece into the melted chocolate, creating a chevron effect. Set on the baking sheet. Chill for 15 minutes or until set. Before serving, allow the fruit to stand at room temperature for 10–15 minutes.

Cognac and Ginger Creams

You will need plastic moulds to create these luxurious chocolates with just the right touch of expertise, but the technique is quite straightforward. All you need is a little patience.

Makes 18–20
300g/11oz/ dark (bittersweet)
  chocolate, chopped into
  small pieces
45ml/3 tbsp double
  (heavy) cream
30ml/2 tbsp cognac
4 pieces of preserved stem ginger,
  drained and finely chopped,
  plus 15ml/1 tbsp syrup from
  the jar
crystallized (candied) ginger,
  to decorate

1 Polish the insides of 18–20 chocolate moulds carefully with cotton wool (absorbent cotton). Melt about two-thirds of the chocolate in a heatproof bowl over a pan of barely simmering water, then remove from the heat. Spoon a little melted chocolate into each mould. Reserve a little of the melted chocolate for sealing the creams.

2 Using a small brush, gently sweep the chocolate up the sides of the moulds to coat them evenly, then invert them on to a sheet of baking parchment and set aside until the chocolate sets.

3 Melt the remaining chopped chocolate over simmering water. Remove from the heat and stir in the cream, cognac, preserved stem ginger and ginger syrup, mixing well. Spoon into the chocolate-lined moulds. If the reserved chocolate has solidified, melt it again, then spoon a little into each mould to seal.

4 Leave the chocolates in a cool place, but not in the refrigerator, until set.

5 To remove them from the moulds, gently press them out on to a cool surface, such as a marble slab. Decorate with small pieces of crystallized ginger. Keep the chocolates cool if not serving them immediately.

Double Chocolate Dipped Fruit Energy 54kcal/227kJ; Protein 0.8g; Carbohydrate 6.8g, of which sugars 6.8g; Fat 2.8g, of which saturates 1.7g; Cholesterol 0mg; Calcium 17mg; Fibre 0.3g; Sodium 7mg.
Cognac and Ginger Creams Energy 93kcal/390kJ; Protein 0.8g; Carbohydrate 10.2g, of which sugars 10g; Fat 5.4g, of which saturates 3.3g; Cholesterol 4mg; Calcium 6mg; Fibre 0.4g; Sodium 3mg.

Chocolate Almond Torrone

Serve this Italian speciality in thin slices.

Makes 20
115g/4oz plain (semisweet) chocolate, chopped
50g/2oz/4 tbsp unsalted butter
1 egg white
115g/4oz/generous ½ cup caster (superfine) sugar
50g/2oz/½ cup ground almonds
75g/3oz/¾ cup chopped toasted almonds
75ml/5 tbsp mixed chopped (candied) peel

For the coating
175g/6oz white chocolate, chopped
25g/1oz/2 tbsp unsalted butter
115g/4oz/1 cup flaked (sliced) almonds toasted

1 Melt the chocolate with the butter in a heatproof bowl over a pan of hot water, stirring until the mixture is smooth.

2 In a clean, grease-free bowl, whisk the egg white with the sugar until stiff. Gradually beat in the melted chocolate, then stir in the ground almonds, chopped toasted almonds and peel.

3 Tip the mixture on to a large sheet of baking parchment and shape into a thick roll. As the mixture cools, use the parchment to press the roll firmly into a triangular shape.
Twist the parchment over and chill until completely set.

4 To make the coating, melt the white chocolate with the butter in a heatproof bowl set over a pan of hot water. Unwrap the chocolate roll and spread the white chocolate quickly over the surface. Press the almonds in a thin even coating over the chocolate, working quickly before the chocolate sets.

5 Chill again until firm, then cut the torronne into fairly thin slices to serve.

Cook's Tip
The mixture can be shaped into a simple round roll instead of the triangular shape, if you prefer.

Fruit Fondant Chocolates

These chocolates are simple to make using pre-formed plastic moulds, yet look very professional. Fruit fondant is available from sugarcraft stores and comes in a variety of flavours including coffee and nut. Try a mixture of flavours using a small quantity of each, or use just a single flavour.

Makes 24
225g/8oz plain (semisweet), milk or white chocolate
115g/4oz/1 cup real fruit liquid fondant
15–20ml/3–4 tsp cooled boiled water

For the decoration
15ml/1 tbsp melted plain (semisweet), milk or white chocolate

1 Melt the chocolate. Use a piece of cotton wool (absorbent cotton) to polish the insides of the chocolate moulds, ensuring that they are spotlessly clean. Fill up the shapes in one plastic tray to the top, leave for a few seconds, then invert the tray over the bowl of melted chocolate allowing the excess chocolate to fall back into the bowl. Sit the tray on the work surface and draw a metal spatula across the top to remove the excess chocolate and to neaten the edges. Chill until the chocolate has set. Repeat to fill the remaining trays.

2 Sift the fruit fondant mixture into a bowl. Gradually stir in enough water to give it the consistency of thick cream. Place the fondant in a baking parchment piping (pastry) bag, fold down the top and snip off the end. Fill each chocolate case almost to the top by piping in the fondant. Leave for 30 minutes or until a skin has formed on the surface of the fondant.

3 Spoon the remaining melted chocolate over the fondant to fill each mould level with the top. Chill until the chocolate has set hard. Invert the tray and press out the chocolates one by one. Place the melted chocolate of a contrasting colour into a baking parchment piping bag, fold down the top, snip off the point and pipe lines across the top of each chocolate. Leave to set, then pack into pretty boxes and tie with ribbon.

Fruit Fondant Chocolates Energy 88kcal/368kJ; Protein 0.7g; Carbohydrate 13.1g, of which sugars 10.8g; Fat 4g, of which saturates 2.4g; Cholesterol 1mg; Calcium 5mg; Fibre 0.4g; Sodium 8mg.
Chocolate Almond Torrone Energy 205kcal/856kJ; Protein 3.5g; Carbohydrate 17.8g, of which sugars 17.4g; Fat 13.8g, of which saturates 5g; Cholesterol 8mg; Calcium 62mg; Fibre 1.2g; Sodium 45mg.

Chocolate Boxes

These tiny chocolate boxes make the perfect containers for handmade chocolates or other sweets. Make them as you need them.

Makes 4
225g/8oz/plain (semisweet), or milk chocolate, melted
50g/2oz white chocolate

For the decoration
handmade chocolates or sweets (candies), to fill
2m/2yd ribbon, 1cm/½in wide

1 Line a large baking sheet with baking parchment.

2 Pour all but 15ml/1 tbsp of the chocolate over the parchment paper and quickly spread to the edges using a metal spatula. Pick up 2 corners of the paper and drop; do this several times on each side to level the surface of the chocolate.

3 Leave the chocolate until almost set but still pliable. Place a clean piece of baking parchment on the surface, invert the chocolate sheet and peel the parchment away from the back of the chocolate. Using a ruler and a craft knife, measure and cut the chocolate sheet into 16 squares each 5cm/2in to form the sides of the boxes. Measure and cut out 8 squares each 5.5cm/2¼in for the lids and bases of each of the boxes.

4 To assemble the boxes, paint a little of the remaining melted chocolate along the top edges of a chocolate square using a fine brush.

5 Place the side pieces in position one at a time, brushing the side edges to join the four squares together to form a box. Leave to set. Repeat to make the remaining three boxes.

6 Melt the white chocolate and spoon into a baking parchment piping (icing) bag. Fold down the top and snip off the point. Pipe 20 chocolate loops on to a sheet of baking parchment and leave them to set. Remove from the parchment with the tip of a brush. Stick them in place on each side of the box using melted chocolate.

Chocolate and Coffee Mint Thins

These coffee-flavoured chocolate squares contain pieces of crisp minty caramel and are perfect for serving with after-dinner coffee.

Makes 16
75g/3oz/scant ½ cup sugar
75ml/5 tbsp water
3 drops oil of peppermint
15ml/1 tbsp strong-flavoured ground coffee
75ml/5 tbsp near-boiling double (heavy) cream
225g/8oz plain (semisweet) chocolate
10g/¼oz/½ tbsp unsalted butter

1 Line an 18cm/7in square tin (pan) with baking parchment. Gently heat the sugar and water in a heavy pan until the sugar has dissolved. Add the peppermint oil, and boil until a light caramel colour.

2 Pour the caramel on to an oiled baking sheet and leave to harden, then crush into small pieces.

3 Put the coffee in a small bowl and pour the hot cream over. Leave to infuse (steep) for about 4 minutes, then strain through a fine sieve (strainer). Melt the chocolate and butter in a bowl over barely simmering water. Remove from the heat and beat in the hot coffee cream. Stir in the mint caramel.

4 Pour the mixture into the prepared tin and smooth the surface level. Leave in a cool place to set for at least 4 hours, preferably overnight.

5 Carefully turn out the chocolate on to a board and peel off the parchment. Cut the chocolate into squares with a sharp knife and store in an airtight container until needed.

> **Cook's Tip**
> *Don't put the chocolate in the refrigerator to set, or it may lose its glossy appearance and become too brittle to cut easily into neat squares.*

Chocolate Boxes Energy 353kcal/1479kJ; Protein 3.8g; Carbohydrate 43g, of which sugars 42.5g; Fat 19.6g, of which saturates 11.8g; Cholesterol 3mg; Calcium 52mg; Fibre 1.4g; Sodium 17mg.
Chocolate and Coffee Mint Thins Energy 118kcal/494kJ; Protein 0.8g; Carbohydrate 13.9g, of which sugars 13.8g; Fat 7g, of which saturates 4.3g; Cholesterol 9mg; Calcium 10mg; Fibre 0.4g; Sodium 6mg.

Chocolate Peppermint Crisps

If you do not have a sugar thermometer, test cooked sugar for "hard ball stage".

Makes 30
50g/2oz/¼ cup sugar
50ml/2fl oz/¼ cup water
5ml/1 tsp peppermint extract
225g/8oz plain (semisweet) chocolate, chopped
unflavoured oil, for greasing

1 Lightly brush a large baking sheet with unflavoured oil. In a pan over a medium heat, heat the sugar and water, swirling the pan gently until the sugar dissolves. Boil rapidly until the temperature registers 138°C/280°F on a sugar thermometer. Remove the pan from the heat and add the peppermint extract and swirl to mix. Pour on to the prepared baking sheet and leave to set and cool completely.

2 When the mixture is cold, break it into pieces. Place in a food processor fitted with a metal blade and process to fine crumbs but do not over-process it.

3 Line two baking sheets with baking parchment. Place the chocolate in a small heatproof bowl set over a pan of gently simmering water. Place over a very low heat until the chocolate has melted, stirring frequently until smooth. Remove from the heat and stir in the peppermint mixture.

4 Using a teaspoon, drop small mounds on to the prepared baking sheets. Using the back of the spoon, spread to 4cm/1½in rounds. Cool, then chill in the refrigerator for about 1 hour, until set. Peel off the parchment and store in airtight containers with baking parchment between the layers.

Peppermint Chocolate Sticks

With their double flavour, these are so much nicer than any kind of chocolate sticks you can buy.

Makes about 80
115g/4oz/½ cup sugar
150ml/¼ pint/⅔ cup water

2.5ml/½ tsp peppermint extract
200g/7oz plain (semisweet) chocolate, chopped into small pieces
60ml/4 tbsp toasted desiccated (dry unsweetened shredded) coconut

1 Lightly grease a large baking sheet. Place the sugar and water in a small, heavy pan and heat gently, stirring, until the sugar has dissolved.

2 Bring to the boil and boil rapidly without stirring until the syrup registers 138°C/280°F on a sugar thermometer. Remove from the heat and stir in the peppermint extract.

3 Pour the mixture on to the prepared baking sheet and leave until set.

4 Break up the peppermint mixture into a small bowl and use the end of a rolling pin to crush it into small pieces.

5 Melt the chocolate in a heatproof bowl set over a pan of gently simmering water. Remove the bowl from the heat and stir in the mint pieces and desiccated coconut.

6 Place a 30 × 25cm/12 × 10in sheet of baking parchment on a flat surface. Spread the chocolate mixture over it, leaving a narrow border all around, to make a rectangle 25 × 20cm/10 × 8in. Leave to set.

7 When the chocolate rectangle is firm, use a sharp knife to cut into thin sticks, each about 6cm/2½in long.

> **Cook's Tip**
> To test for "hard ball stage", drop a little of the syrup into a bowl of ice cold water. Gather it together with your fingertips and if it forms a hard ball, the syrup has reached the required temperature.

> **Variation**
> You can also use dark (bittersweet) chocolate for these sticks.

Peppermint Chocolate Sticks Energy 23kcal/96kJ; Protein 0.2g; Carbohydrate 3.1g, of which sugars 3.1g; Fat 1.2g, of which saturates 0.8g; Cholesterol 0mg; Calcium 2mg; Fibre 0.2g; Sodium 0mg.
Chocolate Peppermint Crisps Energy 45kcal/188kJ; Protein 0.4g; Carbohydrate 6.5g, of which sugars 6.4g; Fat 2.1g, of which saturates 1.3g; Cholesterol 0mg; Calcium 3mg; Fibre 0.2g; Sodium 1mg.

Marshmallows

These light and fragrant mouthfuls of pale pink mousse are flavoured with rose water.

Makes 500g/1¼lb

45ml/3 tbsp icing (confectioners') sugar
45ml/3 tbsp cornflour (cornstarch)
50ml/2fl oz/¼ cup cold water
45ml/3 tbsp rose water
25g/1oz powdered gelatine
pink food colouring
450g/1lb/2 cups sugar
30ml/2 tbsp liquid glucose (clear corn syrup)
250ml/8fl oz/1 cup boiling water
2 egg whites

1 Lightly grease a 28 × 18cm/11 × 7in Swiss roll tin (jelly roll pan). Sift together the icing sugar and cornflour and use some of this mixture to coat the inside of the tin evenly. Shake out the excess.

2 Mix together the cold water, rose water, gelatine and a drop of pink food colouring in a heatproof bowl. Place over a pan of hot water and stir occasionally until the gelatine has dissolved.

3 Place the sugar, liquid glucose and boiling water in a heavy pan. Stir over a low heat to dissolve the sugar completely. Ensure that there are no sugar crystals around the water line; if so, wash these down with a brush dipped in cold water.

4 Bring the syrup to the boil and boil without stirring until the temperature reaches 127°C/260°F on a sugar thermometer. Remove from the heat. Stir in the gelatine mixture.

5 Whisk the egg whites stiffly in a large grease-free bowl using an electric hand whisk. Pour a steady stream of syrup on to the egg whites, constanly whisking for about 3 minutes, or until the mixture is thick and foamy.

6 Pour the mixture into the prepared tin and leave to set overnight. Sift the remaining icing sugar mixture over the surface and over a board. Ease the mixture away from the tin with an oiled metal spatula and invert on to the board. Cut into 2.5cm/1in squares, coating the cut sides with the sugar mixture.

Marzipan Logs

Shiny gold-coated sweets, sometimes called dragées, give these irresistible petits fours an air of luxury. They would make a welcome gift to a dinner-party hostess for serving at the end of a meal.

Makes about 12

225g/8oz marzipan, at room temperature
115g/4oz/⅔ cup candied orange peel, chopped
30ml/2 tbsp orange-flavoured liqueur
15ml/1 tbsp soft light brown sugar
edible gold powder
75g/3oz plain (semisweet) chocolate, melted
gold-coated sweets (candies)

1 Knead the marzipan well, then mix in the chopped peel and liqueur. Set aside for about 1 hour to dry.

2 Break off small pieces of the mixture and roll them into log shapes with your hands.

3 Dip the tops of half of the marzipan logs in the sugar and brush them lightly with edible gold powder.

4 Dip the remaining logs in the melted chocolate. Place on baking parchment and press a gold-coated sweet in the centre of each. Leave to set.

5 Arrange all the logs on a plate and decorate the arrangement with extra gold-coated sweets.

Cook's Tips
• *Store the marzipan logs in an airtight container, interleaved with baking parchment, for a maximum of 2 days. After this, they will start to dry out and become hard and brittle.*
• *Edible gold powder may also be labelled gold lustre or sparkle dust. A silver version is also available, as too are silver dragées.*

Marshmallows Energy 2228kcal/9504kJ; Protein 8.5g; Carbohydrate 584.1g, of which sugars 529.3g; Fat 0.3g, of which saturates 0g; Cholesterol 0mg; Calcium 275mg; Fibre 0g; Sodium 220mg.
Marzipan Logs Energy 137kcal/580kJ; Protein 1.3g; Carbohydrate 23.6g, of which sugars 23.6g; Fat 4.2g, of which saturates 1.2g; Cholesterol 0mg; Calcium 28mg; Fibre 1g; Sodium 31mg.

Marzipan Fruits

These eye-catching and realistic fruits will make a perfect gift for lovers of marzipan.

Makes 450g/1 lb
450g/1lb white marzipan
yellow, green, red, orange and
  burgundy food colouring dusts
30g/2 tbsp whole cloves

1 Line a baking sheet with baking parchment. Quarter the marzipan and cut a quarter into ten equal pieces. Put small heaps of the food colouring dust on a plate. Halve two-thirds of the cloves, making a stem and core end.

2 Roll each of the 10 pieces into a ball. Dip a ball into the yellow colouring and roll between the palms of your hands. Dip it into the green colouring and roll to a greenish yellow. Roll one end of the ball with your finger to make a pear shape. Press a clove stem and core into each end. Make 9 more pears and place on the baking sheet.

3 Cut another marzipan quarter into 10 and roll into balls. Dip each into green colouring and roll in your hands. Add a spot of red and roll again. Indent the top and base of each ball with a ball tool or the end of a paintbrush to make apples. Add stems and cores.

4 Repeat as above using another piece of the marzipan to make 10 orange coloured balls. Roll each over the surface of a fine grater to give the texture of an orange skin. Press a clove core into the base of each.

5 Reserve a small piece of the remaining marzipan, roll the rest into tiny beads and colour them burgundy. Put a whole clove on the baking sheet and arrange a cluster of beads to make a bunch of grapes. Make three more.

6 Roll out the remaining tiny piece of marzipan thinly and brush with green food colouring dust. Using a small vine leaf cutter, cut out 8 leaves, mark the veins with a knife and place 2 on each bunch of grapes, bending to give a realistic appearance. When all the marzipan fruits are dry, pack into gift boxes.

Coconut Ice

A great favourite with both adults and children, the ice is always sweet and juicy. However, if you've only ever eaten sweets made with dried coconut, you are about to experience an unforgettable taste explosion.

Makes 16 squares each 5cm/2in
1 coconut
450g/1lb sugar
120ml/4fl oz/1/2 cup coconut milk
25g/1oz butter
red food colouring
flavourless oil, for greasing

1 Grease a 20cm/8in square cake tin (pan) or brush with a little flavourless oil.

2 Crack the coconut and drain off the milk into a bowl. Break open the shell, remove the flesh and grate it.

3 Put the sugar, reserved coconut milk and butter into a pan and bring to the boil over a low heat, stirring frequently, until the sugar has dissolved and the butter has melted. Gradually stir in the grated coconut and continue to boil, stirring constantly, for 10 minutes, until thickened. Remove the pan from the heat.

4 Divide the mixture between two bowls. Add a few drops of red food colouring to one batch and mix well to colour it pink. Leave the second batch uncoloured.

5 Firmly press the uncoloured coconut mixture into the prepared tin to make an even layer. Cover with the pink coconut mixture, pressing it down into an even layer. Leave to set, then cut into squares with a sharp knife. The squares can be wrapped in individual cellophane parcels, if you like.

Cook's Tip
To crack a coconut, hold it firmly in one hand and pierce the eyes with a skewer. Pour the milk into a bowl. Hit the coconut all around the centre with a hammer and lever apart. Scoop out the flesh with a small knife and peel off the skin.

Marzipan Fruits Energy 1837kcal/7752kJ; Protein 28.3g; Carbohydrate 314.7g, of which sugars 304.2g; Fat 61g, of which saturates 5.2g; Cholesterol 0mg; Calcium 351mg; Fibre 8.6g; Sodium 100mg.
Coconut Ice Energy 162kcal/683kJ; Protein 0.5g; Carbohydrate 30.2g, of which sugars 30.2g; Fat 5.2g, of which saturates 4.2g; Cholesterol 3mg; Calcium 19mg; Fibre 0.9g; Sodium 21mg.

Turkish Delight

You either love or loathe this somewhat chewy sweetmeat – there are no half measures. Fans will certainly welcome this versatile recipe that can be made in minutes.

Makes 450g/1lb
450g/1lb/2 cups sugar
300ml/½ pint/1¼ cups water

25g/1oz powdered gelatine
2.5ml/½ tsp cream of tartar
30ml/2 tbsp rose water
pink food colouring
25g/1oz/3 tbsp icing (confectioners') sugar, sifted
15ml/1 tbsp cornflour (cornstarch)

1 Wet the insides of 2 × 18cm/7in shallow square tins (pans) with water. Place the sugar and all but 60ml/4 tbsp of water into a heavy pan. Heat gently, stirring occasionally, until the sugar has dissolved.

2 Blend the gelatine and remaining water in a small bowl and place over a pan of hot water. Stir occasionally until dissolved. Bring the sugar syrup to a boil and boil steadily for about 8 minutes or until the syrup registers 127°C/260°F on a sugar thermometer. Stir the cream of tartar into the gelatine, then pour into the boiling syrup and stir until well blended. Remove from the heat.

3 Add the rose water and a few drops of pink food colouring to tint the mixture pale pink. Pour the mixture into the prepared tins and leave to set for several hours or overnight. Dust a sheet of baking parchment with some of the sugar and cornflour. Dip the base of the tin in hot water. Invert on to the paper. Cut into 2.5cm/1in squares using an oiled knife. Toss in icing sugar to coat evenly.

Variation
Try substituting the same quantity of orange flower water or crème de menthe or a few drops of lemon extract for the rose water, and using orange, green or yellow food colouring.

Rose Turkish Delight

In the Middle East, these sweets are served with tiny cups of very strong coffee.

Makes 450g/1lb
60ml/4tbsp triple-distilled rose water
30ml/2tbsp powdered gelatine
450g/1lb/1¾ cups sugar
150ml/¼ pint/⅔ cup water

cochineal colouring
9 drops rose essential oil
25g/1oz/¼ cup coarsely chopped blanched almonds
20g/¾oz/scant ¼ cup cornflour (cornstarch)
65g/2½oz/⅓ cup icing (confectioners') sugar

1 Lightly brush a 15–18cm/6–7in square baking tin (pan) with flavourless oil.

2 Pour the rose water into a bowl and sprinkle the gelatine over the surface. Set aside to soften and become spongy.

3 Meanwhile put the sugar and measured water into a pan and bring to the boil over a low heat, stirring until the sugar has dissolved. When the syrup is clear, boil until the mixture registers 116°C/234°F on a sugar thermometer.

4 Remove the pan from the heat and add the gelatine and rose water. Return the pan to a low heat and cook, stirring constantly, until the gelatine has dissolved.

5 Remove the pan from the heat and stir in a few drops of cochineal to colour the mixture pale pink, then stir in the rose oil and almonds.

6 Pour the mixture into the prepared tin and leave to set. Using a sharp knife, cut the Turkish delight into pieces. Sift the cornflour and icing sugar together, then sprinkle it over the pieces.

Cook's Tip
Although it is expensive, cochineal produces the purest red colouring.

Turkish Delight Energy 1944kcal/8295kJ; Protein 2.5g; Carbohydrate 515.4g, of which sugars 501.6g; Fat 0.1g, of which saturates 0g; Cholesterol 0mg; Calcium 257mg; Fibre 0g; Sodium 37mg.
Rose Turkish Delight Energy 2368kcal/10080kJ; Protein 36.7g; Carbohydrate 558.3g, of which sugars 539.2g; Fat 14.1g, of which saturates 1.1g; Cholesterol 0mg; Calcium 336mg; Fibre 1.9g; Sodium 45mg.

Macaroon Candies

These tasty little macaroons, decorated with almonds and cherries, make delightful petits fours to serve with after-dinner liqueurs and coffee or with a glass of sweet dessert wine.

Makes 30
50g/2oz/1½ cup ground almonds
50g/2oz/¼ cup caster (superfine) sugar
15ml/1 tbsp cornflour (cornstarch)
1.5–2.5ml/¼–½ tsp almond extract
1 egg white, whisked
15 flaked (sliced) almonds
4 glacé (candied) cherries, quartered
icing (confectioners') sugar or unsweetened cocoa powder, for dusting

1 Preheat the oven to 160°C/325°F/Gas 3. Line two baking sheets with baking parchment.

2 Place the almonds, sugar, cornflour and almond extract into a bowl and mix together well using a wooden spoon.

3 Stir in enough egg white to form a soft piping consistency. Spoon the mixture into a nylon piping (pastry) bag fitted with a 1cm/½in plain nozzle.

4 Pipe about 15 rounds of mixture on to each baking sheet, well spaced apart. Press a flaked almond on to half the macaroons and quartered glacé cherries on to the remainder.

5 Bake for 10–15 minutes, until firm to touch. Leave to cool on the baking sheets and dust with sugar or the unsweetened cocoa powder before removing from the baking parchment.

> ### Variation
> To make chocolate macaroons, replace the cornflour (cornstarch) with the same quantity of unsweetened cocoa powder. Decorate with pieces of marrons glacés and dust with sifted unsweetened cocoa powder when cold.

Creamy Fudge

A good selection of fudge always makes a welcome change from chocolates and won't melt like chocolate. Mix and match the flavours.

Makes 900g/2lb
50g/2oz/4 tbsp unsalted butter, diced
450g/1lb/2 cups sugar
300ml/½ pint/1¼ cups double (heavy) cream
150ml/¼ pint/⅔ cup milk
45ml/3 tbsp water (this can be replaced with orange, apricot or cherry brandy, or strong coffee)

For the flavourings
225g/8oz/1 cup plain (semisweet) or milk chocolate chips
115g/4oz/1 cup chopped almonds, hazelnuts, walnuts or Brazil nuts
115g/4oz/½ cup chopped glacé (candied) cherries, dates or dried apricots

1 Grease a 20cm/8in shallow square tin (pan). Place the butter, sugar, cream, milk and water into a heavy pan. Heat very gently, stirring occasionally, until the sugar has dissolved.

2 Bring the mixture to the boil and boil steadily, stirring constantly to prevent the mixture from burning on the base of the pan. Boil until the fudge reaches just under soft ball stage, 113°C/230°F for a soft fudge.

3 If you are making chocolate flavoured fudge, add the chocolate at this stage. Remove the pan from the heat and beat thoroughly until the mixture starts to thicken.

4 Alternatively, add the chopped nuts for a nutty fudge, or glacé cherries or dried fruit for a fruit-flavoured fudge. Beat well until evenly blended.

5 Pour the fudge into the prepared tin. Leave the mixture until cool and almost set. Using a sharp knife, mark the fudge into small squares and leave in the tin until quite firm.

6 Turn the fudge out on to a board and invert. Using a long-bladed knife, cut into neat squares. Dust some squares with icing sugar and drizzle other squares with melted chocolate, if you like.

Macaroon Candies Energy 102kcal/426kJ; Protein 2.8g; Carbohydrate 7.8g, of which sugars 7.5g; Fat 6.9g, of which saturates 0.6g; Cholesterol 13mg; Calcium 33mg; Fibre 0.9g; Sodium 5mg.
Creamy Fudge Energy 5886kcal/24635kJ; Protein 40.4g; Carbohydrate 708.8g, of which sugars 704.5g; Fat 340.8g, of which saturates 171g; Cholesterol 540mg; Calcium 874mg; Fibre 14.1g; Sodium 512mg.

Easy Hazelnut Fudge

The sweetness of the nuts combines beautifully with plain chocolate in this truly scrumptious and reliable recipe.

50g/2oz/1/2 cup halved hazelnuts
350g/12oz/2 cups plain
   (semisweet) chocolate chips
5ml/1 tsp hazelnut liqueur
   (optional)

Makes 16 squares
150ml/1/4 pint/2/3 cup evaporated
   milk
375g/13oz/1 3/4 cups sugar
pinch of salt

1 Generously grease a 20cm/8in square cake tin (pan).

2 Combine the evaporated milk, sugar and salt in a heavy pan. Bring to the boil over a medium heat, stirring constantly. Simmer gently, stirring, for about 5 minutes.

3 Remove the pan from the heat and add the hazelnuts, chocolate chips and liqueur, if using. Stir until the chocolate has completely melted.

4 Quickly pour the fudge mixture into the prepared tin and spread it out evenly. leave to cool.

5 When the fudge has set completely, cut it into 2.5cm/1in squares. Store in an airtight container, separating the layers with sheets of baking parchment.

Variation
• For Easy Peanut Butter Fudge, substitute peanut butter chips for the chocolate chips and replace the hazelnuts with the same quantity of peanuts.
• If can't find hazelnut liqueur, suitable substitutes include Cointreau (orange), Drambuie (honey and heather), Galliano (honey and vanilla) or Tia Maria (coffee). For a non-alcoholic alternative, use orgeat (sugar-free) syrup.

Vanilla Fudge

Perennially popular, home-made fudge ends a meal beautifully when served as a petit four. This meltingly good vanilla version is sure to become a favourite.

Makes 60 pieces
175g/6oz/3/4 cup butter
900g/2lb/4 cups soft light
   brown sugar
400g/14oz condensed milk
2.5ml/1/2tsp vanilla extract,
   or to taste

1 Butter a shallow tin (pan), about 18 x 28cm/7 x 11in. Put the butter and 150ml/1/4 pint/2/3 cup water into a large, heavy pan and warm very gently over a low heat until the butter melts.

2 Add the sugar and stir over a low heat until it has completely dissolved. Raise the heat and bring the mixture to the boil. Boil hard until it reaches hard crack stage (168°C/336°F on a sugar thermometer). Test by pouring a small amount into a saucer of cold water to form strands that can be cracked.

3 Remove from the heat and beat in the condensed milk with a wooden spoon. Return to a medium heat, stirring, for a few minutes. Remove from the heat again, add the vanilla extract, and beat again with a spoon until glossy. Pour the mixture into the tin. Leave to cool.

4 Cut the fudge into cubes and store in an airtight tin until required. Place in petits fours cases to serve.

Cook's Tip
It is essential to keep stirring the fudge mixture while it is boiling, as it may otherwise catch on the base of the pan. Even if this does not taint the flavour, the mixture will not set properly and the fudge will be spoiled.

Variations
• For Coffee Fudge, add 30ml/2 tbsp coffee extract.

Easy Hazelnut Fudge Energy 234kcal/987kJ; Protein 2.4g; Carbohydrate 39.5g, of which sugars 39.3g; Fat 8.5g, of which saturates 4.1g; Cholesterol 3mg; Calcium 48mg; Fibre 0.8g; Sodium 14mg.
Vanilla Fudge Energy per piece 103kcal/435kJ; Protein 0.7g; Carbohydrate 19.4g, of which sugars 19.4g; Fat 3.1g, of which saturates 1.9g; Cholesterol 9mg; Calcium 28mg; Fibre 0g; Sodium 28mg.

Index